INSIGHTS:
Readings in Operations Management

Robert E. Markland
University of South Carolina

Shawnee K. Vickery
Michigan State University

Robert A. Davis
Texas A & M University

West Publishing Company
Minneapolis/St. Paul   New York   Los Angeles   San Francisco

WEST'S COMMITMENT TO THE ENVIRONMENT

In 1906, West Publishing Company began recycling materials left over from the production of books. This began a tradition of efficient and responsible use of resources. Today, up to 95% of our legal books and 70% of our college texts and school texts are printed on recycled, acid-free stock. West also recycles nearly 22 million pounds of scrap paper annually—the equivalent of 181,717 trees. Since the 1960s, West has devised ways to capture and recycle waste inks, solvents, oils, and vapors created in the printing process. We also recycle plastics of all kinds, wood, glass, corrugated cardboard, and batteries, and have eliminated the use of Styrofoam book packaging. We at West are proud of the longevity and the scope of our commitment to the environment.

Production, Prepress, Printing and Binding by West Publishing Company.

COPYRIGHT © 1995 by WEST PUBLISHING CO.
610 Opperman Drive
P.O. Box 64526
St. Paul, MN 55164–0526

All rights reserved
Printed in the United States of America
02 01 00 99 98 97 96 95   8 7 6 5 4 3 2 1 0

ISBN 0–314–05803–6

INSIGHTS: Readings in Operations Management

Chapter 1:	Activity Based Systems: Measuring the Costs of Resource Usage, Accounting Horizons, September 1992, Cooper & Kaplan, pp. 1-13.	1
	Do Financial and Nonfinancial Performance Measures Have to Agree, Management Accounting, November 1990, McNair, Lynch, and Cross, pp. 28-36.	14
Chapter 2:	The New Service Class, Time, November 14, 1994, John Greenwald, pp. 72-74.	21
Chapter 3:	Competitiveness: Does It Matter?, Adapted from PEDDLING PROSPERITY: Economic Sense and Nonsense in the Age of Diminished Expectations, 1994, Paul Krugman, W.W. Norton & Company.	23
Chapter 4:	none	
Chapter 5:	New U.S. Factory Jobs Aren't in the Factory, Business Week, November 18, 1994, Stephen Baker and James B. Treece.	27
Chapter 6:	Custom-Made, Direct From the Plant, Business Week, Otis Port, pp. 158-159.	28
Chapter 7:	Ten Mistakes CEO's Make About Quality, Quality Progress, June 1994, Willard Zangwill, pp. 43-48.	30
	Quality Auditing in a Public-Sector Service Environment, Quality Progress, June 1994, Bonnie Holzer, pp. 61-62.	36
Chapter 8:	The Digital Factory, Fortune, November 14, 1994, Gene Bylinsky, pp. 93-110.	38
Chapter 9:	The New Deal, Fortune, June 13, 1994, Brian O'Reilly, pp. 44-52.	45
Chapter 10:	Leading--Edge Distribution Strategies, Journal of Business Strategy, Nov/Dec 1990, Neil Novich, pp. 48-53.	52
Chapter 11:	Brace for Japan's Hot New Strategy, Fortune, September 21, 1992, Thomas A. Stewart, pp. 63-74.	58
Chapter 12:	none	
Chapter 13:	Global Manufacturing Strategies and Practices, International Journal of Operations and Production Management, 12, 9, Young, Kwong, Li, and Fok.	64
Chapter 14:	Capacity Planning Techniques for Manufacturing Control Systems, Journal of Operations Management, Vol. 3 No. 1 November 1982, Berry, Schmitt, and Vollman.	71
Chapter 15:	none	
Chapter 16:	Saturn, Rising Star, Purchasing, September 9, 1993, Ernest Raia, pp. 44-51.	78
	A Thousand Parts Alight, Purchasing, September 9, 1993, Peter Bradley.	81

Chapter 17:	Service is Everybody's Business, Fortune, June 27, 1994, Ronald Henkoff, pp. 48-60.	83
Chapter 18:	none	
Chapter 19:	Reducing Variability-Key to Continuous Improvement, Manufacturing Systems, March 1990, Gregg D. Stocker, pp. 32-36.	89
	What Management Accountants Need to Know, Management Accounting, January 1992, Keys and Reding, pp. 26-30.	93
Chapter 20:	none	

ACTIVITY BASED SYSTEMS:

Measuring the Costs of Resource Usage

By Robin Cooper and Robert S. Kaplan

This paper describes the conceptual basis for the design and use of newly emerging activity-based cost (ABC) systems. Traditional cost systems use volume-driven allocation bases, such as direct labor dollars, machine hours, and sales dollars, to assign organizational expenses to individual products and customers. But many of the resource demands by individual products and customers are not proportional to the volume of units produced or sold.(1) Thus, conventional systems do not measure accurately the costs of resources used to design and produce products and to sell and deliver them to customers. Companies, including those with excellent traditional cost systems,(2) have developed activity-based cost systems so that they can directly link the costs of performing organizational activities to the products and customers for which these activities are performed.

I. ABC SYSTEMS AS RESOURCE USAGE MODELS

Activity-based cost systems estimate the cost of resources used in organizational processes to produce outputs.(3) Many people have attempted to interpret activity-based costs using their more familiar fixed versus variable cost framework, an interpretation inconsistent with an ABC system's measurements of resource usage costs. The conventional fixed versus variable cost classification arises from an attempt to classify the likely change in spending or supply of a resource. The measurement of unused capacity provides the critical link between the costs of resources used, as measured by an ABC model, and the costs of resources supplied or available, as reported by the organization's periodic financial statements.(4) The following equation, defined for each major activity performed by the organization's resources, formalizes this relationship:

Activity Availability = Activity Usage + Unused Capacity

A simple example illustrates the difference between the cost of resources supplied and the cost of resources used to perform activities. Consider a purchasing department in which the equivalent of 10 full-time people (the resource supplied) are committed to processing purchase orders (the activity performed). If the monthly cost of a full-time employee is $2,500,(5) the monthly cost of the activity, "Process Purchase Orders," equals $25,000. Assume that each employee, working at practical capacity, can process 125 purchase orders per month, leading to an estimated cost of $20 for processing each purchase order.(6) Thus, the organization, each month, spends $25,000. This expenditure provides a capability to process up to 1,250 purchase orders (the activity availability) during the month. During any particular month, the department may be asked to process fewer purchase orders, say only 1,000. At an estimated cost of $20/purchase order, the ABC system would assign $20,000 of expenses to the parts and materials ordered by the purchasing department that month. The remaining $5,000 of monthly operating expenses represents the cost of unused capacity in the purchase order processing activity.

This example shows why companies need two different reporting systems. The periodic financial statements provide information on the cost of activities supplied each period (the $25,000 monthly expense in the purchasing department); and the activity-based cost system provides information on the quantity (1,000 purchase orders) and the estimated cost ($20,000) of activities actually used in a period. The difference ($5,000) between the cost of activities supplied ($25,000) and the cost of activities used ($20,000) equals the cost of unused capacity (or capacity shortage) during the period. And this difference is measured for each organizational activity, defined by the ABC system.(7) The two systems provide different types of information for management. The cost of resources supplied is relevant for predicting near-term spending. Spending on many organizational resources will not vary with short-term fluctuations in activity volume and mix. That is why these costs have been classified as "fixed" in numerous accounting systems and textbooks.

But measuring and managing the operating expenses of most organizational resources as fixed in the short-run does not give much insight as to why the resources were acquired, what the resources are currently being used for, and the level of resources that will likely be required in the future. While the cost of supplying the resources may be fixed in the short-run,(8) the quantity of these resources used each period fluctuates based on activities performed for the outputs produced. Activity-based systems measure the cost of using these resources, even though the cost of supplying them will not vary, in the short run, with usage.

The ABC resource usage cost information can be used by managers to monitor and predict the changes in demands for activities as a function of changes output volume and mix, process changes and improvements, introduction of new technology, and changes in product and process design. As such changes are contemplated, managers can predict where either shortages or excesses of capacity will occur. The managers can then either modify their decisions so that activity demand will be brought into balance with activity supply, or they can change the level of activities to be supplied in forthcoming periods.

For example, if newly designed custom products, with many unique parts and materials, are added to the mix, managers may forecast a much higher demand for the purchasing activity, perhaps now requiring that 2,000 purchase orders a month be processed. With no change in the process or efficiency of the processing purchasing order activity, this increase in demand will exceed available supply by 750 purchase orders per month, a shortage that can be relieved by hiring six more purchasing clerks. The ABC model, in addition, will trace purchasing costs directly to the newly designed custom products that are creating the demand for these additional purchasing resources, enabling managers to determine whether the revenues received fully compensate the organization for the cost of all the resources used to produce and deliver these products.

Of course, supplying additional purchasing clerks is only one possible action that the managers can take to the contemplated activity shortage. The engineering department can be asked to redesign the custom products so that they make more use of existing part numbers, an action that would reduce the amount of additional purchase orders required. Or the managers can search for process improvements or technology that would make the purchase order processing activity more efficient, perhaps raising the monthly output per person from 125 to 200 purchase orders.

Thus, measuring the costs of resources supplied indicates to managers the level of current spending (or, more generally, expenses) and the capacity to perform activities that this spending has provided. Measuring the costs of resources used by individual outputs provides information for managerial actions, as will be discussed more fully subsequently in the paper.

II. ISN'T THE UNUSED CAPACITY CALCULATION JUST A NEW NAME FOR THE VOLUME VARIANCE?

The calculation of unused capacity each period looks, at first glance, suspiciously like the traditional cost accounting volume variance. But the formulas:

Activity Availability = Activity Usage + Unused Capacity

or

Cost of Activity Supplied = Cost of Activity Used + Cost of Unused Activity

First, and most obviously, volume variances are reported only in aggregate financial terms since traditional cost systems do not identify the quantity of overhead resources supplied or used. The activity-based approach reports both the quantity (number of purchase orders not written) and the cost of unused capacity. Second, traditional volume variances are often calculated with a denominator volume based on budgeted production, rather than practical capacity. In the activity-based approach, the "denominator volume" must always be the practical capacity of the activity being supplied, not the anticipated volume. And, third, the traditional cost accounting procedure of allocating overhead with a denominator volume is viewed as useful only for inventory valuation, not to provide information relevant for management; e.g.,

> The preselected production volume level of the application base used to set a budgeted fixed-factory-overhead rate for applying costs to inventory is called the denominator volume.
>
> In summary, the production volume variance arises because the actual production volume level achieved usually does not coincide with the production level used as a denominator volume for computing a budgeted application rate for inventory costing of fixed-factory overhead.(9) (emphasis added)

Note how students are instructed that the calculation involves only the application of (so-called) fixed-factory overhead to units of production. Clearly, the volume variance is viewed, at least in textbooks (but not always in practice), as a cost accounting exercise for financial statements that is devoid of managerial significance.

These three differences between volume variances and measurements of unused capacity, while real, are not, however, the most important distinction. The cost accounting calculation that leads to a volume variance uses a measure of activity volume for the period (i.e., the denominator volume, also called the allocation base) that varies with the number of units produced. Direct labor hours, units of production, materials purchases, and machine hours are typical allocation bases used by traditional systems to assign factory expenses to products in production cost centers.(10) Implicitly, this procedure assumes that factory expenses are used by products in proportion to the overhead allocation base, i.e., proportional to volume of units produced. In practice, of course, this assumption is not valid. Activity-based cost systems use separate activity cost drivers (the ABC generalization of an assignment or allocation base) for each activity. The activity cost drivers are not devices to allocate costs. They represent the demand that outputs make on each activity. For example, the activity cost driver for the setup activity could be the number of setups or the number of setup hours; the activity cost driver for processing purchase orders could be the number of purchase orders; the cost driver for administering and maintaining parts in the system could be the number of active part numbers. While some activity cost drivers are unit-related (such as machine and labor hours), as conventionally assumed, many activity cost drivers are batch-related, order-related, product-sustaining, and customer-sustaining.(11)

Because traditional cost systems use allocation bases that do not represent the demands for support resources by activities, the volume variance for a period can be zero even while substantial shortages or surpluses of capacity exist for many individual activities. For example, if actual production includes an unexpectedly high proportion of mature, standard products, produced in large batches, the demands for many batch and product-sustaining activities will be well below the quantity of resources supplied to perform these activities and much unused capacity will exist during the period. Conversely, if the actual production volume includes a substantial and unexpectedly high number of new, customized products, that are made in very small batches, the demand for batch and product-sustaining activities may exceed the quantity supplied. Shortages, delays, and overtime may occur in the batch and product-sustaining activities even though the total quantity of units produced during the period equaled the budgeted or anticipated amount.

The distinction between the measurement, by activity-based cost systems, of the cost of activities used (and unused) and the traditional cost accounting emphasis on fixed versus variable costs can be reconciled by examining closely the way managers contract for and supply resources to perform organizational activities

III. RESOURCES THAT ARE SUPPLIED AS USED (AND NEEDED)

Some resources are acquired as needed. For these resources, the cost of resources supplied will generally equal the cost of resources used. For example, materials are usually ordered as needed so that materials expense equals the cost of materials used. And the cost of energy supplied to operate production machines also equals the cost of using that energy. Temporary employees hired on a aily basis from employment agencies and employees who are paid on a piece-work or overtime basis are additional examples. The company contracts with these workers to produce output and the workers are paid only when they are needed to produce output. Capital supplied by lenders is another example where the supply and the usage cost are identical (equalling the interest expense on the amount borrowed).(12)

In general, when the organization acquires a resource from outside suppliers, without long-term commitments, the cost of using the resource can equal the cost of acquiring (and supplying) the resource; for example, when the organization acquires the resource in spot markets. The costs of supplying such resources are apparently what many people have in mind when they refer to "variable costs." Such resources have no unused capacity. Whatever is supplied is used, or, alternatively, whatever is needed is acquired. This causes the costs of supplying the resource to be strongly correlated with the quantity (and hence the cost) of the resource used.

IV. RESOURCES THAT ARE SUPPLIED IN ADVANCE OF USAGE

Organizations commit, however, to making many other resources available whether or not the resources will be fully used for current and future activities. This commitment can take several forms. The organization can make a cash expenditure to acquire a resource that provides service for several periods into the future. The most common example occurs when the company acquires or overhauls buildings and equipment. Such a transaction leads to an expense being recognized in each period during the useful life of the resource, with the organization gaining the capacity provided by the resource during each such period. The expense of supplying the resource will be incurred, each period, independent of how much of the resource isused.(13)

As a second example, the organization can enter into an explicit contract to obtain the use of a resource for several periods in the future For example, a company leases buildings and equipment, or it guarantees access to energy or key materials through take-or-pay contracts. In this situation, a cash payment will occur and an expense will be recognized in each future period. Again, the amount of the cash payment and associated expense are independent of the actual quantity of usage of the resource in any period.

The third, and most important, example occurs when an organization enters into implicit contracts, particularly with its salaried and hourly employees, to maintain employment levels despite short-term downturns in activity levels. In this case, the spending (and expenses) associated with these employees will remain constant independent of the quantity of work performed by the employees.(14)

In each of the three contracting mechanisms, the organization acquires units of service capacity before the actual demands for the service units are realized. Consequently, the expenses of supplying the service capacity from these resources are incurred (or recognized) independent of usage. This independence in the short-run between the supply (or expense) of these resources and their usage has led this category of expense to be considered 'fixed' with respect to current production volume and mix.

The separation between the acquisition of resource capacity and its actual usage arises from economies-of-scale in contracting for resources. For example, some service units come in lumpy amounts (e.g., physical capacity of machines, or the services provided by individual employees). Managers also find it less expensive to acquire some resources on a long-term commitment basis rather than to contract continually in spot markets to acquire resource capacity as needed.(15) These issues have been discussed at some length by scholars, such as Coase, Chandler, and Williamson.

Through any or all of these three contracting mechanisms, the organization acquires a capability or capacity to perform activities, and an associated expense of providing that capacity. The first step, therefore, in an activity-based analysis is to estimate both the expense of providing the capacity to perform an activity (the $25,000 monthly expense to process purchase orders), and the capacity or number of units of service activity that can be practically delivered (the 1,250 purchase orders per month) by the resources supplied. The expense of providing the activity capacity is divided by the number of available service units to obtain an estimate of the cost of supplying a unit of service of the activity (the $20 per purchase order cost).

V. MEASURING COSTS OF RESOURCES USED IN A PERIOD: THE ROLE FOR ACTIVITY-BASED COST SYSTEMS

The distinction between resources supplied as needed and resources supplied prior to (but in anticipation of) usage suggests that a relatively simple system can be used for the periodic measurement of actual expenses (see Exhibit 1). In this system, short-term contributionmargin is measured as price (or revenues) less the cost of resources acquired as needed: materials, energy, and short-term labor (and overtime). By assumption, the remaining operating expenses represent resources that have been acquired prior to actual usage. The costs of these resources should be unaffected by actual activity levels during the period. The periodic income statement can report, for each activity, the costs of resources used for outputs and the costs of resources unused during the period.

For management purposes, flexible budgets and variance analysis become unnecessary for these expense accounts. A simple comparison of actual to budgeted expenses, account by account, will suffice to provide feedback.(16) Basically, the authorized expenses have been determined either by prior commitments (acquiring plant, property, and equipment; (signing take-or-pay contracts) or during the annual budgeting process. One manufacturing manager expressed this point quite forcefully:

Cost variances are useless to me. I don't want to ever have to look at a cost variance, monthly or weekly. Once you've decided to run a product, you don't have many choices left. Resources are already committed regardless of how the cost system computes costs among alternative processes.

Monthly, I do look at the financial reports. I look closely at my fixed expenses and compare these to the budgets, especially on discretionary items like travel and maintenance. I also watch headcount. But the financial systems still don't tell me where I am wasting money. I expect that if I make operating improvements, costs should go down, but I don't worry about the linkage too much. The organizational dynamics make it difficult to link cause and effect precisely.(17)

Managers may be encouraged to modify their use of resources in the short-run based on information on unused capacity. For example, when excess setup capacity exists, they can temporarily decrease batch sizes. Alternatively, managers may be expected to adjust downward the quantity of resources supplied when substantial amounts of unused capacity persist for several periods.

Several organizations, however, not understanding the important distinction between measuring the costs of resources supplied (and expensed) and the costs of resources used, have attempted to use their activity-based systems to budget monthly expenses. A good example of the problems arising from using an activity-based system for monthly performance measurement was documented in the Hewlett Packard: Queensferry Telecommunications Division case.

HEWLETT PACKARD: QTD Case(18)

QTD had recently installed a new activity-based cost system. The system accumulated expenses at each process and assigned these expenses to products with a cost driver defined for each process (e.g., number of axial insertions). The system was developed primarily to provide process cost information to product engineers to help them design products that would be less expensive to manufacture. The system, however, was also used to monitor production performance. The two functions soon came into conflict when production volume dropped due to the postponement of a major contract. The lower production volume

EXHIBIT 1
Example of ABC Income Statement

	SALES			20,000
Less:	EXPENSE OF RESOURCES SUPPLIED AS USED			
	Materials	7,600		
	Energy	600		
	Short-term labor	900		
	CONTRIBUTION MARGIN			9,000
Less:	ACTIVITY EXPENSES: COMMITTED RESOURCES	Used	Unused	
	Permanent direct labor	1,400	200	
	Machine run-time	3,200		
	Purchasing	700	100	
	Receiving/Inventory	450	50	
	Production runs	1,000	100	
	Customer administration	700	200	
	Engineering changes	800	(100)	
	Parts administration	750	150	
	TOTAL EXPENSES OF COMMITTED RESOURCES	9,000	700	9,700
	OPERATING PROFIT			1,200

---

led to large monthly volume variances because operating expenses could not be reduced proportionately to the decline in volume. The controller commented:

In a perfect world, spending would drop to offset lower production volumes. However, in environments like ours, where we retain our employees, it isalmost impossible for spending to be cut back when volume drops in a period.

Higher cost driver rates were calculated, based on the lower production volumes, so that the accounts would "clear" each period without large volume variances. This change, however, negated the primary purpose of the newly designed system. With unused capacity expenses now loaded on to cost driver rates, the system no longer provided product designers with accurate information on the expenses of activities performed to manufacture their products.

Companies like QTD, that attempt to budget expenses each month from their activity-based resource usage model, will end up, each month, with a variance representing the unused capacity for every activity and resource for which usage and availability are not perfectly correlated. The unused capacity variance signals only that managers did not adjust the resource availability level to the amount actually required for the volume and mix of outputs produced that period. It is not helpful, however, to predict spending or expense changes.

Once decisions get made on resource availability levels in the organization, typically in the annual budgeting and authorization process, the expenses of supplying most resources will be determined for the year (unless managers deliberately act to eliminate or add to the resources). For example, the resources committed to the purchase-order processing activity will be determined annually as a function of the expected number and complexity of purchase orders to be processed. We would not expect, however, the size of the purchasing department to fluctuate weekly or monthly depending on how many purchase orders get processed during a week or a month. Therefore, even when usage of a resource drops, the expense associated with that resource continues at its previous level. The difference between the costs of resources supplied and the costs of resources used for producing products equals the cost of unused capacity for the period.(19) The difference should not be interpreted as a change in the cost of performing the activity.

VI. RELEVANCE FOR MANAGERIAL DECISIONS: USING ABC TO INCREASE PROFITS

An improved costing system is a means to an end. The goal is to increase profits, not to obtain more accurate costs. How do activity-based cost systems help companies improve their profitability? We attempt to answer this question through the simple profit equation:

Profits = Revenues - Expenses

PRICING AND PRODUCT MIX

Some companies use their ABC information to reprice their products, services, or customers so that the revenues (resources) received exceed the costs of resources used to produce products for individual customers. For example, prices are lowered to customers ordering standard products in high volumes, and prices are raised to customers ordering highly customized products in low volumes. Pricing strategies are part of a broader set of actions taken by managers to improve profits through changes in product and customer mix. For example, some companies, experiencing declining demand for their standard products, proliferated their product line to offer customized, low-volume varieties. This strategy was influenced by their belief that many costs were 'fixed' and that the lost volume in standard products needed to be replaced with customized products that could "absorb overhead" and even sell at price premiums. With this traditional view, the labor hours, machine hours, and materials purchases could be approximately the same between the old product and the new product mix. But the new product mix included many customized, low volume products that made many more demands on resources performing batch and product-sustaining activities. Because sufficient unused capacity did not exist to perform these activities, the companies had to increase their spending so that more resources could be supplied to perform batch and product-sustaining activities. After the product proliferation had occurred, and the companies were incurring higher expenses for support resources, ABC models revealed that many of the newly-added products were unprofitable.(20)

Once this situation has been discovered, managers have typically first attempted to raise prices on the unprofitable products. If this action does not generate sufficient revenues to cover all their product-specific costs, managers contemplate eliminating unprofitable products. Or they consider outsourcing products to suppliers whose total cost of acquisition is below the cost of resources required to make the product internally. Of course, before outsourcing or dropping products, managers should verify that they can eliminate the resources no longer needed or can replace the lost volume with more profitable business. Thus before any decision is taken from activity-based product or customer costs, managers must assess the incremental revenue and spending consequences.

Critics of ABC have stated:

> Isn't this what we have been teaching (or practicing) as relevant costing or incremental analysis? Students in introductory cost and managerial accounting classes are already taught that costs unaffected by whether a particular product is retained or eliminated are irrelevant for that decision and should be excluded from the analysis. Why do companies need an ABC system? Why not just calculate the changes in spending that would occur for any contemplated decision, such as dropping or outsourcing a product, and make a decision based on that analysis? What purpose is served by building, maintaining, and attempting to interpret a generalized activity-based cost model?

Perhaps one can understand the demand for a generalized (activity-based) resource usage model from a similar situation that arises in physics. Introductory physics courses teach Newton's laws of motion, such as conservation of angular momentum or gravitational attraction. The principles are illustrated with problems that require calculating the interactions among two or three objects. Students who survive to more advanced physics courses encounter a subject called statistical thermodynamics, which provides predictions of the aggregate behaviors of large numbers of particles. A naive student might ask, "Why do we need to study thermodynamics as a separate subject? Don't

Newton's laws of motion still apply to these particles? "The answer is, of course, they do, but to apply Newton's laws to the large numbers of particles being studied would exceed the lifetime and computational power of the universe. Therefore, physicists have devised laws to describe and predict the aggregate behavior of large numbers of interacting particles.

"Relevant costing" or "incremental analysis" situations are illustrated in introductory courses and books by simple examples with two or three products and simple overhead structures. An activity-based resource usage model can be viewed as the thermodynamic equivalent to the three product examples of introductory cost accounting courses. Consider, for example, the analysis that arises in the Bridgeton Industries case.[21] The plant initially produced five product lines. Because of competitive pressures, the plant's profitability had declined. Special studies were performed and eventually two product lines were outsourced. As the case proceeds, students learn that the total spending on resources declined by less than the loss in revenues so that the economics of the plant had deteriorated further. From a "relevant costing" perspective, how many special analyses would have been required to determine which product lines or combinations of product lines should have been dropped. Certainly each product line individually could have been analyzed. But because most resources come in lumpy amounts, perhaps substantial reductions in resource supply (and therefore spending) would occur only if at least two product lines were dropped, as was actually done. But why stop at two? Why not consider dropping all combinations of three, or four, or even all five product lines? In total, 25 or 32 combinations would have to be analyzed, with the relevant costs calculated for each of the 32 possible maintain/drop combinations.

The 32 possibilities may not seem insuperable, but for companies with hundreds and thousands of products, customers, processes, and facilities, the combinations, while still finite, would, as in thermodynamics, exceed the lifetime and computational power of the universe to enumerate much less evaluate And retain versus drop is a relatively simple binary decision. What about shifts in product mix, improvements in production processes, and changes in product designs? Managers cannot possibly apply introductory cost accounting relevant cost calculations to all possible product and customer mix decisions. The activity-based cost model, like the thermodynamics model, provides an aggregate view of the economic laws of motion of a complex enterprise, with thousands of individual products, customers, and facilities.[22]

Borrowing another analogy, integral calculus teaches us that the sum total of doing lots of little things can amount to something substantial. An activity-based resource usage model forecasts the changes in aggregate demands for activities from making decisions on many products, services, and customers. In effect, the activity-based cost model performs the integral calculus function of adding up a lot of small effects into something quite substantial. It approximates the changes in resource demands that will occur from implementing new decisions on pricing, product mix, and customer mix. Before actually implementing the proposed decisions, of course, managers must assess the cash flow consequences by forecasting, as well, the increases and decreases in resource supply (including revenues) that they anticipate will occur. An activity-based cost model serves to direct managers' attention to where more detailed analysis will likely yield the highest payoffs. The ABC model reduces the dimensionality of decisions to where the cash flow consequences from only a few alternatives need to be examined closely.

CHANGE RESOURCE USAGE

In addition to pricing, product and customer mix changes, which affect profits directly through changes in the margins earned between revenues received and resources expended, ABC models can help managers reduce resource usage, while holding revenues constant. When resource usage is reduced, some unused capacity will be created which can then be either managed away (enabling lower spending to occur) or used to process more throughput (enabling more revenues to be earned). Demands on support resources can be reduced by taking two types of actions:

* Reducing the number of times activities are performed, and

* Increasing the efficiency with which activities are performed.(23)

REDUCING NUMBER OF TIMES ACTIVITIES ARE PERFORMED:

Changing from unprofitable to profitable product and customer mixes, as described above, enables companies to earn the same or even higher revenues while performing fewer activities. Managers can take additional actions to reduce the number of times activities are performed, especially activities performed by support resources. Marketing and sales executives in some companies have set minimum order sizes to reduce the large number of activities triggered by many small orders. As engineers improve the design of products, fewer engineering change notices are required. Other change activities are reduced when engineering managers discourage their employees from excessive tinkering with existing product designs, and marketing managers discourage or charge premiums for customer-requested changes in products and delivery schedules. In addition, design engineers, informed about the resource expenses associated with introducing and maintaining a large number of parts in the system, can develop product designs that use fewer and more common parts.(24) All these actions, individually and in combination, reduce the number of demands for activities performed by support resources, while maintaining existing (unit-driven) production volume.

INCREASING EFFICIENCY (LOWERING THE COST) OF ACTIVITIES PERFORMED:(25)

A complementary set of actions can be taken to increase the efficiency of performing activities. The increased efficiency enables the same quantity of activities to be performed with fewer resources. Continuous improvement programs, such as total quality management and cycle time reduction (just-in-time), reduce the resources required to inspect products, changeover and setup machines, and move and store materials. Successful implementation of continuous improvement programs produces major reductions in the demands for resources to perform batch and product-sustaining activities.

Introduction of advanced information technology reduces by substantial amounts the expenses of many batch and product-sustaining activities. Computer-Aided-Design and Engineering(CAD/CAE) equipment reduces the expenses of designing products and making changes to existing products. They also standardize the maintenance of routings and bills-of-materials. Flexible Manufacturing Systems (FMS) and Computer Integrated Manufacturing (CIM) essentially eliminate many batch activities through automatic scheduling, materials movement, inspection, and tool positioning, gauging, and maintenance, plus instantaneous changeovers between operations. In the theoretical limit, a CIM system requires the same resources to make 1 unit of 1,000 different products as it does to make 1,000 units of 1 product.(26) Electronic Data Interchange (EDI) and Electronic Funds Transfer (EFT) link companies with suppliers and customers, greatly reducing the expenses associated with purchasing, scheduling, receiving, shipping, invoicing, and paying for materials and products.

IMPROVING PROFITS

Through a combination of reducing the quantity of activities performed and increasing the efficiency of performing the remaining activities, companies can maintain production throughput and, hence, revenues while reducing their demands for indirect and support resources. Ideally, managers can now obtain additional business, many of whose demands would be handled by resources currently in excess supply. This would enable the company to enjoy substantially higher profits because revenues would increase with only modest spending increases.(27) Alternatively, the unused capacity created can be reduced in the next budgeting cycle.

BUDGETING: CHANGING THE SUPPLY OF RESOURCES TO MATCH RESOURCE DEMANDS

As managers adjust their product and customer mixes, introduce new products, phase out mature products, improve operating processes, and introduce new technology, they change the demands for activities performed by indirect and support resources. The revised demands for resources to perform support activities can be estimated with an activity-based model. Differences etween the demand for and the supply of resources can then be translated into expected changes in future spending on resources. Used in this way, the activity-based model becomes a central tool for management planning and budgeting. The budgets for each resource are determined based on the activities required for the forecasted product volume and mix, and existing production processes. For resources forecasted to be in short supply, the analysis provides a justification for additional spending to increase resource availability. For a resource forecasted to be in excess of predicted demands, managers can be requested to reduce the availability and hence the expenses of that resource. They can reduce the unused capacity by selling or scrapping machinery without replacement, by not replacing employees who retire or leave the organization voluntarily, by redeploying employees from activities where they are no longer needed to activities where capacity shortages exist, or, more drastically, by laying off now redundant employees. These actions enable the company to generate the same revenues with fewer resources, thereby allowing profits to increase.

Alternatively, companies may not exploit the profit opportunities from having created unused capacity. They may keep existing resources in place, even though the demands for the activities performed by the resources have diminished substantially. In this case, and only in this case, will the actions that reduced activity usage not yield any tangible benefits. Profits will remain the same, since revenues have remained constant and the expenses of resources supplied have also remained fixed. But the failure to increase profits is not due to costs being intrinsically "fixed." Rather, the failure is the consequence of managers being unable or unwilling to exploit the unused capacity they have created. The activity-based cost model focuses managers' attention on decisions that affect the resource demands by activities. If the decisions lead to lower demands for some resources, the company can then realize increased profits by either using these resources to generate higher revenues or by reducing spending on these resources. The costs of these resources are only "fixed" if managers cannot or do not exploit the opportunities from the unused capacity they helped to create.

VII. SUMMARY AND CONCLUSIONS

Activity-based cost systems contain two important insights. First, the activities performed by many resources are not demanded in proportion to the total volume of units produced (or sold). The demands arise from the diversity and complexity of the product and customer mix.

Second, activity-based cost systems are not models of how expenses or spending vary in the short-run. ABC systems estimate the costs of resources used to perform activities for various outputs. During any given period, the production of products and services, and their marketing, sale, and delivery to customers, create a demand for organizational activities. The quantity of each activity supplied to outputs is estimated by activity cost drivers such as the number of setup hours, number of purchase orders processed, number of receipts, number of direct labor and machine hours, and number of parts maintained. By summing across the costs of all resources supplied to perform activities for individual outputs, the ABC model estimates the costs of resources used during the period by all the organization's outputs.

Activity-based systems model how activity usage varies with the demands made for these activities. If activity usage exceeds the quantity available from existing resource supply, then higher spending to increase the supply of resources will likely soon occur. If, however, activity usage is below available supply, spending or the expenses of resources will not decrease automatically. Management, to obtain higher profits, must take conscious actions either to use the available capacity to support a higher volume of business (i.e., by increasing revenues) or to reduce spending on resources by eliminating the unused capacity. Costs and profits are fixed only if management takes no action, and leaves the unused capacity undisturbed. Management behavior, not cost behavior, determines whether reductions in resource demands become translated into higher profits.

APPENDIX
Separate Systems For Measuring Resource Expenses And Resource Usage: A Case Study

The Union Pacific case study illustrates well how a service organization developed a system for measuring the costs of resource usage quite different from the system used for operational and expense control.(28) During the 1960s, the company had developed an extensive system for monitoring spending and expenses in its more than 5,000 cost centers around the country. Cost centers included freight and locomotive repair yards, switching yards, transportation crews, and maintenance of track and right of way. Expenses were recorded in up to 1,200 different account codes.(29) Each month, a cost center manager received a report on actual and budgeted expenses for each of these accounts, supplemented with data on Year-to-Date actual expenses compared with budget and with a similar period in the previous year. The 5,000 individual cost center expense control reports were aggregated into summary data for higher level managers all the way to senior vice-presidents in Omaha who received a one page summary of operations under their control. This extensive system of monthly reports was used to monitor and control cost center expenses and measure efficiency improvements.

In the deregulated environment of the 1980s, the company realized that despite extensive reporting of cost center expenses, it had no information to estimate the costs of resources used to move a carload of freight from one point to another. This gap occurred for two reasons. The railroad environment provides a vivid example of where almost complete separation exists between resource spending and resource usage. The monthly spending to maintain track and right of way and to repair locomotives and freight cars has no relation to the amount of traffic run that month. The monthly spending reflects the millions of gross ton miles hauled in many preceding months, and management's decision to replenish the supply of these resources so that they will be available for the future. The cost of using those resources occurred in the past; the spending to revitalize the depleted resources was occurring today.

Even apart from the temporal separation between resource usage and resource spending, the railroad like many other service organizations did not measure the use of resources by individual products within each cost center. For example, the railroad supplied switching yards and measured the expenses of operating switching yards. But it did not measure the quantity of use of switching yards by individual freight cars as they moved from shipper to customer.

The railroad had to develop entirely new analytic systems to measure the costs of activities performed to supply its customers with products and services. The costs of resources used to move a carload of freight from shipper to destination could not be estimated based on incremental spending since virtually no incremental spending occurred when the company picked up a freight car from a shipper, scheduled it, connected it to a train, switched it to several different trains, and finally delivered it to the customer. Yet available. And the actual running of the freight car placed incremental demands on several resources that would require additional spending sometime in the future. The company understood that it could not wait until the freight car, locomotive, or track was repaired to send out bills to all the shippers that made use of these resources in the past. It also understood that the amounts spent to supply train crews, scheduling and information systems, and switching yards were justified by the expected volume and mix of traffic to be carried. The company developed a system that estimated, move by move, the quantity and cost of all the resources used by individual carload moves, even though short-run spending was almost completely independent of these moves.

The railroad example provides a vivid example of the difference between resource usage and resource spending (or resource expenses). The power of the case, however, extends beyond railroads or even service companies since most manufacturing companies' resources are also now characterized by large distinctions between the use of the resources and the amount of current expenses to supply the resources.

1 Early versions of the transactional demand for resources appeared in J.Miller and T. Vollman, "The Hidden Factory," Harvard Business Review (September-October 1985), 142-150, and Robin Cooper and Robert S. Kaplan, "How Cost Accounting Systematically Distorts Product Costs," Management Accounting (April 1988), pp. 20-27. A more comprehensive explanation of the impact of diversity and complexity on indirect costs was presented in the series of Journal of Cost Management articles by Robin Cooper, "The Rise of Activity-Based Cost Systems: Parts I-IV" (Summer 1988, Fall 1988, Winter 1989, and Spring 1989).

2 See, for example, Robert S. Kaplan, "John Deere Component Works (A) and (B), HBS Cases # 9-187-107 and -108; Robin Cooper and Karen H. Wruck, "Siemens: Electric Motor Works (A)," HBS Case # 9-189-089.

3 We will use the term "outputs" to refer generically to products, services, customers, projects, facilities or any object that creates a demand for or benefits from organizational activities. Activity-based cost systems as-sign the organization's operating expenses to outputs based on the activities performed for these outputs.

4 We have adopted the terminology of unused capacity, as suggested by Alan Vercio of Texas Instruments, rather than our initial term of "excess capacity." Not all "unused" capacity represents "excess" capacity.

5 This cost includes the costs of fringe benefits. secretarial and administrative support, equipment costs, and space charges associated with each purchasing department employee.

6 Note that this calculation does not use actual activity levels during the period; the denominator represents service capacity not actual usage of this capacity.

7 Later in the paper, we will show how to develop a new format for the periodic income or expense statement that highlights the costs of resources used and unused.

8 More accurately, the spending on (or expenses assigned to) these resources will be independent of the volume and mix of outputs produced during the period.

9 Charles T. Horngren and George Foster, Cost Accounting: A Managerial Emphasis, Seventh Edition (Prentice-Hall, 1991), pages 258 and 265.

10 More complex traditional systems that use multiple allocation bases within the same cost center will have multiple volume variances, but each allocation base is still unit-level, driven by the volume of output.

11 The hierarchy of factory expenses was introduced in Robin Cooper, "Cost Classification in Unit-Based and Activity-Based Manufacturing Cost Systems" (Fall 1990), pp. 4-13, and discussed further in Robin Cooper and Robert S. Kaplan, "Profit Priorities from Activity-Based Costing," Harvard Business Review (May-June 1991), pp. 130-137.

12 Of course, the commitment fee associated with a line of credit is a counterexample, because the cost of supplying the resource (the right to borrow) is incurred whether the resource is used or not.

13 We are using the word "expense" in its traditional accounting sense; e.g., an outflow or other using up of assets or incurrence of liabilities (or a combination of both) during a period from delivering or producing goods, rendering services, or carrying out other activities that constitute an enterprise's ongoing major or central operations (W. W. Cooper and Yuji Ijiri, Kohler's Dictionary for Accountants, Sixth Edition (Prentice-Hall: Englewood Cliffs, NJ, 1983; pp. 203-204). To avoid confusion associated with financial accounting inventory valuation procedures that shift some period expenses forward in time to be matched against future revenues generated, we will assume, for purposes of this paper and without loss of generality, that units produced always equal units sold. This enables all period expenses to be recognized as expenses in the period they are incurred.

14 The actual expenses of providing this capability in a given period can even exceed the cash outlays in that period. This situation arises when cash payments made in much later periods, such as for vacations, pensions and other post-employment benefits, are attributed to the supply of the resource during the given period.

16 This distinction between the financial system required for performance measurement (reporting on actual period expenses) and the activity-based system reporting on the costs of resource usage underlay the arguments in R. S. Kaplan, "One Cost System Isn't Enough," Harvard Business Review (January-February 1988). A good example of a company that separated its monthly reporting system from the system used to estimate the cost and profitability of its products is provided by the Union Pacific case study described in the Appendix.

17 Quote taken from Robert S. Kaplan, "Analog Devices: The Half-Life System," HBS # 9-190-061.

18 Robin Cooper and Kiran Verma, "Hewlett Packard: Queensferry Telecommunications Division," HBS Case # 9-191-067.

19 During a period when usage exceeds normal capacity, the difference will represent a "favorable" over-utilization of capacity.

20 Unprofitable products are those for which the expenses assigned to maintain, produce, and deliver them exceed the net revenues received from their sale.

21 Robin Cooper, "Bridgeton Industries: Automotive Component and Fabrication Plant," HBS Case # 9-190-085.

22 And even the thermodynamic extension is now known to be an approximation that ignores relativistic and quantum mechanical phenomena. Similarly, the activity-based resource usage model, as currently formulated, is likely just a first order, linear approximation to what may require stochastic, nonlinear formulations in certain situations.

23 These actions are iterative, not sequential, as managers continually adjust the volume and mix of their outputs, and manage the efficiency with which their activities are performed.

24 These design activities were the focus of the ABC systems described in the Tektronix and Hewlett Packard cases: Robin Cooper and Peter Turney, "Tektronix (A)," HBS Case # 9-188-143; and "Hewlett-Packard Roseville Networks Division," HBS Case # 9-189-117.

25 Using activity-based information to focus improvement activities was discussed in H. Thomas Johnson, "Activity-Based Information: A Blueprint for World-Class Management Accounting," Management Accounting (June 1988), pp. 23-30. Using an activity-based cost system for performance improvement was a central focus in the system described in Robert S. Kaplan, "Maxwell Appliance Controls," HBS Case # 9-192-058.

26 In effect, CIM transforms batch and product-sustaining activities into unit-level activities so that product variety costs approach zero.

27 Spending will increase for resources for which availability and usage are tightly coupled (e.g., materials, energy), and for resources where unused capacity does not exist (perhaps direct labor or machine time). Also, it would be preferable for the added volume to generate revenues excess of the expenses of resources used so that the new business can be sustained in the long run.

28 Robert S. Kaplan, "Union Pacific: Introduction, (A), and (B)," HBS Cases 9-186-176, -177, -178.

29 The larger number of account codes arose from regulatory reporting requirements specified by the Interstate Commerce Commission for Railform A.

Robin Cooper is a Professor at the Claremont Graduate School and Robert S. Kaplan is a Professor at the Harvard Business School.

Cooper, Robin and Kaplan, Robert S., "Activity Based Systems," *Accounting Horizons*, September 1992, pp. 1-13. Reprinted with permission from Accounting Horizons and the author, Copyright 1992.

Do Financial and Nonfinancial Performance Measures Have to Agree?

The key to this question is knowing when agreement matters.

BY C.J. MCNAIR, CMA, RICHARD L. LYNCH, AND KELVIN F. CROSS

Certificate of Merit, 1989-90

In reviewing an operational manager's proposal for a new nonfinancial measurement system, a vice president of finance asked, "What happens when these nonfinancial measures look good but the company's financial measures disagree?" The operating manager quipped, "My resume will look great and yours won't."

The issue is no laughing matter. The conflict causes tension, clouds action, and often polarizes factions within companies. Unfortunately, much time is wasted trying to reconcile the different messages, and focus on continuous improvement gets sidetracked.

New manufacturing methods, such as just-in-time manufacturing, have exposed the informational and motivational shortcomings of traditional accounting systems. Feedback in the form of standard cost variances has been counterproductive. Other financial reports, such as profit and loss statements, budgets, and margin analyses, have been too aggregated, too late, and too one dimensional to be useful to operating managers. Managers need clear, timely, and relevant signals from their internal information systems to understand root causes of problems, to initiate corrective actions, and to support decisions at all levels of the organization.

Faced with an information gap, many companies, such as Caterpillar, Wang Laboratories, and Analog Devices, are creating new performance measurement systems that address customer satisfaction, flexibility, and productivity.[1] For the most part, these systems are being designed outside the world of management accounting. Frustrated with the limitations of traditional accounting measures, operating managers are designing separate measurement systems as part of strategic planning or quality improvement efforts. One school of thought says that's all that is needed: simply disconnect the financial accounting information systems from the operational.[2] We don't think that this is the answer. Most senior managers we know won't take this leap of faith. They continue to watch both the financial and nonfinancial scorecards. After all, they're held accountable for both.

SYMPTOMS OF TENSION

Signs of tension are common. Consider the following workplace scenarios:

- An operating manager in a computer company implements a just-in-time work cell and witnesses a dramatic improvement in quality, cycle time, and work-in-process inventory—but gets whacked over the head with a stack of financial reports telling him that he has large volume variances, underabsorbed costs, and poor productivity.
- A general manager at a high-tech facility sees significant, steady improvement in yields but is puzzled that the results haven't surfaced on the company's financial scorecard.
- Line supervisors learn to serve two masters. In the first two months of the quarter they're driven by their delivery, quality, and cycle-time

goals. But in the last few weeks of the quarter they're asked to pull in big orders to make revenue targets and absorb more costs into inventory, ruining their performance against nonfinancial measures.
- A seasoned line manager asks to be taken off the distribution list for the plant's financial reporting package because he considers it totally useless and would rather rely on his instincts.
- In allocating scarce resources a division controller hears "trust me" from the operating manager. The manager tells him that there is a cause-and-effect relationship between the proposal and the financials, but both are unsure of the linkage.

A specific case study will clarify the cause of this tension. Although everyone involved is trying to do what's best for the company, they're looking at different decisions, with different time spans, even though they are using the same basic information. The result is foreseeable: confusion, tension, and disagreement on what actions to take.

CHANGING THE PERFORMANCE YARDSTICK

Until 1985, company "A" operated under a batch production philosophy, utilizing a full absorption, standard cost system.[3] Artificial buffers were set up on the plant floor (i.e., work-in-process inventory), but the accounts used to track them were hiding problems and promoting local optimization. The result was a disjointed production process with irregular delivery performance, high levels of waste, and no organizational learning/feedback on the realities of the production process. The accounting system modeled the complexity and confusion on the plant floor. The systems were matched; they were equally inadequate for supporting competitive manufacturing.

In 1985, the company adopted just-in-time (JIT) practices in its manufacturing operations. Early JIT cells were treated as an experiment, giving management the flexibility to suspend the usual set of performance measurements in measuring the cell's progress. Removed from confusing and often conflicting responsibility for variances beyond their control, the managers set about achieving the objective of JIT: continuous improvement in terms of reduced defects, decreased throughput time (e.g., increased responsiveness), and inventory reductions.

JIT-based successes on the plant floor were striking: Work-in-process inventory decreased 85%, while throughput time went from 20 days to under three. When measured in the traditional manner, however, the successes were recorded as failures in the accounting reports. Why? Because the

The successes are recorded as failures in the accounting reports.

traditional labor efficiency and utilization measures did not match the characteristics of the new process. In a JIT cell, resources are activated only when needed (i.e., balancing the line), and direct labor begins performing both direct and indirect tasks, two events that penalize the JIT cell in terms of low utilization and poor productivity. If the accounting measures were interpreted correctly, management would see that they now had idle capacity in the cell that could be used for further production. If sales were to pick up, then unit costs would go down.

SHORTCOMINGS OF STANDARD COST SYSTEMS

Standard costing system measures were deficient in three important ways. First, labor efficiency was measured crudely—total output per person; second, quality levels were not considered in the analysis; and third, management's use of the "absorption"-based variances from the accounting system encouraged the production of more output than was needed. Overproduction was encouraged rather than identified as waste of the highest level.

JIT was calling for production of the right number of units, when they were needed, and with no tolerance for waste or defects. The standard costing system, however, ignored these changes, thereby building all types of waste (e.g., scrap, rework) *directly into* the benchmarks used to evaluate the system.

The primary themes of JIT are "continuous improvement" and the "elimination of waste." In a standard cost environment, these characteristics mean that in each and every operating cycle there should be a positive variance in the cell, as performance improves (i.e., actual cost per unit decreases as volume grows). Over time, the variance grows. The variance reporting system, though, is designed to provide a warning signal when such patterns occur. It signals "problem" when in fact problems (such as poor quality) are being eliminated.

Operating results should be used to update the standards. Instead, variances are fed into the accounting system; they are used to balance the ledger—no more, no less. Translation: The standard costing system used in most U.S. companies today is a *broken control loop*. Feedback concerning improvements is disregarded, allowing the system to move totally out of sync with reality.

Standard cost-based reporting systems are static; standards are not updated every period. To overcome this obstacle, the real issue companies must first decide is—who owns the performance measure? If it is not manufacturing, and part of continuous improvement, then the critical linkage between performance and evaluation is broken. Some companies are responding to this problem by replacing engineered standards with rolling averages of historical actual costs, using the theoretical optimum as the long-range performance target. Dynamic standards for dynamic systems.

TIME TO QUIT FLOGGING A DEAD HORSE

Recognizing the problems that would occur if the JIT cells were evaluated on the existing measures, company A's vice president of manufacturing assigned the task of developing a new measurement system to two senior managers, one from industrial engineering and one from finance. The basic assumptions underlying the development of the new performance measurement system are presented in the right-hand column of Table 1.

The new system was to be focused on strategic issues, which translated to a "customer" orientation. First and foremost was the requirement that the new measures had to make sense to the marketplace customer. Second, cross-functional activities were mapped out as a single business sys-

TABLE 1/TRADITIONAL VS STRATEGIC MEASUREMENT SYSTEMS

- **Financial focus**
  - Financially driven (past focus)
  - Limited flexibility; one system serves both external and internal needs
  - Not linked to operations strategy
  - Used to adjust financials
- **Locally optimized**
  - Decrease costs
  - Vertical reporting
- **Fragmented**
  - Cost, output, and quality viewed in isolation
  - Trade-offs unknown
- **Individual Learning**
  - Individual incentives

- **Strategic focus**
  - Customer-driven (future focus)
  - Flexible; dedicated system for operational control
  - Tracks concurrent strategies
  - Catalyst for process improvements
- **Systematically optimized**
  - Improve performance
  - Horizontal reporting
- **Integrated**
  - Quality, delivery, time, and cost evaluated simultaneously
  - Trade-offs addressed
- **Organization Learning**
  - Group incentives

tem. Performance of the entire business system replaced the focus on local optimums. Third, at each stage in the internal process a supplier and customer were identified. Quality and delivery measures were installed where the two functions met. Finally, cycle time and waste measures also were tracked to make sure customer needs were being met efficiently.

In keeping with JIT characteristics, a "pull" rather than "push" mentality was used to shape the new measures. The objective was to change the orientation of the system from tracking incurred costs (i.e., cost control) to supporting the drive for process improvements (i.e., strategic cost information). As part of this effort, accounting was transformed from a nonvalue-adding, or scorekeeping, function to a value-adding one that provided strategic information to management.

The second key element of the approach was the clear recognition of interdependence in the manufacturing process. A customer order puts a demand on final assembly, which pulls the various subassemblies needed for the final product. The subassembly department, in turn, pulls materials required through material services. The order fulfillment business system could perform only as well as its weakest component.

BUILDING A STRATEGIC INFORMATION SYSTEM

The performance pyramid depicted in Figure 1 represents the structural framework for this new measurement system. It's based on concepts of total quality management, industrial engineering, and activity accounting. The pyramid provides the structure for a two-way communication system that is required to institute the strategic vision in the organization. Objectives are translated down, and measures are translated up. The objectives start from the corporate vision (a statement about what markets the company will compete in and on what basis—price, quality, or delivery). These objectives then are translated into more specific market and financial goals and objectives at the business unit level, such as market share, revenue, and profit goals. Strategies are set, and financial forecasts and budgets are put in place to make them happen.

Success at the business operating system level (i.e., order fulfillment or new product introduction) means supporting the business strategy through tangible operating objectives that apply to cross-functional activities. Translating the business unit goals into measures useful at the operating level is a critical step. In order for the company to achieve its strategic and financial goals, it must focus on making sure that daily activities support these goals.

The performance pyramid in Figure 1 incorporates three factors at the business operating system level: customer satisfaction, flexibility, and productivity. Customer satisfaction is defined as meeting customer expectations. Flexibility refers to the responsiveness of the business operating system as a whole. Productivity refers to how activities and resources are managed in meeting customer satisfaction objectives. These three criteria in turn are supported by four focused areas of performance measurement in the individual departments and work centers: quality, delivery, cycle time, and waste:

At the local department level, specific day-to-day measures capture the feedback information that supports continuous improvement. The first set of measures is tied directly to the marketplace customer. Quality and delivery are externally driven. Quality means more than conformance to specifications; it means meeting cus-

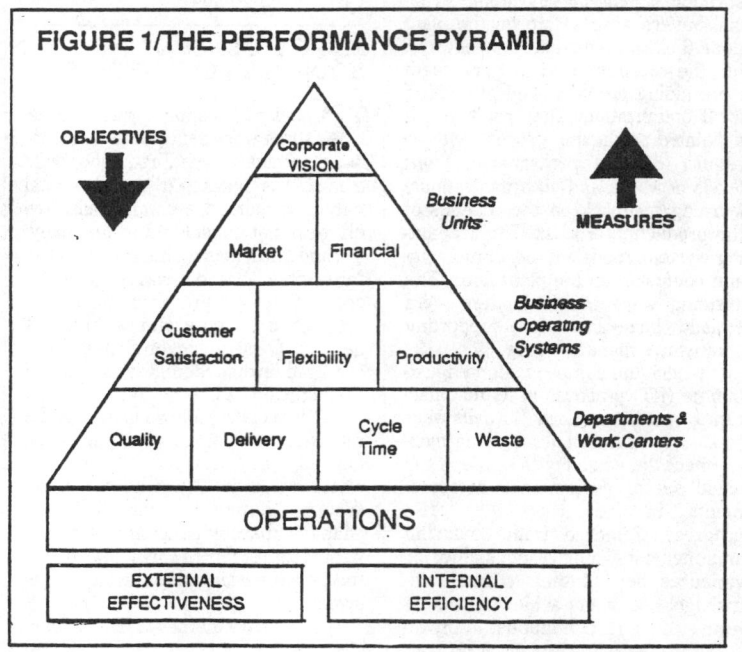

FIGURE 1/THE PERFORMANCE PYRAMID

tomer expectations. Delivery covers both quantity and timeliness—the delivery of the right amount of product on time.

Internal measures (cycle time and waste) do not have a direct tie to the customer's expectations but can be thought of as the "internal levers" that must be moved in order to provide quicker response time and better value for the customer. They are also of strategic importance. Decreasing waste (e.g., nonvalue-added activities or resources) and total cycle time from order release to finished goods shipment translates to improved productivity and flexibility for the plant itself.[4] Increasing the velocity of material through the plant, the result of improvements on these measures, also translates to improved financial performance when sales increase. Asset turns accelerate—the company gets more use out of each dollar of investment in its asset base.

Here's how the system works. A semiconductor company adopts a vision: to provide high-quality solutions for customer needs in real-world signal processing. After the company has made significant improvements in customer service measures, its focus shifts to productivity, that is, satisfying customer requirements more efficiently than the competition. At the business unit level, goals are set to increase yields. Each department supports that objective through specific measures aimed at improving quality and reducing cycle time, thereby eliminating waste.

In this example, the measurements are part of a consistent, focused, and integrated system. It channels efforts that support the achievement of corporate goals by translating upper management objectives into precise performance measurements for individual departments or work centers. The system described here implicitly incorporates the accounting system. The next step is to tie the performance pyramid directly to defined accounting structures: to close the control loop. Otherwise, managers could receive mixed signals on their performance, and tension will persist, as suggested in Table 2.

MAKING MANAGEMENT ACCOUNTING MORE USEFUL

Management accountants should be participating in the information revolution. One obvious role is to periodically audit the nonfinancial metrics. Another role is to help op-

TABLE 2/THE TENSION ZONE

	Yield	# of Lots Released	Accounting Story	Operational Impact Inventory	Operational Impact Scrap	Accounting Verdict
The Tension Zone	1. 30%	Many	Variations normal, costs absorbed	High	High	OK
	2. 50%	Many	Favorable variances	High	Lower	OK
	3. 50%	Fewer	Overhead underabsorbed, efficiency variance	Low	Low	Bad
4.	50%	Fewer	Standard changed, no pressure to overproduce	Low	Low	OK

erating managers quantify nonfinancial information as needed in support of improvement activities. More important, management accountants should be providing strategic cost information. Here are some ways to do it.

Suggestion No. 1: Provide the Right Information at the Right Time. Accountants need to understand that the information they provide is part of the management control system. Control systems direct behavior, evaluate performance against preset goals, and provide information for adjusting the goals themselves through the feedback process. In current accounting-based performance measurement systems, this loop usually is not completed. Rather than updating goals (i.e., standards), variances are merely bled off to the general ledger. The underlying assumption, of course, is that the standards are right and that reality is wrong. As noted above, this assumption is at odds with the goals of JIT manufacturing.

Figure 2 illustrates a series of performance loops embedded in the measurement system. Essentially, the base of the pyramid is a plan-do-check-act circle (loop 1). *Nonfinancial measures* such as on-time delivery, quality, cycle time, and waste (e.g., number of accidents, percent rework, and scrap)

FIGURE 2/THE PERFORMANCE LOOPS

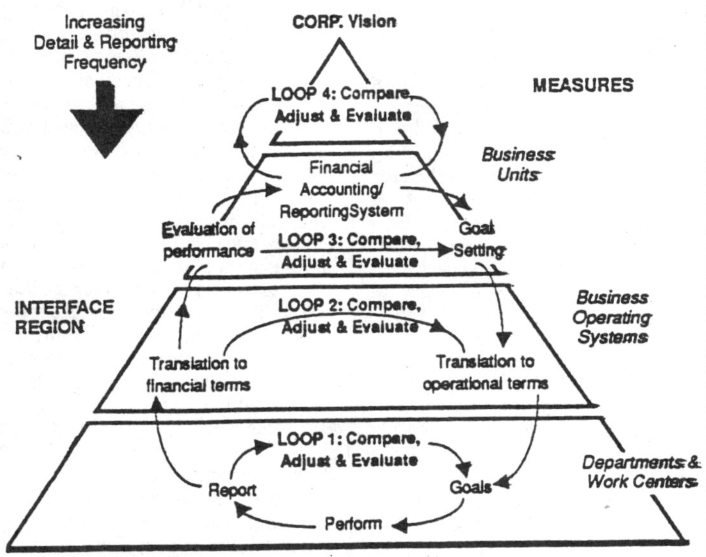

provide a complete control loop, whether for an individual operation or the whole department. Targets are set (e.g., reducing waste or cycle time, improving quality), action takes place, and results are chartered. Process adjustments are made, based on the results, to keep the system on track. These measures are timely, stated in the language of operations, and close to the point of action. That means feedback can be used to adjust current activities accurately—the definition of a complete control loop.

The business operating system level (see loop 2) actually consists of a double set of controls: operating and financial. The former is used to evaluate how departments work together in meeting business system objectives. As far as the end-customer is concerned, the business performed only as well as the quality, delivery, and performance of the last department in the business system. Financial reporting completes the control loop used at this level, translating the operating data into summary cost data for top management.

For example, as improvements in cycle time are made at the department level, this information is passed up to the business system in the second performance loop; overall cycle time in the business unit is reported as an aggregate measure. Adjustments are made to inventory to satisfy external financial reporting needs, and the information is fed back into the goal-setting process in loop 1 (i.e., the goals are set more aggressively).[5] Another example of how operating data are linked to the accounting system can be seen in the way costs are handled. At the department level, nonvalue-added costs or waste are captured. These indicators typically are stated in terms of percent or numbers. At the plant level, the finance department can add value by translating waste items into dollars for upper management (e.g., cost of rework, late delivery penalties, rescheduling penalties, and inspection costs). This conversion need not be perfect. A Pareto analysis of the waste dollars will help operations to focus on the significant cost improvement activities.

The feedback in loop 2 is not as timely as in loop 1. The time span of decision making at this level is longer.[6] Most plants are evaluated on monthly or quarterly performance. Managers at the business operating level need only enough feedback to know when a problem exists that is going to affect total period performance so that they can put appropriate programs in place to improve performance.

While forewarned is forearmed, there is no way that the same level of intense feedback can be available at this level. Nor should it be. The focus of decision making—the relationships that managers at this level can affect—is mid-range. Not by the minute but by the week or month. New resources, improvement activities, or major production shifts cannot be implemented at a moment's notice. In fact, if the integrity of management tools such as the master production schedule are to be maintained, these responses must be constrained by the existing "frozen" time fence.

Management accountants should be participating in the information revolution.

Moving up the pyramid, the level of detail decreases markedly, as do the definition and realities of the timeliness and frequency of reporting cycles. For example, the performance of the major business systems such as new product introduction or order fulfillment is passed up to the business unit level to evaluate how well strategies have been executed (loop 3). The operating measures (and exceptions) provide a signal that financial and marketing objectives may not be reached. The financial control loop verifies this after the fact. Here nonfinancial data are recorded, for example, as market share or product quality ratings, and financial performance of the business unit is reflected in the unit's profit and loss numbers and return on assets. Again, the financial results are translated back into operational imperatives at the business system level. For example, if asset turn objectives for the business unit were not met, new programs are developed, or emphasis is added to the cycle time measures in the business system to help improve the financial metric.

In this loop, the financial and nonfinancial measures may not agree. This may seem somewhat paradoxical, but quality improvements, better delivery, and faster cycle time may not translate immediately into improved profits. Why not? There are several reasons. First, and most obvious, has to do with volume and mix changes. Second, if the competition has been making similar or better improvements, the yardsticks have been moved. The nonfinancial improvements were needed just to stay in the game. Management accountants can add value to this analysis by conducting benchmarking studies.

Third, the operational improvements may be benefiting a future financial period. For example, yield improvements may increase a plant's effective capacity, postponing the need for additional space and equipment. Similarly, cycle time improvements may reduce the size of the required workforce. However, the company's policy may be to redeploy workers or to fund excess capacity until the volume in future periods picks up. Fourth, quality and delivery improvement could have resulted in market share gains that were made inefficiently. For example, quality was inspected in and delivery objectives were met by carrying everything in inventory.

The final feedback loop (loop 4) provides feedback on the corporate vision itself. Top management receives information over time on how effectively strategies have been executed and resources deployed. Total corporate performance is compared to expectations. Markets and competitive tactics are evaluated and adjusted as necessary.

In summary, the information system can support whatever type of reporting upper management wants. The detail is there, ready to be passed up through the reporting hierarchy on demand. Each level has its own tightly defined control loop as well as the means to obtain information from lower levels through the integrated system. Management accounting plays a key role in translating the nonfinancial data into the language of money for senior management.

FROM SCOREKEEPER TO COACH

Suggestion No. 2: Switch from Scorekeeper to Coach. In the goal-setting process, financial goals need to be translated into operating terms, a procedure that requires strategic cost information. After the fact, the general ledger needs to be brought into line with operating realities. This is the world of cost control. It requires a different view and a change in emphasis from "relevance" to "balance."

"Strategic cost information" has one overriding objective: providing relevant, timely information to support decision making. It builds from prior results, serving as a database of trended results. The translation of financial accounting data into good management data is the world of *activity accounting*. This term captures the essence of the tie between costs and the activities that cause those costs. For each pool of activity-based costs, a number of causal factors, known as drivers, can be identified. These drivers are the cause of downstream costs. They also are the basis for developing the operating control system.

If you think about activity accounting, it is a financial measure divided by an operational one. It is the metric that provides the linkage between the financial budget and operating plans. By understanding activity costs managers can: focus improvement on specific problems; make better business decisions about make, buy, and pricing; and, more important, prevent waste from occurring in the first place by analyzing bills of activity for new products before costs are committed in volume production.

Suggestion No. 3: Focus on What Counts the Most. Three types of waste costs (nonvalue-added activities) can be identified: defect detection, internal failure, and external failure. The existing general ledger structure of most companies can provide information about costs incurred for each of these types. In terms of detection, account codes for incoming inspection personnel and test equipment, in-process inspection, reliability testing, and so on, can be grouped together. Dividing this total by the number of units produced in the same period provides a benchmark of the cost of detection. Based on the analysis of historical trends, then the operating system is given goals to reduce the underlying activities that generated the costs.

In this setting, accounting adds value by focusing management attention on what needs to be done. As Dr. J.M. Juran says in several of his books, one must pay attention to the vital few, not the trivial many. Accounting-based precision and balance are not important. For practical reasons the calculations will consist of approximations and assumptions, but the output (i.e., Pareto analysis) will be relevant to the decisions at hand. The accountant's primary task is to re-pool existing account structures to match a new set of cost objectives.

It also is important to remember that this information does not have to be recreated every day. In fact, the information is necessary only when plans are being made or the operating system signals that existing cost estimates are out of line.

DOING WHAT'S BEST

Suggestion No. 4: Know When to Play Second Fiddle. Most accountants, when facing these new concepts, become alarmed. Accounting is a simple science built on the balance of the sources and uses of funds. There is no "just about right" in the system: it either balances or it doesn't. Accounts have to be balanced, but general ledger maintenance is a back-office task that should not pervade the organization. Overemphasizing this task would be like stopping the check processing in a bank every time an incorrect date appeared on a check.

The challenge for today's accountant is how to maintain the equity of debits and credits without unduly distorting the reporting system. Some say just to ignore the problem. But if top-level reports are built off accounting data, the treatment of the balancing issue is critical to ensuring that top management gets consistent signals about performance in the plant. If balance is constantly forced in, distortions may occur whenever actual results don't match estimates (as with volume variances). As any practicing manager knows, this is more the rule than the exception.

Two types of problems can occur in matching estimates to actuals: output variances and cost shifts. Output variances mean that the actual mix or volume of sales may not match expectations, a situation that can be due to changes in the market, errors in forecasts, or process problems. By year-end, though, most of these problems work their way out of the system. Output variances are, in a global sense, *compensating* (i.e., offsetting). A compensating variance is a "mean regressing" phenomenon — over the operating period the estimate and the actual performance should be closely aligned.

In contrast, cost shifts cannot be controlled, nor is there any reason to believe they will reverse. Cost shifts, then, are *noncompensating* variances (i.e., they're not expected to wash out). In the noncompensating case, the mean has shifted. For example, products will always cost more if material or labor prices have risen. Similarly, if quality improvement efforts result in permanent yield enhancements, then the cost standards need to be updated.

Once these two events have been separated, the appropriate accounting treatment emerges. For the noncompensating variances, the traditional accounting approach of writing the costs off to the appropriate inventory and expense accounts on a monthly basis makes sense. Is there a need to signal the variance back to top management? Yes. Should it be done through accounting reports or through the operating reports? It would seem operating managers know before accounting does. The accountant, though, is the one charged with maintaining the integrity of the standards used to give credit to production for good units completed. The data, then, should be used to adjust the cost standards more frequently. The feedback loop on non-compensating variances is short.

What about compensating or offsetting variances? If they are passed immediately through to the ledger and up to management, attention is focused on the past. The company may break the budget forecast into monthly buckets, but in reality seldom will orders arrive in the same mix, volume, and period as the plan suggested. This simple fact of life is the source of immense friction between production and marketing.

While JIT can solve a lot of the problems on the plant floor, if the accounting system perpetuates the tension through monthly volume and mix variances, total performance improvements will be stunted. A yearly adjustment, though, serves the underlying responsibility structure of an organization. For example, top management is charged for "idle capacity" through the reconciliation entry. This is feedback to upper management and marketing on the quality of their strategic plan and forecast, not monthly feedback to line managers.

Efficiency variances really make no sense in a JIT setting because the primary concern is with good output per cell, not per worker. If the cell does not produce its needed output, the operating system is sending messages up the reporting hierarchy long before accounting gets involved. Cost is caused by the activities in the cells. Accounting's job is to make sure that any unrecoverable cost variances are passed through immediately to inventory and that recoverable ones do not interfere with the integrity of the operating system.

The accounting treatment of the compensating variances is straightforward. Just as "buffers," or contra accounts, are used to store reserves for bad debts and related events, an inventory contra account can be developed to hold output variances. The final performance for the year is the important factor, so monthly reconciliation just doesn't make sense. According to GAAP and the 1986 Tax Recovery Act, these costs eventually must be put into inventory, but the requirements of the law can be handled through an end-of-period adjustment. It is an accounting technicality that should *not* be passed on to management.

It is the actual output measures concerning quality and delivery to the downstream customer that are important. All the information, compared with planned output, is readily visible to top management. The accounting variance does not add information to the analysis—it takes it away. Forcing balances to compensating variance accounts is nonvalue-adding activity of the worst kind because it trickles through the organization, promoting improper decisions and discord between functional units. Should compensating variances be fed back immediately into the standard cost system? No. Should they be used to provide strategic cost information in the next planning period? Definitely. Their value lies in letting management know what effect volume and mix variances have on annual performance. The time span of the reporting process is matched to the decision-making cycle.

A LOOK TO THE FUTURE

In answer to the question raised in the title, the simple answer is "it depends." When permanent changes have occurred in capacity, methods, or costs, then all systems should be synchronized. If, instead, the differences reflect volume-based effects or changes that will smooth out over the long run, there's little value in forcing them into balance. At this point accountants need to understand that their numbers have an impact on behavior—if the numbers are wrong in the short run, don't report them.

Our suggestions can benefit operating managers by:

- Providing strategic cost information on products and resource allocation decisions.
- Quantifying productivity improvement proposals.
- Suppressing meaningless variances.
- Getting management accountants to focus on the vital few.
- Modifying the accounting system to bring it in line with operational realities.
- Mitigating the potential for mixed signals.
- Helping accountants and operations agree on what constitutes continuous improvement.

Interpreting the financial and nonfinancial signals of the business and responding to them, even when they disagree, is a management issue, not an accounting issue. As part of the management team, management accountants can be an invaluable source of information. They can help operating managers focus on the right activities for continuous improvement and provide feedback on how well those activities were managed. ■

Carol J. McNair, Ph.D., CMA, is assistant professor of accounting at Babson College, Wellesley, Mass. Her major research efforts have focused on the impact of technology on the management accounting system as well as the effects these accounting systems have on behavior in organizations. She is a member of the Providence Chapter, through which this article was submitted.
Richard L. Lynch is a manager of quality and productivity improvement at Analog Devices in Wilmington, Mass. He is a member of the Merrimac Valley Chapter.
Kelvin F. Cross is a vice president with Gray, Judson and Howard, Cambridge, Mass. Lynch and Cross are co-authors of Measure Up! Yardsticks for Continuous Improvement, *Basil Blackwell, Inc., Cambridge, Mass., 1990.*

---

[1] Examples include Lou Jones, "Competitive Cost Analysis at Caterpillar," MANAGEMENT ACCOUNTING®, October 1988; K. Cross and R. Lynch, "Accounting for Competitive Performance," *Journal of Cost Management for the Manufacturing Industry*, Spring 1989; and Ray Stata, "Organizational Learning—The Key to Management Innovation," *Sloan Management Review*, Spring 1989.
[2] J. Robb Dixon, Alfred J. Nanni, and Thomas E. Vollmann, *The New Performance Challenge: Measuring Operations for World-Class Competition*, Dow-Jones Irwin, Homewood, Illinois, 1990.
[3] The basic information used in this section was first published in "Wang Scores EPIC Success," by K. Cross, *Industrial Engineering*, January 1988, and K. Cross and R. Lynch, "The SMART Way to Define and Sustain Success," *National Productivity Review*, Winter 1988/1989.
[4] If total cycle time per order decreases, the effective capacity of the plant is increased. This is one of the hidden benefits of JIT.
[5] Leading-edge firms are not eliminating standard costing. They are changing the definition of "standard." Expenses are debited to the cell, and credit is given for good units at standard costs. However, standards are based on historical performance, not engineered standards.
[6] John Deardon coined this term in 1968. The basic concept is that the frequency of feedback information should match the characteristics of decision making at the various levels of the organization. If decisions are made weekly, then weekly feedback is necessary. More frequent reporting is a waste of resources.
[7] A good source for understanding the cost of quality is *Measuring, Planning, and Controlling Quality Costs*, Wayne Morse et al., National Association of Accountants, Montvale, N.J., 1987.

Is this article of interest to you? If so, circle appropriate number on Reader Service Card. Yes 76 No 77

The New Service Class

The once lowly sector creates plenty of good-paying jobs, but workers with few skills are still left behind

By JOHN GREENWALD

IT SOUNDS AT FIRST LIKE ANOTHER cruel tale from the world of corporate layoffs. Young IBM personnel specialist, 36, loses his job last July in cutbacks at the troubled computer giant. In dismay over leaving IBM—the company where both his parents spent their careers—young man plunges into the harsh job market. But there the miraculous happens: after a flurry of interviews, he is hired by Electronic Payment Services, a start-up Delaware company that processes credit-card transactions, for substantially more than his old salary. "I never knew how marketable I was," says Peter Dychkewich, the hero of this story. "But then I floated my résumé, and the job I have now came up rather quickly."

His good fortune reflects the astonishing strength and diversity of U.S. service industries, which account for 70% of the country's economic activity. Even as manufacturers such as IBM and General Motors shed workers by the tens of thousands, service providers from banking to health care are taking on new employees. Just last week the Labor Department reported that service companies created 153,000 new jobs in October. That dwarfed the 40,000 positions that manufacturers added and helped reduce the unemployment rate to 5.8%—the lowest in four years.

Not only does hiring by service firms represent nearly 90% of the 2.7 million jobs that the U.S. economy has produced this year, but many bear little resemblance to the low-paying gas-pumping and fast food-making positions that the word "services" has often brought to mind. Indeed, nearly half the new service jobs have gone to people with managerial, professional or technical skills, which has helped raise the average income of all service workers to close to the level of their manufacturing brethren.

Mark Strassman, the president of Don Richards Associates, a Washington-based firm that places middle managers and consultants in jobs, offers a useful illustration of the more elaborate ways in which the service sector has accommodated refugees from other parts of the economy: "There are so many complex choices in the mutual-fund world that you need an investment counselor," he says. "Computers change quickly, so you have to hire consultants. Law firms need more attorneys and the Arthur Andersens and KMPG Peat Marwicks are adding more accountants."

Of course, the growing demand for professionals tends to mask the fact that millions of service workers remain stuck in jobs like waiter or sales clerk that pay little more than the $4.25-an-hour minimum wage. "All you have to do is hire two Goldman Sachs partners and you probably distort the average wage scale throughout the service sector," quips Bruce Greenwald, a management professor at the Columbia Business School.

Put more precisely, work throughout the $6 trillion U.S. economy is skewing more sharply than ever along educational lines. "We're getting the good jobs and the bad jobs, but the middle jobs we're losing," says David Wyss, an economist at the DRI/McGraw Hill consulting firm. "Take something like health care. It pays great if you're a doctor or a nurse, but in both cases you need a special degree. Without one, there aren't any good wage jobs in that sector. Those who aren't well educated are still flipping hamburgers at McDonald's or working as janitors."

While that may be grim news for many, the demand for skills provides great flexibility for managers and professionals who suddenly find themselves out of work in manufacturing industries. And even though many of the displaced may be less fortunate than Dychkewich, having to take pay cuts in their new positions, experts say they still stand to be handsomely rewarded by service-industry standards.

For manufacturing workers with less adaptable skills, the wage gap between industries is still daunting. Two years ago, the Pequot Indians opened their now-packed Foxwoods casino in Ledyard, Connecticut. So profitable have such gambling dens become that the Pequots could afford to staff the casino with 9,000 craps dealers, bartenders and other workers. But fully 56% of the nearly 1,300 employees who arrived after losing their jobs at local defense contractors like Electric Boat had to take pay cuts of at least $2,500 a year, according to Donald Peppard, a Connecticut College economist. One welder-turned-security guard was making $23,000 less than he had been earning. The workers who came from service jobs fared considerably better. Peppard found most earning at least $2,500 more than in their old positions.

The irony, of course, is that the layoffs that have bedeviled workers like those at Electric Boat are now providing job opportunities in service industries. Four years ago, accountant Greg Smith, 36, lost his $55,000-a-year position as an audit manager for a food-service firm that trimmed its payroll. After a succession of part-time work and other jobs, Smith joined the consulting firm Grossberg Co. in Maryland last summer as an auditor who sniffs out financial fraud for clients who have pared back their own accounting departments. Today Smith figures that between his salary and his cut of hourly billings, he has nearly doubled his old income. Because of downsizing, he says, "a lot of companies eliminated internal controls and positions, and that's worked in my favor because now these companies have to come to me."

Greenwald, John, "The New Service Class," *Time*, November 14, 1994, pp. 72-74. Reprinted with permission from *Time*, November 14, 1994, Copyright 1994.

The temporary-work sector is mirroring a growing sophistication in the upper ranks of the service economy. No longer solely providers of secretaries and clerical workers, these agencies now routinely send out doctors, lawyers, scientists and senior executives. As a result, the wage levels of temporary workers have been steadily climbing.

Such changes show up sharply at agencies like On Assignment in Calabasas, California, which places chemists, biologists and other scientists in temporary jobs. Thanks partly to layoffs at pharmaceutical companies, revenues at On Assignment have grown from $7 million in 1989 to an estimated $48 million this year. On any given day the company has 1,400 scientists working in jobs around the country for hourly wages of up to $35. (Pharmaceutical firms seem to thrive on outsiders. In New York City last week, an agency called the Cantor Concern swiftly filled a drug company's order for a specialist to help the firm decide whether to keep its in-house printing facilities. The pay rate: $2,000 a day.)

Meanwhile, the service sector itself is constantly generating new jobs. Realizing that personal computers were changing the way people work and play, Bob Zyontz and Larry Trink quit comfortable jobs in advertising agencies in 1986 to try to cash in on the new technology. Today their New Jersey-based firm, Princeton Direct, has $6 million in revenues and 14 employees engaged in the business of putting multimedia catalogs and other marketing material on diskettes and CD-ROMs. To keep up with the workload, Zyontz and Trink two years ago brought in computer expert and psychologist Jeff Friedman as a third partner.

Other new firms are helping to repair crack-ups in the financial industry. Tim Scala and Ken Jingozian left banking jobs last year to become self-styled derivatives investigators—experts who advise clients on how to cope with the risks of those securities. Their timing was uncanny: soon after Scala and Jingozian created their New York City–based firm, Treasury Resources Consulting and Investigations, the Federal Reserve raised interest rates and sent the value of many derivatives plunging. Their phone has hardly stopped ringing. Says Jingozian: "The entire derivatives market has taken a quantum leap in complexity and sophistication. As a result, the ability of senior management and the back office to understand it has become more difficult."

As financial services have become more complex, companies have created new jobs requiring new skills. Fidelity Investments, the mutual-fund giant with more than $200 billion under management, has been opening as many as four new investment centers a year and bringing in about 100 people to staff them. Many are recent college graduates. The newcomers learn to field virtually any question about Fidelity products and can double salaries that start at about $20,000 within four years.

Retailers too are hunting for skilled sales personnel to explain sophisticated products. Home Depot is increasingly turning to design-school graduates to work in its new line of Expo stores, which will cater to customers building new houses. The company has already hired armies of carpenters, electricians and other craftsmen to take the angst out of shopping as the do-it-yourself chain has expanded to more than 300 outlets. Home Depot went farther afield to hire Larry Wells, 43, who lost his $60,000-a-year job as an Eastern Airlines pilot when that carrier went out of business in 1991. A do-it-yourself remodeler, Wells started as a floor salesperson in Atlanta for less than a third of his pilot's salary and has since become a district installation manager. Of his current salary he will only say that it is "certainly reasonable."

Some of the growth in service jobs has helped narrow the pay gap between men and women. While women made 34% less than men in median weekly earnings in 1983, the differential closed to 25% last year. That's partly because expanding fields such as health care and education have added numerous nurses, teachers and librarians—jobs that are still mostly held by women.

In fact, the real divide in the U.S. economy is no longer between services and manufacturing, or even between men and women. The real split separates those with the education to get good jobs from those who lack it. Professor Michael van Biema, who has studied these trends at the Columbia Business School, predicts that in fields such as banking and finance "you will see many of the lower-end service jobs disappearing and being replaced by technologies." That's the bad news for some. The good news is that the same technologies will help wounded IBMers with management and professional skills make their way back up the pay scale. —*Reported by Bernard Baumohl and Jane Van Tassel/New York, Sophfronia Scott Gregory/Atlanta and Suneel Ratan/Washington*

JOB GROWTH
Annual employment in millions

In 1983 wages for business services lagged behind manufacturing 17%

WAGE GAP
Average hourly earnings in seasonally adjusted dollars

Last year this wage gap narrowed to 8%

*Includes hotel employees, accountants, lawyers, and educators, but not salespeople.
Source: DRI/McGraw-Hill TIME Graphic by Steve Hart

COMPETITIVENESS: DOES IT MATTER?

A lot for companies—but hardly at all for countries, argues a top U.S. economist in a new book. Raising *domestic* productivity, not capturing global markets, is what lifts living standards.

by Paul Krugman

Almost nobody—in business or government—would disagree with this statement: "Today America is part of a truly global economy. To maintain our standard of living, we must learn to compete in an ever tougher world marketplace. That's why high productivity and product quality have become essential. We need to move the economy into high-value sectors that will generate jobs for the future. And the only way we can be competitive is if we forge a new partnership between government and business."

The problem is: It's baloney. In reality, there is almost nothing to our fixation with national competitiveness, or its central idea—that every country is like a giant corporation slugging it out against rivals in global markets. The U.S. and Japan are simply not competitors in the same way that, say, Ford competes with Toyota. Any country's standard of living depends almost entirely on its own domestic economic performance, and not on how it performs *relative* to other countries. That's not just my view; it's what most economists think.

Why should you care? One important reason: Countries that wrongly think they are in a competitive struggle over who gets the spoils are more likely to fall into a major trade war. Such conflicts don't destroy economies the way real wars do, but they harm everyone—and it takes a long time to recover from them. When protectionist measures like the infamous Smoot-Hawley tariff shattered the global trading system between the two world wars, trade among industrial countries didn't regain its 1914 peak until 1970.

The other risk is that true believers in competitiveness—I call them strategic traders, to point up their obsession with winning export battles—often advocate pouring huge sums of taxpayer money into projects they hope will create jobs or build prestige but that make almost no economic sense. Example: the billions of dollars France has spent propping up its computer industry. Leading American strategic traders—among them, Labor Secretary Robert Reich, Clinton health policy adviser Ira Magaziner, and MIT economist Lester Thurow—have argued for similarly extravagant (and misguided) investments to enhance national competitiveness.

To understand why the doctrine of strategic trade drives economists into a fury, go back to that imaginary quotation. It was carefully constructed to illustrate six fundamental misconceptions. Let's do the numbers.

♦ **"Part of a truly global economy."** Strategic trade rhetoric implies both that the typical U.S. business or worker is now producing for global markets and that the extent of globalization is historically unprecedented. Neither is true.

In 1992, exports were 10.6% of U.S. GDP, imports were 11.1%. This was substantially more than the 4% on both sides of the ledger in 1960. Surprisingly, however, the numbers haven't changed much since 1980: The big increase in the importance of international trade to the U.S. economy took place in the 1970s, not the '80s. Even so, the numbers remain modest.

Now remember the strategic traders' favorite analogy: that a country is merely a corporation writ large. As we've just seen, the theoretical corporation called America Inc., even after globalization, sells almost 90% of its output to its own workers and shareholders. How many companies do anything close to that? None. Clearly countries are not at all like corporations.

One might argue that while most U.S. output is still sold to ourselves, a much larger proportion is sold in domestic markets that are newly subject to international competition, such as automobiles or computers. This is, however, only a little bit true. More than 70% of U.S. output consists of services rather than goods, and most services are effectively insulated from international competition because they are hard to transport. Collectively, services account for only about 20% of U.S. trade.

Nor is the degree of U.S. dependence on world trade without precedent—or even unusual. Most historians of the international economy date the emergence of a truly global economy to the Forties—the 1840s, when railroads and steamships reduced transport costs to the point where large-scale shipments of bulk commodities became possible. International trade quickly surged. By the mid-19th century, the leading economy of the day, Great Britain, was exporting more than a third of its GDP—three times as much as U.S. exports today. Britain eventually invested about 40% of its savings overseas every year. An era of mostly open borders was marked by international migration that dwarfs anything recent. (Where was your great-grandmother born?)

Why does this matter? Strategic traders reject conventional economic wisdom on the grounds that it is no longer relevant in a global economy—but even classical economic theory, developed mostly by English economists in the 19th century, applied to an economy that was far more dependent on international trade and investment than the U.S. is today. So what looks like wisdom to the unwary looks like ignorance and shoddy thinking to anyone who knows some economic history.

♦ **"Competing in the world marketplace."** Again, strategic traders hold that countries compete with each other in the same way that Nike competes with Reebok; they attribute the long stagnation of middle-class living standards in the U.S. to a failure to do this effectively.

What's wrong with their thinking? At a conceptual level, the most basic point about international trade is that it is not a zero-sum game. Companies like Nike and Reebok are almost purely rivals: Only a tiny fraction of Nike's sales are to Reebok workers, and vice versa. So one's success tends to be at the other's expense. But the major industrial countries, while they sell products that compete with each other, are also each other's main export markets and main suppliers of useful imports. If anything, a successful European or Japanese economy helps the U.S. by providing us with larger markets.

Moreover, the purpose of international trade—the reason it is useful—is to import, not to export. That is, what a country really gains from trade is the ability to import things it wants. Exports are not an objective in and of themselves; the need to export is a burden that a country must bear because its import suppliers are crass enough to demand payment.

But isn't it a fact that the stagnation of U.S. living standards has been in large part due to a failure to compete effectively on world markets? No, it's not a fact. From 1979 to 1989 the real compensation of all U.S. workers rose 5.8%, while productivity rose 5.1%. These are purely domestic variables—that is, productivity is not measured relative to other countries, and no data about global market shares or anything that involves the global economy are taken into account. Yet the two series rose by almost exactly the same (disappointing) amount. So we got almost exactly the growth in living standards we would have gotten if the U.S. were alone in the world and we had no international trade at all.

♦ **"High productivity."** Just about everyone now agrees that the U.S. economy needs higher productivity. Most people, however, are confused about why. The most popular explanation is that we need to be productive in order to compete in the global economy. That was the explanation President Clinton gave in February 1993, when he tried to justify an economic package that included painful tax increases. But it's wrong. We need to be more productive in order to produce more, and this would be true even if the U.S. were completely without foreign competitors or customers.

To illustrate, let's consider three questions. First, what happens to a country whose productivity is inferior to that of the countries it trades with? The common view is that it will suffer. After all, if you aren't better than your rivals in *something*, how can you sell anything on world markets? The right answer is that being less productive than your trading partners poses no special problems. Of course, a country whose productivity is low across the board is not going to have a high standard of living; but that has nothing to do with the fact that it must coexist with more productive nations. In fact, the option of exporting to those superior "competitors" the things you don't make too badly, and importing from them the things you do, delivers a somewhat higher living standard than a country with very low domestic productivity might otherwise enjoy. This is the basic point David Ricardo made in 1817 when he first expounded the principle of comparative advantage—a principle that every student learns in Economics 101 and that most politicians persist in ignoring.

Second question: What happens to a country whose productivity growth lags behind that of its rivals? The common view is that it is in big trouble—after all, a corporation that systematically fails to match competitors' productivity gains is not going to stay in business. The right answer is that how fast productivity is growing abroad, and whether we're ahead of or behind the pack, is irrelevant.

From World War II until 1973, productivity in the U.S. rose 2.8% annually. After 1973, it rose only 0.9% annually, a rate generally slower than in other advanced nations. If the rest of the world did not exist, this slowdown would have reduced growth in U.S. incomes by 1.9% per year. Any effects from lagging behind foreign competitors contributed at most another 0.1 percentage point. The moral: What matters for the trend in U.S. living standards is our domestic rate of productivity growth—*period*.

Third question: Which is more important, productivity growth in industries that must compete with foreigners, or productivity growth in sectors that produce for sheltered domestic markets? Most people would answer that productivity growth among companies that compete internationally is more important. The right answer, again, is that what matters for the U.S. standard of living is the overall productivity of American workers. It doesn't matter whether they are competing with foreigners or producing only for the domestic market. This has one major result that runs counter to much conventional wisdom: Service productivity matters more than manufacturing productivity. To be exact, since about 70% of the value added in the U.S. economy is in services, vs. 20% in manufacturing (with the remainder in agriculture, construction, and mining), a percentage point gain in service productivity is worth 3 1/2 times as much as an equal gain in manufacturing.

♦ **"High-value-added sectors."** Strategic traders claim the best way to improve living standards is to encourage investment in sophisticated industries like computers and aerospace, which provide high value added per worker. Wrong again. Why is value added per worker in some businesses higher than in others? It isn't enough to assume they are just better businesses. If they were, capital and labor would flood into them, competing those high returns away. (Markets may be imperfect, but they aren't stupid or sluggish.) In fact, the usual reason value added per worker is high in some industries is that other inputs, such as capital or skill, are high there as well. Since the economy has limited supplies of capital and skill, encouraging industries that use those scarce resources intensively may well lower instead of raise per capita income.

What is most striking, however, is that advocates of "high value" industries, like Robert Reich and Lester Thurow, apparently haven't bothered to check which industries actually *do* have high value per worker. As the table on this page reveals, it turns out that the real high-value industries in the U.S. are extremely capital-intensive sectors like cigarettes and oil refining. High-tech sectors that everyone imagines are the keys to the future, like aircraft and electronics, are only average in their value added per worker.

♦ **"Jobs."** Many strategic traders blame America's failures in international competition for the loss of "good jobs" in manufacturing, with the unfortunate workers forced either into unemployment or into much lower-paying service jobs. The image of the former steelworker now earning minimum wage flipping hamburgers is deeply embedded in popular perceptions.

In fact, the U.S. economy has been the great job engine of the advanced world, with a 38% increase in employment from 1973 to 1990, compared with 19% in Japan and only 8% in Europe. Now it is true that real wages have stagnated. But is this because workers have been forced out of good manufacturing jobs into low-paying service jobs? No, for two reasons. First, manufacturing jobs are not all that well paid (the hourly wage in manufacturing is only 10% higher than in other jobs). The stagnation in real wages was not because good jobs in manufacturing were lost, but because real wages for *all* jobs that didn't require a college education stagnated or fell, as technological change reduced demand for less skilled workers. And second, the widespread belief that the U.S. has lost its manufacturing base in the face of foreign competition is simply wrong.

Deindustrialization and the "hollowing out" of the economy never happened. True, the share of manufacturing in U.S. value added and employment has been falling for many years. But this trend is common to all industrial countries. In fact, manufacturing's share of the economies of Germany and Japan has declined as fast as or faster than that in the U.S. Nor is there any mystery about the trend. Essentially, it is driven by the combination of relatively fast productivity growth in manufacturing and limited demand for manufactured goods. The general public prefers to spend most of the annual increase in its income on services. The result: Demand can be satisfied by a static or even falling number of factory workers.

The story should sound familiar: It's exactly what happened to agriculture 50 years earlier. Very few Americans live on the farm, not because our farmers are uncompetitive, but because they are so productive we don't need many of them. And America's "deagriculturalization" has proceeded in spite of consistent trade surpluses in farm products.

What appears to make the manufacturing story different is that since 1980 the U.S. has consistently run trade deficits in manufacturing, and there is no question that some industries, such as shoes and apparel, have shrunk under the impact of import competition. But is this mainly because of a failure to be competitive in manufacturing?

The answer is an overwhelming no. In 1992 the U.S. trade deficit in manufactured goods was $62 billion. Now, remember that much of a dollar of "manufactured" exports indirectly represents services such as health care purchased by the manufacturer. (GM's largest supplier is not a steel company but Blue Cross/Blue Shield.) Input-output studies of the U.S. economy give us a pretty good estimate of the hidden service component of manufactures trade: Only 60% of a dollar of manufactures sales represents manufacturing value added. Thus, we should scale down the merchandise deficit by 40% to estimate the impact of trade on the industrial base. This suggests that, at most, competitive problems in U.S. manufacturing, as measured by our trade balance, reduced value added in these industries by 60% of $62 billion, or $37 billion, in 1992.

That may sound like a big number, but keep in mind that even a supposedly "deindustrialized" America in 1992 still had a value added in manufacturing of more than $1.1 trillion. We have just suggested that in the absence of a trade deficit that number might have been about $37 billion larger; that's a difference of only 3.3%.

♦ **"A new partnership."** This is, of course, the bottom line. Unfortunately, as we've just seen, a government-business partnership guided by the tenets of strategic trade would almost certainly lead to bad policies, since it would be founded on excruciatingly bad economics—as bad, in its own way, as the extreme supply-side doctrine popularized by a different set of policy entrepreneurs during Reagan's presidency.

My advice is to consider a proper understanding of the real relationship between productivity and competitiveness as a kind of test of the reliability of supposed experts, in and out of government. The issues involved are not hard to sort out—we're not talking quantum mechanics here. So if you hear someone say something along the lines of "America needs higher productivity so that it can compete in today's global economy," never mind who he is, or how plausible he sounds. He might as well be wearing a flashing neon sign that reads I DON'T KNOW WHAT I'M TALKING ABOUT.

Adapted from PEDDLING PROSPERITY: Economic Sense and Nonsense in the Age of Diminished Expectations by Paul Krugman, with the permission of W.W. Norton &Company, Inc. Copyright (c) 1994 by Paul Krugman.

NEW U.S. FACTORY JOBS AREN'T IN THE FACTORY

by Stephen Baker and James B. Treece

An hour's drive east from Pittsburgh in the hills of Westmoreland County, Pa., stands a symbol of America's manufacturing renaissance. In 1988, the sprawling former auto assembly plant was abandoned, a Rust Belt relic, its workers scattered to other jobs or the unemployment rolls. Then two years ago, Sony Corp. arrived. Today, Westmoreland is one of the world's most advanced electronics plants, churning out thousands of big-screen television sets. And this is no border-style *maquiladora*, with Americans merely snapping together Japanese-made parts. Fully 80% of the components are U.S. made.

Why does Sony make televisions in Pennsylvania? The U.S. is the world's largest TV market by far, especially for big-screen versions, and the closer Sony gets to its customers, the less it has to spend on shipping.

Moreover, the U.S. has a strong industrial infrastructure—wide roads, clean water, educated workers, and plenty of suppliers—and a superb technical base. Drawing on resources at nearby Carnegie-Mellon University helped Sony engineers build a robot that automatically fine-tunes the televisions before shipping.

Sony's plant is part of a fundamental shift in manufacturing—one that will leave the U.S. well positioned for global competition in the coming decades. Taking advantage of great economies of scale, manufacturers long built huge mass-production plants, then shipped their products to distant markets. But today, the trend is toward smaller, more flexible, less labor-intensive operations near the customers.

That's as true for steel and autos as it is for TV sets. Built close to their industrial customers, the low-cost U.S. minimills run by Nucor Corp., Birmingham Steel Corp., and others are among the world's most efficient steel plants. In autos, U.S. production this year will surpass Japan's for the first time since 1979, thanks in part to more than a million Hondas, Nissans, and Toyotas pouring out of factories in Ohio, Tennessee, and Kentucky.

And it's not just currency swings and local-content concerns that lure manufacturers to the U.S. In no other market in the world do American, Asian, and European manufacturers compete so directly and freely. "If you are successful in the U.S., you are proving that you are a global player," says Helmut Werner, chairman of Mercedes-Benz. The company is setting up an assembly plant in Alabama.

♦ **Manuals in German.** Don't expect the manufacturing renaissance in the U.S. to spark a boom in factory jobs, however. Just as the mechanization of agriculture a century ago all but emptied the farms, the new factory model means fewer workers are needed to put the final product together. The number of U.S. workers employed in manufacturing has fallen by 3.2 million since the peak of 21 million in 1979. Yet manufacturing output has remained stable as a percentage of gross national product. "We did not see any trends toward lower manufacturing activity," says economist Gordan Richards of the National Association of Manufacturers.

Yet as these factory jobs vanish, a new manufacturing-driven economic sector will emerge—industries such as computer software, robot making, and countless services that will add jobs to supply the leaner manufacturers. At Carnegie Group Inc. in Pittsburgh, technicians are putting together software to guide Ford Motor Co.'s engineers through circuit board design. And they devise programs that translate Caterpillar Inc.'s mountains of technical manuals into German, Russian, and other languages.

Carnegie Group is expanding from 125 to 200 workers this year alone. Says Chief Executive Dennis Yablonsky: "It's a wide universe of technology companies that service manufacturing. The jobs add up pretty quickly."

These support industries, with their high component of knowledge skills, constitute nothing less than a second tier of the manufacturing industries. "A smaller percentage of our workforce will be in production," comments Carnegie-Mellon University professor Richard L. Florida. "But a much larger percentage will be supporting that."

These U.S. systems analysts, robot makers, and software engineers will increasingly be selling their wares around the globe. Indeed, 20 years after the much-ballyhooed deindustrialization of America, the U.S. keeps discovering new ways to make things.

Reprinted from November 18, 1994 issue of Business Week by special permission, copyright (c) 1994 McGraw-Hill, Inc.

CUSTOM-MADE, DIRECT FROM THE PLANT

The newest manufacturing combines state-of-the-art fabrication and product-delivery technologies with the old-world artisan's aim to please

by Otis Port

It is 2010, and you need a new suit—fast—for an overseas business trip. No problem. You head to the department store at the mall. You step into a kiosk-like contraption, and an optical scanner automatically measures your body. Seconds after you record your choice of style and fabric, the information is relayed to a plant where lasers cut the cloth precisely to your size. A few days later, the suit is ready.

You may not have to wait 15 years for this kind of high-tech couture. Manufacturing is fast entering a new age of industrial excellence: mass customization. Not only clothes, but a huge variety of goods, from autos to computers, will be manufactured to match each customer's taste, specifications, and budget. Mass customization will mark the culmination and synthesis of agile manufacturing, virtual companies, and total quality management. If ever the term "paradigm shift" was appropriate, "this is it," says Roger N. Nagel, deputy director of Lehigh University's Iacocca Institute, the Bethlehem (Pa.) think tank where the notion of agile manufacturing was born three years ago.

Customized products will be made as fast and as cheaply as mass-produced products. "But factories won't sell things—they'll sell customer gratification," says Nagel. The price of products will be determined not by adding up the costs of all the parts in a finished product, but by the value of the knowhow and services that a company musters to assure utmost customer satisfaction. Once customers realize that agile suppliers can provide exactly what's needed on a tight schedule and eliminate the costs of maintaining inventories of parts, "price is no longer a factor," says David L. Ross, marketing director at Ross Operating Valve Co., a private 350-employee maker of pneumatic valves in Troy, Mich. "It is literally the last thing discussed."

This isn't just fantasy. More than 200 companies have joined the Agile Manufacturing Enterprise Forum, which Nagel co-founded. AMEF members include such heavyweights as Air Products & Chemicals, Chrysler, FMC, Honeywell, Milliken, Texas Instruments, and Westinghouse. This past summer, the National Science Foundation and the Pentagon's Advanced Research Projects Agency helped set up three agile manufacturing research institutes: at the University of Illinois, the University of Texas, and Rensselaer Polytechnic Institute. And the apparel industry's research consortium, the Textile/Clothing Technology Corp. in Cary, N.C., is leading the development of the optical-scanning "tailor" described above.

Agile manufacturing might do more for U.S. employment than the post-industrial work that was supposed to supplant manufacturing. Some of the production work that went offshore in the 1980s has been returning in the 1990s. One reason: Companies striving to become agile are forced to slash cycle time—the period between receiving an order and delivering the goods—and they often discover that moving products through an international pipeline eats up more time than the labor savings are worth. Items that have come back to agile wannabes range from some of Caterpillar Inc.'s huge earthmoving equipment, for a while made in Korea, to computer modems from U.S. Robotics Inc., which used to outsource the production of components in Mexico.

♦ **Valves by Phone.** Nobody expects blue-collar jobs to hold the line, much less grow. Building on the pioneering work of Allen-Bradley Co. and others, tomorrow's factories will be smaller, with fewer but smarter machine tools that need only token human care—yet they'll turn out a far richer variety of goods. So, shop-floor employment is heading the way of farm labor. However, agile technology is also spawning new white-collar jobs in support industries, just as modern agriculture has created myriad jobs in package design, food engineering, marketing, and other services.

However, such growth is taxing agile companies. Take Ross Operating Valve. "I cannot train people quick enough to take care of all the potential new business," says Ross. At the Ross/Flex plant in Lavonia, Ga., customers phone to discuss what valves they need with company engineers called "integrators." The specs are entered into a CAD/CAM system to design a one-of-a-kind valve, and automated machine tools grind out the metal parts overnight. Finished valves are delivered in as little as 72 hours, at a typical cost of $3,000. That's about one-hundredth the time and one-tenth the cost of traditional methods.

Richard K. Dove, a consultant on agile manufacturing in Oakland, Calif., believes this new method may be the ticket to surpassing the Japanese. He sees a future where the U.S. exploits its lead in information technologies. "The Japanese miracle was based on the exquisite refinement of manufacturing," notes Steven L. Goldman, a Lehigh professor of humanities who is an expert in the history of technology. "But agility moves the center of value away from manufacturing itself. What counts now is the software, the knowledge—and that expertise is outside Japan."

♦ **Roving Robots.** The goal is to link customers, suppliers, and manufacturers into a kind of superefficient confederation. What a factory produces today will be driven by yesterday's retail sales—or an order received moments ago from an on-line partner. By 2000, says Carl P. McCormick, president of electronics maker Group Technologies Corp., many factories will be tightly interlinked via nationwide networks such as the Enterprise Integration Network. EINet is being developed by Microelectronics & Computer Technology Corp. (MCC), a consortium of high-tech companies in Austin. Networked manufacturers will be able to dump their orders directly into their suppliers' factory computers, and these will in turn relay the suppliers' needs to their own suppliers.

Ultimately, the communications web may extend the connection down to individual machines on the shop floor. Already, researchers at Massachusetts Institute of Technology and Purdue University are jointly developing software for smart machine tools.

Under the MIT-Purdue scheme, mobile robots would carry parts around the factory. When a robot rolled onto the floor, it would broadcast to the machine tools what work its part requires. The affected machine tools would then consult their production schedules to determine when they could be available, and the computers would collectively calculate which combination of machines would most efficiently polish off the necessary work.

Computers negotiating production schedules with other computers, taking care of routine business transactions without human intervention, and even programming each other: This agile world will take some getting used to. And it's coming faster than anyone expected. "Fundamental transformations of the terms of commerce have always been measured in decades," says Lehigh's Goldman. "In 1991, I figured it would take 15 years for agile manufacturing to become common practice. But now, I think it will be the norm within five years."

Reprinted from November 18, 1994 issue of Business Week by special permission, copyright (c) 1994 McGraw-Hill, Inc.

Ten Mistakes CEOs Make About Quality

THE WINNERS OF THE MALCOLM BALDRIGE National Quality Award and other firms noted for excellent quality programs think differently about quality than most firms. A professor of management science and students at the University of Chicago interviewed executives at a number of firms that have excellent quality programs. These interviews revealed 10 mistakes that many corporate executive officers (CEOs) make that might prevent their companies from developing excellent quality programs.

Mistake 1: Failing to lead

When CEOs strive to be leaders and to inspire their employees to excel, many adopt an approach that almost always fails. They recall movie scenes in which great leaders give powerful and highly motivating speeches, such as Knute Rockne inspiring his football team or Gen. George Patton spurring his troops to success. Leadership to these CEOs becomes management by exhortation and inspiration. Speeches, high goals, slogans, and campaigns are supposed to motivate employees and propel the organization toward competitive victory.

This misguided Hollywood style of leadership almost always fails. Jack Stack, CEO of Springfield Remanufacturing, which remanufactures engines in Springfield, MO, recalls when he took over a division and gave a powerful speech designed to rouse and inspire the workers.[1] At the end of the speech, he asked if there were any questions, and one worker in the back yelled out, "How old are you, anyhow?" The workers had often been exhorted with motivational speeches and campaigns, slogans, and goals. They were cynical because of repeated failures and knew from experience that little real change would occur.

Although speeches and exhortations might produce a brief flurry of activity, soon people go back to the same management, systems, and procedures as before. Repeatedly, CEOs make speeches, set goals, wage a big campaign, and then wonder why this leadership produces little lasting change.

Movies, in an effort to create a dramatic effect, confuse the issue. Prior to their speeches, Rockne and Patton thoroughly planned, organized, equipped, trained, and prepared their men. That was the main substance of their leadership and created the success. The motivational speech was the final encouragement and, perhaps, was not even necessary.

Good leadership must produce results, which means that the actual work done in the offices or factory must change. Exhortations rarely accomplish that. Change requires a new infrastructure in which the organization's steps, procedures, and techniques are improved. This requires new systems, planning, incentives, and training. Improvement in the way work is done is what quality systems accomplish and is the substance of real leadership.

Mistake 2: Thinking that planning devolves from financial or marketing goals

Planning, in many organizations, starts with top management setting goals for financial growth (profit, earnings per share, and return on investment) and market growth (sales). These overall financial and sales goals then get broken down into specific goals and budgets for each department or area.

What is often neglected in these goals, however, is the customer, who makes the purchase and pays the bills. Planning should start with the customer, and the centerpiece of planning should be customer satisfaction. This is true of the Baldrige Award winners. Westinghouse Commercial Nuclear Fuels Division, for example, has quality goals that directly relate to customer satisfaction issues. The senior management level has eight goals, which are divided into subgoals in lower levels of the organization. Even the individual worker or work team has goals that relate to the overall customer satisfaction goals. Each month, Xerox Business Systems sends out 40,000 surveys to its customers and to people who bought from the competitors, and the data from these surveys strongly influence corporate goals. Motorola has overarching goals for improving quality and cycle time, which are directly derived from customer satisfaction issues. All of the Baldrige Award winners examined, such as Globe Metallurgical, IBM Rochester, and Federal Express, have systems to ensure that customer satisfaction drives their goals.

Peterson Products, a metal stamping firm near Chicago, IL, was about to launch a marketing campaign to elevate sales. Instead, it decided to improve on-time delivery to the customer. When the percentage of on-time delivery went up, the salespeople were ecstatic because for the first time they could promise delivery. Sales rose 25% because the customers were getting what they wanted, and Peterson was able to drop the plan for the marketing campaign.

Another example is Cooper Tire in Findlay, OH. Building a reputation as a reliable supplier with modern plants, it aimed its marketing directly at the customers. It has doubled its market share and enjoys a profit growth rate of 22% per year. According to the *New York Times*, it is the envy of giants like Goodyear, Bridgestone, and Michelin.[2]

In most firms, planning is a vertical process that is driven from the top down or from the bottom up. Planning should be a horizontal process, however, starting from the customer and working inward. Financial goals are also necessary, but the customer should drive the goal-setting process, and every department and functional group should have goals that positively affect customer satisfaction. As Bob LaBant, IBM vice president, said, "My goal is to make our customers successful. If I had one measure, it would be their success."

Mistake 3: Believing that being close to the customer and planning for customer satisfaction is sufficient

The top executives at many companies believe that their firms have a strong customer focus. They might have oriented their planning systems to better satisfy the customer. They might also maintain complaint hotlines, have extensive warranties, and conduct customer satisfaction surveys. These techniques, while helpful, still do not constitute a total customer focus because customer satisfaction is not something that concerns only some parts of the firm. Each and every group in the firm should have goals and incentives that are tied into enhancing customer satisfaction. This requires a carefully conceived management system that involves all parts of the firm in improving customer satisfaction.

Why is this done so infrequently? Perhaps the most pervasive reason is that many companies lack a systematic approach to customer satisfaction. The executives believe that a system isn't needed and that they already understand the customers and know what they want. Almost always, however, that belief is false. Motorola, for example, is well aware of this fact and requires its executives to visit its customers' firms. The executives are required to speak not just to the firms' executives, but also to the workers who actually use the Motorola product. Experience has shown that almost everyone has distorted ideas about what customers truly think, and a systematic approach is needed to overcome this.

Steps to overcome the problem

How should such an approach be developed? The first step is to conduct an analysis of all of the interactions a customer might have with the organization. Most organizations collect customer satisfaction information on the products or services they provide, but an organization provides far more than just a product or service. It also provides a complicated set of interactions with the customer, all of which should be top notch. For example, a firm must have knowledgeable salespeople, on-time delivery, accurate information, error-free invoices, courteous and helpful employees who quickly answer phones, and accurate and understandable technical manuals. Data should be collected on all customer interactions because total customer satisfaction means meeting or exceeding customer expectations in all areas.

Once the data are collected, the information must be used to improve the system. For example, the complaint department might handle a customer's complaint well, but once the customer's specific problem is resolved, a deeper issue arises about what happens next. Many firms do not try to find the cause of the complaint and change the system to prevent the problem from recurring. Using customer information merely to resolve the immediate problem or error is not sufficient; the underlying system must be improved.

The failure to properly use customer information often occurs in the design of a new product. The marketing department might collect a great deal of customer-related information, but the design engineers might not use it. For instance, marketing might discover that customers want a car with good acceleration, but the engineers need to know whether that means acceleration for passing on a highway, acceleration from 0 to 60 miles per hour, or acceleration to make the tires squeal. Each situation requires different engineering design choices, but marketing often does not obtain information in a form that the engineers can use.

One way to overcome this problem is to give the right people direct access to the customers. Ingersoll Rand in Pittstown, NJ, did this in the design of a new hand-held air grinder. A cross-functional new product development team was formed consisting of people from the marketing, engineering, and manufactur-

Zangwill, Willard I., "Ten Mistakes CEO's Make About Quality," *Quality Progress*, June 1994, pp. 43-48. Reprinted with permission from *Quality Progress*, June 1994, Copyright 1994.

ing departments. This team conducted focus groups with customers throughout the country. It was able to develop the new grinder in one-third the usual development cycle time. The grinder has sold well and won an award from the Industrial Design Society of America.[4]

While exposing decision makers to customers is a good first step, more formal techniques should be developed to drive the customer information throughout the company. Quality function deployment (QFD) is used by a number of companies, including Hewlett-Packard, Ford, and General Motors. QFD obtains detailed lifestyle information from the customer. This information is then deployed throughout the product design process to ensure that the final product fits the lifestyle of the customer, who then will feel comfortable with it.

A good customer satisfaction system does far more than obtain information. It gets the right information to the right people and ensures that the information is used not just to correct a specific error, but to improve the underlying process.

When the system breaks down

Even a very good system might not be sufficient under times of stress and strain. The system is often abandoned and customer-oriented goals are sacrificed to achieve other business objectives. To meet end-of-period goals, for example, a great rush often takes place in which defective products are shipped or services are cut. This happens because executives are driven to reach their numerical goals, to ship a specified amount of product, or to make a certain profit. When a crunch comes and the numbers might not be reached, the customer-oriented standards are likely to be abandoned first.

What can be done about this? Robert Galvin, chairman of Motorola's executive committee, said one of his most important roles was to stand up for quality.[5] He served as the guardian and maintained the status of quality and customer focus even in times of stress and pressure, when others would have sacrificed them. That is a role that top management cannot delegate, and it is the foundation of any successful total customer satisfaction system. Only the CEO can ensure, even in times of great pressure, that quality and customer satisfaction are preserved.

Mistake 4: Believing that quality means inspection

Many executives view quality narrowly and believe that it refers only to manufacturing process control and inspection. Inspection, however, is the antithesis of quality. In fact, quality's ultimate goal is to eliminate inspection. Inspection should not be needed if the process is successful in producing the product without defects. Inspection is only necessary if the production process is faulty and producing defects. In this circumstance, final inspection might be necessary, but it should be viewed only as an interim procedure.

There are three problems with inspection. The first is that inspection only eliminates a percentage of the defects. Joseph M. Juran, W. Edwards Deming, and others suggest that inspection will, as a rule of thumb, eliminate 80% of the defects, and 20% of the defects will still get through to the customer.[6]

Second, an inspector might be able to find defects when the defect rate is at a few percent, but when there is one defect per 25,000, he or she cannot hope to find a defect. Today's marketplace demands such high quality levels, often a few defects per million, that final inspection is not a practical method for achieving those levels.

The third major problem with final inspection is that it is expensive; the cost of inspectors, equipment, and correcting the defects at the final stage is high. At worst, the defective product must be scrapped, totally wasting the item. Even when the item can be salvaged, the rework and repair adds substantially to the cost.

Quality improvement efforts in many companies have shown that inspection is an inadequate approach. It is much better and less expensive to produce the product correctly in the first place. The key to this is error cause removal, which means identifying the cause of the defect or error and then eliminating it. Once the cause is eliminated, the defect cannot occur. Systematically done, this approach is far less expensive and is the best way to achieve virtually zero defects.

For example, billing invoices for domestic pagers from Motorola had 450 errors out of 22,000 total invoices. The errors included wrong or omitted serial numbers, freight amounts, or carriers. In just one year, the error rate was cut to nine out of 20,000. This would have been impossible to do by inspection. Instead, the causes of the defects were rooted out one by one. The team working on this problem noticed that some of the information was already in the computer and did not need to be recopied, which eliminated the possibility of error in that step. Other information was available from the bar coding system, and form simplification cut the remaining errors.[7]

Another example is from the People's Bank of Bridgeport, CT, which had a high error rate for its tellers in the proofing department. For each error found, a special correction notice had to be issued, which was expensive. To solve the problem, extra inspection, training, and management encouragement were attempted, but that did not help the situation. Finally, the bank tried to eliminate the root causes of the errors. It discovered that the tellers had to know how to do 78 operations. The bank standardized documents and reorganized the system so that the tellers needed to do only 12 operations. The errors virtually disappeared.

Whether in manufacturing or service activities, defects are rarely cut by increasing inspection. Getting rid of the root causes of the errors is usually cheaper and more effective.

Mistake 5: Believing that quality improvement is too expensive

Many executives believe that quality improvement is too expensive when, in fact, the opposite is true—quality cuts costs. Quality requires doing the right job right the first time, and doing the right job is cheaper than doing the wrong job. Any task that must be redone or product that must be reworked adds cost. Any information that is incorrect and must be revised adds cost. Any waste of people's time, such as having to wait an excessively long time for top management to make a decision, adds to the cost. The more right things that are done right the first time, the more money that is saved. That is why quality saves money, and all of the Baldrige Award winners have documented proof of this.

One of the curious facts about quality is that costs tend to go down more rapidly than expected. This is because quality improvement in one area often cuts costs in other areas, thereby reaping multiple savings. For example, a firm decided to improve the quality of the information generated by its computerized inventory system.[8] Its computers would show that a product was in inventory when, in fact, there was no such product on the shelf, or they would show that a product was unavailable when there were still several in stock. Even though this happened only a small percentage of the time, people often had to call the warehouse to check whether an item was in stock or not.

To improve this system, the firm set up a special team to get rid of the defects. Any time a problem arose, the team would count the inventory and check out what had gone wrong. Many problems were found and resolved. Part numbers were simplified and corrected, storage was rearranged, and the computer software was improved. After a couple months of effort, the computerized inventory system was made reliable, dependable, and accurate. An immediate savings was in the elimination of phone calls checking whether an item was in stock.

Then came an unexpected twist. Twice a year the firm took physical inventory and counted everything in stock. Soon after the computerized inventory system was corrected, a physical count was made. The numbers from the physical count, however, were different from those that the computer reported. The physical count showed the computer count to be wrong. The quality team was upset and felt demoralized. After all of the effort to improve the computerized inventory system, the team members thought that it had failed.

The quality team, however, decided to check the physical count. Since everyone in the firm helped do the physical count, it turned out that many people made errors because they did not understand the parts number system or the storage system. The physical count, therefore, was wrong, and the computer count of the inventory was more accurate. The biannual physical inventory was stopped, since it was not as accurate as the computer system, and the computer data were then used for all financial reporting.

In addition, the accounting department had two computer programmers developing software for the physical count, which was necessary because of the firm's changing product mix, consisting of a variety of electronic test and computer equipment. Now, with the physical count eliminated, the programmers were no longer needed for that task.

The people who had started the project of correcting the errors in the computer system had no concept that other savings would result. Phone calls from people trying to find out what was in stock, physical counts of inventory, and the need for revisions to the inventory computer program were eliminated.

Most systems consist of many parts or steps in which one part feeds information or material to the next. As the quality of one part of the system improves, it sends higher-quality information or material to the subsequent steps in the process. That higher-quality input produces a cost reduction in those steps. Since the interconnection of systems is often complex, sometimes, as in the inventory example, it is difficult to foresee exactly where the cost reductions will occur. But as quality improves in one operation, costs almost always drop not only in that operation, but also in other operations.

Mistake 6: Managing by intuition and not by fact

Most CEOs strongly believe in their judgment. After all, that is the essence of being a CEO—having the background, judgment, and intuition to make good decisions. Research, however, tells a different story. Many behavioral science studies have verified that intuition and judgment are not nearly as sound as we are led to believe. In effect, people's brains "lie" to them and tell them their judgment is much better than it really is.

The book *Decision Traps* by J. Edward Russo and Paul J.H. Schoemaker, for example, details some of the fallacies that people's brains tell them.[9] In December of one year, executives were asked to predict sales for the following year. More than a year later and after the actual annual sales figures were shared with everyone, the executives were asked to recall their predictions, and they remembered them as being much closer to the actual outcome than they really were. In essence, once the actual figures were known, the brain subconsciously distorted and recalled the predictions as closer to the actual outcome.

Once a person knows an outcome, his or her brain adjusts its memory. The person then thinks that his or her judgment was far better than it actually was. Judgment also gets distorted because the brain tends to pay more attention to recent, unusual, or emotional events.

Management by fact, not intuition, strives to surmount this predicament. One of the most common areas for misjudgment is in assuming to know the needs of customers. Almost all presumptions about customers are wrong. Whitman Corporation in Chicago, IL, was concerned that its customers were upset because of damage to goods during shipment. It launched a project to reduce the shipping damage and succeeded after some effort. Only later did it learn that the customers were disappointed and thought the old shipping method was better. Although the new packaging protected the contents well, it was extremely hard for the customers to open.[10]

> One of the most common areas for misjudgment is in assuming to know the needs of customers.

At First National Bank of Chicago in Illinois, the managers thought that the most important thing to customers was fast, courteous service. When the customers were surveyed, however, that item ranked fourth in importance. The customers' biggest concern was employees who said they would get back to them on an issue, but then did not.[11]

The need for management by fact extends not just to customers, but to any action or decision that can be made, as demonstrated in the following examples. A firm was proud that it had reduced its defect rates to 5% from 15%. When asked for the facts, it produced some charts that showed a 5% defect rate for several months. There was no indication, however, that the defect rate was previously 15%. When pushed further, someone recalled that someone else had said the defect rate was at least 15% at some point last year. Someone else then recollected that when new machines were installed the defect rate shot up briefly, and perhaps, that unique occurrence accounted for the 15%.[12]

Another firm was proud of the new sales techniques its salespeople were using. When questioned, however, they could produce no proof of increased sales and justified it by replying that the salespeople had only recently been trained so it was too early for proof. When the training was investigated, it was discovered that only 60% of the salespeople had attended the training session. When those attendees were questioned, most thought the training was useless and too theoretical, so they never implemented it.[13]

Compaq computer also searches for facts and, according to Vice President Hugh Barnes, continually uses sanity checks and cross-checks.[14] Just because an executive says something, that does not mean the statement is gospel. Suppose an executive predicts that the sales for a product will be 5,000 units. That statement is questioned, and the facts are sought. Is it the person's surmise? Is it based on market surveys? Is it based on firm orders? The degree of validity of the statement is thereby determined.

The mind, behavioral scientists know, searches for evidence to confirm its beliefs and denies the validity or existence of contrary or additional evidence. The best antidote to these distortions is management by fact. The facts are usually easier to obtain and considerably more useful than most people believe. Baldrige Award winners tend to collect a great deal of information and use it extensively in their decision processes.

Mistake 7: Using misguided incentives and developing a distorted culture

CEOs often sincerely try to institute beneficial changes, such as launching a quality program. They allocate resources, train people, and establish goals. But after a year of waiting, they have gained little in return for their time and money. Why does this occur?

Obtaining a sizable change in an organization requires a major revision in the culture, and a CEO's program to improve quality will have little impact if the incentives are wrong for the culture. This frequently occurs, for example, when managers are encouraged to attain monthly production quotas, even if it means shipping poor-quality products.

Another common incentive is the promotion of managers who are deemed good crisis or fire-fighting managers. The manager who is considered a star is the one who marshals the resources, gets everyone to work overtime, and resolves crises. Top management hears of these heroics and promotion occurs. Rarely does anyone ask, however, why this manager permitted so many crises to happen.

One important tenet of quality is to keep the system under control so that defects or crises rarely occur. The best executives follow this philosophy and work to reduce the number of crises. Without the crises to get top management's attention, however, these people might work with little honor or promotion.

Trouble might also ensue if the overriding culture is based on cost reduction. Some managers will cut back on training, maintenance, and new product development. Those actions cut cost, but they have no chance to positively influence the company. This manager will keep costs very low, look good to top management, and receive a promotion in 18 to 24 months. The manager after him or her, however, is left with depleted resources and the inability to compete. Implementing a quality program often means making careful investigation of the cultural aspects of the organization that might defeat it.

Mistake 8: Changing targets each year

Most CEOs have an annual planning process, similar to management by objectives, in which goals are established for the next year. The overall goals are set by top management, and then lower levels get their goals after some debate and discussion in a cascading process. In theory, if managers have reasonable goals and incentives, then most goals will be accomplished. In actual practice, however, high levels of accomplishment rarely occur.

To achieve any really important and challenging goal requires training, investment, management reviews, incentives, worker involvement, and cultural changes. All of this takes time and effort to implement. If new goals are instituted annually, management gets involved with new goals and directions before it can get fully underway on the old goals.

How can a CEO overcome this? Although some of the annual goals can change yearly, a few should be so fundamental and crucial that they persist into the foreseeable future. Motorola has instituted three such goals for the entire firm: quality, cycle time, and cost reduction. It took years to develop and implement the systems to ensure progress on these goals and for some people to realize that the CEO was really serious about them.[15]

Although some goals will have to be revised annually, changing too many goals too fast will confuse middle management and employees. Instead, top management should identify the fundamental factors that underpin the firm's success. To implement these factors, top management should include a few cardinal goals as well as the systems to achieve them (training, management reviews, and incentives).

Mistake 9: Failing to follow the best practices

Near the end of the 1970s, Xerox was confronted by formidable competition from Japanese firms. The Japanese were selling copiers at a cost comparable to Xerox's manufacturing cost. Xerox's market share was plunging. After years of disregarding its Japanese competition, Xerox had to confront reality.

Although Xerox launched several programs in its counterattack, perhaps the most crucial was benchmarking. With benchmarking, employees in the organization determined the best practices in the industry. They learned about these best practices, implemented them, and became the best at them. All functions of the firm, not just manufacturing, were required to benchmark, including shipping, internal auditing, treasury, and training. Xerox, like most manufacturing firms, had most of its costs not in manufacturing, but in overhead and general administration. Therefore, all parts of the firm had to benchmark and learn how to become the best at what they did.[16]

An important aspect of benchmarking is to look for the best practices not just inside one's industry but also outside. For warehousing, for example, Xerox benchmarked against L.L. Bean. Going outside one's industry might, in fact, be easier because direct competitors are less likely to share information. IBM Rochester, a Baldrige Award winner, for example, benchmarks itself against 200 other leading firms from both inside and outside its industry.[17]

Benchmarking is a powerful concept. But despite the obvious value of learning from the best, many managers will perceive the process as threatening and deny its value. They will object that other firms are different and not comparable and argue that what another firm does is not relevant. At Xerox, people gave repeated rationalizations and justifications for not benchmarking, such as the fact that the Japanese have a different culture, get government support, and have a better school system. Denial of the situation was rampant, and Xerox leadership had to convince people that they could learn and improve by studying other organizations.[18] The most difficult part of benchmarking is not the process itself, but in getting people to do it.

Benchmarking requires leadership to help people face the

fact that they are not the best and must therefore improve. It also requires hard work to know one's own process thoroughly and to understand and learn from the benchmarking process. Most of all, it requires a CEO who knows that world-class success cannot be achieved with second-class operations.

Mistake 10: Believing Baldrige Award examiners are stupid

The Baldrige Award is an award given for outstanding quality to companies applying in three categories: manufacturing, service, and small business (no more than 500 employees). To apply, companies must complete the Baldrige Award examination process, which requires making detailed descriptions of the company's total quality systems. Many firms, however, make the mistake of submitting material that resembles a public relations piece. This might occur because of the company's natural enthusiasm for its achievement. More likely, it is because the company lacks well-defined, well-documented, and measurable quality systems.

A rule of thumb for determining whether a good quality system exists is to audit the process. An audit will determine whether the company is making progress in a particular area and what to do if it is not. A poor system, for example, will likely have one or more of the following problems: no clearly established goals, no means to measure progress toward the goals, and no well-defined process of identifying and correcting problems.

Most Baldrige Award applicants have fairly good systems in the processes that directly generate the products and services. The weak systems are generally seen in leadership, planning, product development, and administrative activities. The lack of systems in these areas often becomes apparent in applicants' responses to questions asking how these processes are improved. The companies might respond by indicating that they have meetings or that a particular person, such as the division manager, has responsibility for the activity. Or they might try a public relations approach such as, "We at the XYZ company are always looking for ways to improve our strategic quality planning process. We believe that quality is one of the most important components of our business plan, and thus, quality is an integral part of our strategic planning process." The company, however, never directly describes how the process is systematically improved.

Another example is an organization's description of a "process that ensures that customer service requirements are understood and responded to throughout the company."[19] An inadequate response would be: "We believe that a customer focus is a key element in our continued success. Every customer contact department has signs posted stating 'Service and courtesy are our business.' In addition, all internal stationery for memos has 'Treat the Customer Right' imprinted prominently in the letterhead." Again, there is no discussion of the system.

Virtually every issue addressed in the Baldrige Award criteria asks for a description of the management system or process the company uses for that issue. This means how the process is monitored, how it is improved, and what the results have been both in terms of improvements over time and in comparison to competitors and world-class companies. When no system exists, it is tempting to resort to public relations statements about the importance of quality and customer satisfaction. The Baldrige Award examiners, however, are not stupid enough to be fooled.

Acknowledgment

The author wishes to thank George Easton, University of Chicago, for his extensive help in writing this paper.

References

1. Lucien Rhodes with Patrica Amend, "The Turnaround," *Inc.*, August 1986, p. 42.
2. Johnathan P. Hicks, "A Tire Outdistances Its Rivals," *New York Times*, May 8, 1990.
3. "IBM Rochester, 1990 Winner of the Malcolm Baldrige National Quality Award," IBM, Rochester, MN, 1990.
4. N.R. Kleinfield, "How 'Strykeforce' Beat the Clock," *New York Times*, March 25, 1990, p. 1.
5. Robert Galvin, chairman of the executive committee, Motorola, Guest Lecture at Graduate School of Business, University of Chicago, Feb. 13, 1991.
6. Joseph M. Juran, editor in chief, and Frank M. Gryna, associate editor, *Juran's Quality Control Handbook* (New York, NY: McGraw-Hill Book Company, 1988), Section 18.
7. Paul Noakes, vice president, Motorola, private conversation, March 18, 1991.
8. J. Timothy Fuller and Willard I. Zangwill, "Repealing the Law of Diminishing Returns for Quality," Report, University of Chicago, Graduate School of Business, Nov. 3, 1989.
9. J. Edward Russo and Paul J.H. Shoemaker, *Decision Traps* (New York, NY: Simon and Schuster, 1989).
10. William Naumann, vice president, Whitman Corporation, Guest Lecture at Graduate School of Business, University of Chicago, Nov. 30, 1992.
11. Aleta Holub, vice president, First National Bank of Chicago, personal interview, Jan. 18, 1992.
12. William Naumann, vice president, Whitman Corporation, Guest Lecture at Graduate School of Business, University of Chicago, Nov. 30, 1992.
13. Tim Fuller, lecturer, Special Seminar, University of Chicago, Winter 1991.
14. Hugh Barnes, vice president, Compaq Computer, personal interview, May 18, 1992.
15. Paul Noakes, vice president, Motorola, private conversation, March 18, 1991.
16. Barry Bebb, retired vice president, Xerox, personal interview, Jan. 29, 1992.
17. "IBM Rochester, 1990 Winner of the Malcolm Baldrige National Quality Award," IBM, Rochester, MN, 1990.
18. Barry Bebb, retired vice president, Xerox, personal interview, Jan. 29, 1992.
19. George Easton, professor, Graduate School of Business, University of Chicago, personal interview, May 18, 1991.

Willard I. Zangwill is a professor of management science at the Graduate School of Business, University of Chicago. He has a doctorate in operations research from Stanford University in California. Zangwill is an ASQC member.

Quality Auditing in a Public-Sector Service Environment

AT THE INTERNAL REVENUE SERVICE (IRS) Manhattan District Office, virtually every manager will say that he or she is reviewed to death. Managers are regularly reviewed by the IRS North Atlantic Regional Office, IRS National Office, Internal Audit area, and Equal Employment Opportunity and Problem Resolution offices. In addition, first-level managers are visited about twice a year by their immediate supervisors, and mid-level managers are regularly reviewed by a top-level manager.

Needless to say, when the quality improvement coordinator announced that she was planning to conduct functional quality process assessments, the initial reaction was not one of great enthusiasm. What came to pass, however, was an unequivocally positive experience for all concerned, from the district director to the first-line manager.

According to former District Director Robert E. Mirsberger, "The original intent of performing assessments was to enable me to gauge my organization's progress toward full integration of quality principles. I felt that we were still a long way from being a total quality organization, and it was clear to me that some quality baselines had to be established (see the sidebar "IRS Quality Update"). I also thought the assessments would give me insight into the thoughts and perceptions of the first- and mid-level managers. It was very important for me to have an idea of how my more than 200 managers personally felt about total quality management (TQM)."

Mirsberger discussed his thoughts with the district quality coordinator, and together they developed the quality process assessment. Basically, the assessment would use the corporate and functional critical success factors and fiscal year functional objectives as guidelines. The assessment would focus on the influence of various levels of district management on efforts toward creating a total quality organization. It would also serve to establish a baseline measure to be used in follow-up and future assessments.

Step 1: Assemble items needed to develop the assessment model

The first step taken by the quality coordinator was to assemble the servicewide strategic business plan, function business plans, and other fiscal year functional objectives. These are all significant items employed by the IRS to drive its programs, and they were key for developing an assessment model.

Before actually developing the functional portion of the model, the quality coordinator devised some generic questions that pertained to all first- and mid-level managers in all functions. These questions would be used as discussion topics in focus groups consisting of a sample of first- and mid-level managers to assess the current degree of managerial involvement. The discussion questions included:

- What is your perception of the quality process?
- How would you define your role and responsibilities in the quality process?
- Who are your customers and suppliers?
- Are you familiar with your uniform performance standards related to quality?
- What steps have you taken to meet these standards?

- Do you use any additional standards that relate to quality?
- Are managerial achievements in quality recognized in performance appraisals?
- What weight is given to these managerial achievements?
- Is personal management influence reflected?
- Have any manager contributions to quality been recognized with awards?

The quality coordinator developed specific functional models by culling quality- and productivity-related items and issues from the business plans and objectives.

Once the model was complete, the quality coordinator shared it with the division chiefs, requesting their input regarding the content and any proposed additions, deletions, or changes. After the division chiefs responded, she incorporated their comments into the models. She chose the Taxpayer Service Division for the pilot assessment because of its historical emphasis on quality and customer service. The quality coordinator contacted the chief of the division to review the process and its mechanics and to schedule the assessment. The assessment began with a general discussion between the quality coordinator and the chief and assistant division chief regarding their thoughts on TQM.

Step 2: Discuss quality and productivity issues

The second, and perhaps most enlightening, step was for the quality coordinator to hold two separate focus group meetings with the first- and mid-level managers to discuss the generic questions and any other quality or productivity issues the participants wanted to address, including barriers to TQM. The participants were told to be as candid as possible because their comments would serve as feedback to their division chief, district director, and assistant district director.

Step 3: Discuss functional goals

In the third step, the quality coordinator had discussions with individual managers on their efforts and influence toward achieving specific functional quality and productivity goals.

In the Taxpayer Service Division, these goals are related to areas and programs such as walk-in taxpayers, tax counseling for the elderly, practitioner education, and written taxpayer correspondence.

Purpose of the visit

Throughout the assessment visit, the quality coordinator stressed that the goal of the assessment was to establish baselines, not to evaluate. She was, however, aware of human nature and knew that the visit would be construed to some degree as evaluative. This made the quality coordinator's task of writing a visit report a critical step in the process. It would be disastrous for the openness and honesty of the managers to backfire because it would probably leave them distrustful of the entire process. Moreover, a report with a negative tone could turn the entire division off and set back the district TQM effort.

After completing the report, the quality coordinator arranged a meeting with the division chief and provided him with a draft copy of the report. At the meeting, the quality coordinator's conclusions and recommendations were discussed. Recommendations that the division chief did not agree with were noted, and a date for a follow-up visit was set.

Step 4: Discuss report and visit

The final step of the process was to meet with the district director and assistant district director to discuss the report and the visit in general. Gordon B. Manchester, former Taxpayer Service Division chief, and his division had served as process pioneers. Manchester said, "The quality assessment process is a valuable tool for management to improve the quality of customer service. It provides an objective external perspective focused not only on the work products but also on the methods used to achieve the end results. The follow-up assessment can also prove the validity of the process by measuring the progress toward objectives established during the original review."

Assessments of other divisions

The process was subsequently repeated in both the Examination Division and the Collection Division using the previously mentioned generic questions and appropriate functional items.

Reactions to assessments

In the final analysis, there was an overwhelmingly favorable reaction to the quality process assessments. The director, assistant director, and division chiefs were able to gain valuable insights; the district quality coordinator felt a sense of accomplishment and influence on the quality process; and most important, first- and mid-level managers sensed that their voices were being heard. Many truly believed they were, for the first time, a part of the quality process. Before the assessments, most did not have a firm grasp of the concept of TQM. A number were involved in quality initiatives but were unaware that they should be applauded for their efforts. The assessment not only enlightened them, but also helped them acknowledge their own contributions.

Joseph Jelonek, chief of the Examination Division, told the quality coordinator, "The assessment you made of the Examination Division was, and continues to be, very helpful. It was invaluable to me in making the point that intradivision communication is extremely important. In addition, your assessment was very comprehensive because it covered managerial items such as the Performance Management Recognition System and operational items such as critical success factors."

The former chief of the Collection Division, Terry O'Brien, said, "The best way that we can find out how committed our organization is to quality improvement is to reach down to the grass roots. The quality process assessment did just that."

Assessments are being expanded to include more functions in the district, and the models will be modified based on experience and changes in fiscal year objectives. Overall, the district looks back on the assessment process as one that was well worth the time and effort it took. District officials know they have only begun to realize the benefits of the assessment process and are excited about what the future will bring.

Bonnie Holzer is the career advisor and former quality coordinator at the Internal Revenue Service Manhattan District Office in New York, NY. She received a master's degree in education from Brooklyn College in New York. Holzer is an ASQC member.

What did you think about this article?

Quality Progress needs your feedback. On the postage-paid reader service card inserted toward the back of this magazine, please circle the number that corresponds with your opinion of the preceding article.

Excellent	Circle #333
Good	Circle #334
Fair	Circle #335
Poor	Circle #336

Holzer, Bonnie, "Quality Auditing in a Public-Sector Service Environment," *Quality Progress*, June 1994, pp. 61-62. Reprinted with permission from Quality Progress, June 1994, Copyright 1994.

THE DIGITAL FACTORY

With speed and flexibility that leave the Japanese agog, U.S. manufacturers have come roaring back after years in eclipse. The secret? It's the software, stupid.

by Gene Bylinsky

At one end of a cavernous IBM plant in Charlotte, North Carolina, 40 workers toil at an assembly line unlike any you'll find in Japan. The team is building 12 products at once—hand-held bar-code scanners, portable medical computers, fiber-optic connectors for mainframes, satellite communications devices for truck drivers—a typical morning's output on a line designed to simultaneously make as many as 27 different products, a virtual catalogue of IBM wares.

Around each worker are "kits" of parts that people in a nearby parts cage have assembled to match production orders; more kits arrive as the day progresses. To keep things moving efficiently, each worker has a computer screen hooked into the factory network. It displays an up-to-the-minute checklist of the parts he must install on the product in front of him and will guide him through the assembly steps if he asks it for help. As soon as he finishes his tasks, the worker punches a button and the computer system moves the product via conveyor to the next bench on the line.

Welcome to the new American factory—an information age marvel that is enabling U.S. manufacturing, declared dead more often than a lathe turns, to come storming back. In industries as diverse as construction equipment, cars, PCs, and electronic pagers, Japanese and European producers are scrambling to copy American techniques. The new automation paradigm they're looking to involves an ingenious balancing in which software and computer networks have emerged as more important than production machines, in which robots play a mere supporting role if they're present at all—and in which human workers are back in unexpected force. Call it the digital factory, for its dependence on information technology, or the soft factory, for its mix of the human and the mechanical. Whatever you call it, it's likely to set the tone of manufacturing for years, even decades, to come.

Soft manufacturing brings unheard-of agility to the plant: Companies can customize products literally in quantities of one while churning them out at mass-production speeds. Soft manufacturing also blurs the boundaries of the traditional factory by tying production ever closer to both suppliers and customers. It is weaving a fabric of highly automated job shops, or microfactories, across the American landscape and bringing new life to the beleaguered U.S. machine-tool industry. Perhaps most astounding is soft manufacturing's effect on employment: It could stabilize or even increase the number of production-worker jobs in the U.S.

Make no mistake about the importance of this trend: In potent combination with the economic recovery and the weakness of the dollar relative to other currencies, soft manufacturing has helped the U.S. leapfrog Germany and Japan to regain the No. 1 spot in manufactured exports for the first time in a decade. Says Blair LaCorte, director of data-management products at Autodesk in Sausalito, California: "The near paralysis of the early 1980s is long gone. We're seeing the beginnings of a revolution in American manufacturing."

How quickly things change. Just ten years ago, authorities such as the National Academy of Engineering were sounding alarms about America's manufacturing future. In particular, observers feared Japan for its ability to capitalize on an American innovation known as flexible manufacturing systems (FMSs). Priced as high as $25 million each, such systems typically included computer-controlled machines to sculpt a large variety of complicated metal parts, robots to carry out complex handling chores, and remotely guided carts to deliver materials to the production line. FMSs were widely hailed, especially by the Japanese, as harbingers of "lights out" automatic factories that would be able to operate around the clock almost without workers.

Nearly every major U.S. manufacturer fell under the spell. But years of costly efforts to install flexible manufacturing systems taught them a bitter lesson: Too much automation can actually lose you money. For one thing, despite engineers' efforts to build in safeguards, large, complex systems are inherently vulnerable to failure. Robots, in particular, turned out to be a disappointment: They couldn't hack it as assemblers because they would dumbly try to jam a nut into an opening even if it didn't fit.

As businesses struggled to escape the FMS trap, soft manufacturing was born. Engineers broke down mammoth FMS installations into more manageable "cells"—smaller constellations of machines that are just as versatile but less apt to fail. Robots have been relegated to simple jobs at which they excel, like spot-welding; humans, with their unmatched dexterity and judgment, are back in assembly jobs where the robots floundered. And to help the humans, engineers have spread computers and networks liberally around the plants. Explains IBM manufacturing executive L. Ray Mays: "We're not as enamored with automation as we were in the early 1980s. We did a lot of research about what's reasonable to automate and what isn't. We found that it's much more cost efficient to use hand labor with software networks than to use robots, for example. We've learned that in dealing with odd-size components and tight tolerances, humans are more efficient than robots."

Result: soft factories that perform beyond the wildest dreams of 1980s automation mavens. Take the plant in Boynton Beach, Florida, where Motorola makes pagers. Orders for the pocket-size gizmos stream in from resellers and Motorola salesmen, typically via an 800 line or e-mail. As the salesman spells out what the customer wants—"one Sizzling Yellow pager that goes ding-dong, five in Bimini Blue that beep, ten in Vibra Pink that play a little arpeggio," and so on—the data are digitized and flow to the assembly line. So-called pick-and-place robots select the proper components, but humans assemble the pagers. Often the order is complete within 80 minutes, and depending on where the customer lives, he can have his pagers that same day or the day after.

Motorola thinks of the process not as manufacturing but as rapidly translating data from customers into products; its aim is to do so even faster. Says Sherita Ceasar, director of manufacturing: "Our vision is simultaneous manufacturing, to make the pager even as the customer talks. We're getting close."

IBM's PC Direct operation in Research Triangle Park, North Carolina, follows a similar pattern. Rows of sales reps answer 800-426-7102 calls from customers—about 5,000 a day—and take orders for various models of IBM PCs. As they talk, the sales reps enter the particulars of the order on-screen—the new PC will incorporate, say, a 486 DX66 chip, 16 megabytes of RAM, a built-in fax modem, and so on—and check to make sure the parts are available. Finished orders are zapped to a nearby assembly plant where computers check them every ten minutes.

Those same computers automatically set production in motion. From a small control room, they send a radio signal to workers called "kitters" on the floor below, like Ron Robinson. He receives the data on his hand-held bar-code reader and then walks from one bar-coded location to another, picking up a hard disk from a bin here, a memory board from a bin there. When he has gathered the complete kit that will become a PC, Robinson takes it to an assembly station.

There assembler Tisha Hyman scans the bar code on each part as she builds the machine, and checks her assembly-control screen to make sure the factory system has subtracted each part from inventory. Soon the new PC travels down the line to be automatically tested and packaged—for delivery to the customer the next day by Airborne Express, if the customer so requests. "We call this software-controlled continuous flow manufacturing," says Barry W. Eveland, vice president for fulfillment. "Where you get an advantage is in your ability to take information from your customer and apply it behind the scenes to control the flow of goods." Marvels Charles Duncheon, vice president of marketing and sales at Adept Technology, a Sausalito, California, robot maker: "We may be seeing the merger of a manufacturing plant with a retail store."

No wonder U.S. manufacturers have begun outdistancing foreign competitors in such crucial measures as time to market and manufacturing flexibility. What's equally striking is that the joy of making things for a substantial profit is back. "The executive suites of manufacturers I visit are a lot happier places than they were as recently as three years ago," says Arthur Fury, vice president for sales and marketing at Semtech Corp. of Newbury Park, California, who crisscrosses industrial America selling semiconductors. GE CEO Jack Welch tells subordinates that the 1990s is becoming "the decade of manufacturing." At Hewlett-Packard, CEO Lew Platt calls manufacturing and distribution simply the "core competences" of his company. H-P recently embarrassed its Japanese rival NEC by beating it to market with a line of ink-jet color printers. H-P's units are so good that NEC was forced to withdraw its own printers as uncompetitive only four months after they belatedly hit the market.

Other examples of America's manufacturing resurgence abound. Locomotives are among GE's latest successes: The company has been gaining market share abroad because of the superior time-to-market and customizing capability of its plant in Erie, Pennsylvania. Says Richard Segallini, vice president for manufacturing and engineering at the plant: "We have traditional automation at the start of the line to do repetitive, harsh work, such as building locomotive platforms. But where you customize the locomotive—with different cabs, propulsion, motors, and paint schemes—you need flexible cells that can be programmed. That's where software becomes more important than hardware. In fact, sometimes you have to take automation out—it can slow you down." The plant has more than tripled its output since 1992 and has cut the time it needs to build and customize a locomotive from two years to six months.

A $1.8 billion overhaul of its factories has enabled Caterpillar to regain preeminence in earthmoving machines. This year it vaulted into the No. 3 position, after Boeing and Intel, among the top 50 U.S. industrial exporters, in percentage of sales derived from abroad. Cat makes two-thirds of its products in the U.S., but nearly half its $12 billion in sales last year came from abroad. The company now has a larger market share in Japan than its Japanese archrival, Komatsu, has in the U.S. The most visible sign of soft automation at Cat's assembly plant in Aurora, Illinois: unmanned vehicles, each the size of an office desk, that scurry from one milling machine to another, delivering and picking up gears. Unlike the carts in Japanese FMS installations, which travel in rigid patterns along wires embedded in the factory floor, the carts at Cat run around like animals. Atop each one is a cup-size range finder that bounces laser beams off large bar-coded panels on the factory walls and tells the cart where it is; computer-directed radio signals from a control center direct its pickups and deliveries.

U.S. manufacturing is becoming so good that once again platoons of earnest-looking Japanese can be seen touring U.S. plants. Nothing resembling soft manufacturing is to be found in Japan, where Toyota has been the sole company even to talk about mass-producing customized products. What's more, experts say, copying the Americans will be difficult this time around for most Japanese manufacturers. That's because customizing items for individual buyers runs against the grain: Japan's factories are engineered to mass-produce high-quality identical products and aren't easily reprogrammed. The nation's cumbersome multilayer distribution system works against supplying customized products in the home market. "You get the sense among Japanese business people that they aren't sure what's going on," says Peter Mills, director of intercontinental sales for Adept Technology and a frequent visitor to Japan.

What's going on is that the U.S. is seizing back the global lead as software rather than traditional, noncomputerized hardware begins to dominate manufacturing. Patrick J. Toole, an IBM executive vice president, echoes a widespread view when he says, "The computer has become more important than the production tool." Daniel Frayssinet, president of DP Technology Corp. of Camarillo, California, a supplier of leading-edge manufacturing software, estimates that U.S. manufacturers now use three times as much software as the Japanese, and better software at that. PCs are proliferating in American factories just as they did in offices a decade ago: linked in powerful networks, they open the way toward the use of information technology as a great, unifying communications tool—a kind of superbrain hovering over the factory floor.

The pace of innovation is dramatically increasing. For example, computer-aided design (CAD) has evolved far beyond its original embodiment as an electronic drafting board. The best CAD software, from suppliers like Autodesk, Structural Data Research Corp., Parametric Technology, and IBM, now lets engineers plan products, test them onscreen, and even design tools to make them—all from the same data. CAD has been extended to factory planning, where software from companies like Deneb Robotics, of Auburn Hills, Michigan, lets users design and simulate entire assembly lines. At Chrysler Corp., some 10,000 engineers, designers, and manufacturing experts share a Catia factory database; Catia was developed by Dassault, the French aerospace company, and is sold by IBM. The software includes 48 "modules"—applications ranging from early modeling of a design concept to the management of data on the production line. A designer can call up on his screen a semitransparent view of a car door he's working on, operate the latch and run the window up and down to check how they work, experiment with lighter materials by adjusting the underlying equations, and use the same data to direct machinery to make prototypes of the parts. Catia helped Chrysler complete its Neon subcompact in a record 33 months—lopping a year off the company's usual development cycle.

Designers at Caterpillar use a system that's even more exotic: a virtual-reality proving ground where they test-drive huge earthmoving machines before they are built. Known as a CAVE (short for cave automatic virtual environment), the system is the brainchild of Thomas A. DeFanti and Daniel J. Sandin of the University of Illinois at Chicago. It is a surround-screen, surround-sound cube about ten feet on each side that creates the illusion of reality for anyone inside by projecting supercomputer-generated 3D graphics onto the walls. Unlike users of video-arcade virtual reality systems, CAVE dwellers do not have to don bulky helmets; instead, they wear lightweight stereo glasses that enhance the vividness of the displays. They can walk around inside the CAVE and operate imaginary controls; the system monitors head and hand motions and adjusts the sights and sounds accordingly.

Only three CAVEs exist today, two at University of Illinois campuses and one at the Argonne National Laboratory near Chicago. Corporate partners at the National Center for Super-computing Applications (NCSA)—Caterpillar is one—can use the CAVE in Champaign-Urbana to test their products.

In Caterpillar's simulation you sit in a mockup of an earthmover and put the huge machine into motion just as you would in real life at the company's Peoria, Illinois, proving ground, which the CAVE mimics. The engine roars convincingly and backup signals sound as you scoop up virtual gravel and dump it on a pile. The experience has its uncanny aspects: You can drive with impunity through walls of buildings and stick your hand through the windshield without ill effects. The woman who runs the demonstration waves her control wand in a final flourish; the images on the CAVE walls change as you are transported through the side of the cab to the ground, where you can look up at the big Cat and walk around it. Then she flies you, feeling weightless, back into the driver's seat.

Caterpillar's CAVE program isn't just for thrills. Two machines the company will introduce next year, a backhoe and a wheel loader, will incorporate visibility and performance improvements based on data from virtual test drives. Explains Kem D. Ahlers, the Caterpillar engineer who heads the project: "We took CAD data that describe the vehicles, put them in the virtual environment, and instead of using iron, we manufacture our machines in electrons and light."

Sophisticated computer programming has sparked a revival among U.S. machine-tool makers, who supply the gear for manufacturing lines. They lost their No. 1 position in the $4-billion-a-year industry in 1982 and now are a distant third behind the Japanese and the Germans. But American companies dominate the new, fast-growing market for so-called rapid prototyping machines, computer-driven units that fabricate parts directly from design data, much as a laser printer spits out a spreadsheet. One such machine, developed by 3D Systems, a startup in Valencia, California, builds prototypes by precisely depositing layer upon layer of powdered metal, a process known as stereolithography. Using a 3D machine, Mercedes-Benz recently checked the fit of 50 parts for a new engine, cutting development time by 80% and saving a lot of money. Another rapid prototyping system from 3D shapes parts by aiming a laser beam at a vat of photoreactive resin that congeals wherever the beam lingers.

By far the most spectacular computer-controlled tools are hexapods, which are just now hitting the market. These lightweight machines represent the biggest advance in machine tools since Englishman Henry Maudslay perfected the industrial lathe in 1800.

Hexapods, which resemble ordinary machine tools about as much as a spaceship resembles a train, are capable of handling unprecedentedly complex machining tasks. Embodying the same mechanical principles as a flight training simulator, a hexapod has six legs with computer-controlled motors, which enable the machine's spindle platform to bring tools to bear from any angle in three-dimensional space. Unlike conventional machinery, in which the spindle follows the path of a mechanical guideway, the spindle in a hexapod maneuvers through the air as prescribed by software. On the factory floor, hexapods look like giant hula dancers in motion as they carve out intricate metal parts.

The new machines will bring unheard of agility and mobility to manufacturing. A hexapod can weigh one-tenth as much as a conventional machine tool of comparable power, and unlike the standard tool, incorporates its own frame and needs no special foundation or external support. It can be moved easily and rapidly on the back of a truck and will work anywhere parts need to be made—even on a lawn. Just as highly mobile, truck-launched Soviet Katyusha rocket artillery helped win World War II, hexapods promise to serve as powerful competitive weapons in the manufacturing wars. Giddings & Lewis introduced its Variax machining center this September; the hexapod weighs 15,000 pounds, one-third the weight of a comparable conventional tool; its price has not yet been set. Early next year, Ingersoll will introduce a much bigger hexapod, while Geodetics Inc. will offer a compact version to sit on a desk.

How can manufacturers take advantage of such technological wonders? Not surprisingly, the businesses best suited for soft manufacturing techniques are those that have already broken themselves into smaller units, flattened the bureaucracy, and organized workers on the factory floor into teams with real decision-making power. In planning factories, soft manufacturing pioneers have taken the step-by-step functions of traditional manufacturing—conception, design, tooling, manufacturing, distribution, and field maintenance—and telescoped them radically. When Motorola set up its customized pager plant, for example, it insisted that product designers, process developers, computer specialists, and automation engineers all work side by side in the same lab.

The objective, explains Glenn Urbish, one of the factory's founders, was to scrutinize the production cycle in unprecedented ways. To learn how to make pagers stronger, for example, he and his colleagues dismantled dolls and toy trucks—"some of the toughest products made," says Urbish. They quizzed suppliers to pinpoint causes of delay, the most common of which turned out to be the repeated handling of data. When you order parts and your supplier enters your order into his system, explains Urbish, "you lose time. We want a production machine that takes data and starts churning out a tool or a product. Seamlessness is the secret of timeliness." Motorola engineers helped suppliers upgrade their information systems to accept orders electronically; of one supplier Urbish says, "His machines became an extension of our plant."

Like the pager plant, most soft factories depend heavily on outside suppliers—a fact reflected in the rise of a new generation of job shops, nicknamed microfactories, across the U.S. Unlike traditional job shops, which usually specialize in stamping out parts or making prototypes, microfactories are high-tech establishments that supply ready-made assemblies, such as automated wafer handlers for chipmakers.

A thriving example: Westt Inc. in Menlo Park, California, which builds materials handling systems for Conner Peripherals, defense contractor Watkins Johnson, and other Silicon Valley companies. In 1991, Brian J. Westcott, 37, a Stanford Ph.D. engineer who had worked in manufacturing at GE, started the company with three friends: Gregory S. Lewis, 41, another Stanford Ph.D.; Thomas M. Stepien, 33, a software expert; and Mark Muenchow, 40, a former Morgan Stanley investment banker. The four wanted to test their belief that fortunes can still be made by manufacturing in the U.S. In spacious, airy quarters on an industrial side street, Westt currently operates two $120,000 Cincinnati Milacron milling machines and a $120,000 turning center from the same company; the plan is to expand into a set of regional microfactories. All will be linked by electronic networks so Westt can make the most efficient use of its employees' knowledge and its expensive machines.

There are obstacles to the new factory revolution, to be sure. There are obstacles to the new factory revolution, to be sure. Machine-tool makers still complain bitterly that not enough capital is going into factories and factory equipment. Says Ingersoll chairman Edson Ingersoll Gaylord: "As a country, we're still spending 17 times as much capital on shopping centers and insurance companies as on capital equipment." Dennis E. Wisnosky, CEO of Wizdom Systems of Naperville, Illinois, a maker of PC-based shop-floor controllers, laments that it's still difficult for a new manufacturing company to go public.

The spread of new technology and know-how across the country is uneven at best. Just as farmers still plant corn in rows 40 inches apart—the right width to accommodate a plow horse—old ways in manufacturing are slow to die. Lutz F. Hahne, general manager of IBM's manufacturing-industry sales, reports that he recently ran across a medium-size company that still keeps its records on handwritten three-by-five cards. Factories that try to shift to soft automation, meanwhile, find that making various brands of computer hardware and software work together can be an unexpected challenge; interchangeable "open systems" are just beginning to emerge. And snafus afflict even factories that succeed at installing the latest, whizziest computers to link up with their suppliers. Jim Fortunes, who manages PC production for IBM in North Carolina, tells of a supplier that, without notifying IBM, changed the alloy it used to line certain electrical contacts. IBM would have turned out thousands of faulty computers had an alert assembler at the PC plant not noticed that the contacts no longer worked.

The greatest roadblock to a U.S. manufacturing renaissance is a shortage of qualified workers. It encompasses not just Ph.D. manufacturing engineers but also skilled laborers to work in busy job shops, like Industrial Modern Pattern & Mold Corp. in Rosemont, Illinois. The 13-employee, $1.5-million-a-year business, tucked away on a commercial side street, turns out prototypes for Motorola, GM, and other companies. Owner Louis Daniel has just ordered a $250,000 fast-prototyping machine, but today Industrial Modern looks exactly as you'd imagine a conventional job shop: it occupies rather crowded quarters, uses standard machine tools, and has just one PC in the back for design work and a few more in the modest front office. Daniel likes to hire young people and train them as machinists, eventually paying them as much as $20 a hour plus benefits. But he's at a loss to find qualified applicants: "I've been advertising in the papers without results for months. If I could find qualified workers, I could enlarge my operation to 100 people tomorrow." To help fill similar job gaps in their own areas, companies like Ingersoll Milling Machine Co., in Rockford, Illinois, have been pumping money into nearby junior colleges and bringing in local high-schoolers for tours of the plant.

Despite such headaches, the advent of soft manufacturing represents a potent tonic for America's economy. Some experts see an end at last to the steep decline in the number of production workers employed, which in the past 15 years has plunged from more than 15 million to 12 million. Already, in the past 12 months, the Labor Department has recorded a gain—some 214,000—in the number of workers employed. Even a slight rise has an outsize economic effect: Studies show that each new high-paying manufacturing job creates 4.5 additional jobs in the community. Craig Giffi, associate national director of manufacturing consulting for Deloitte & Touche in Cleveland, expresses a belief held by some experts when he predicts that factory employment will either remain constant or increase by up to two million jobs in the next five years.

Ken Goldstein, who studies factory employment at the Conference Board in New York, says that the most substantial growth will be in high-end jobs, those that require skills far beyond those of the traditional factory operative. That's because in the shift to soft manufacturing, companies will need high-tech factories no matter what product they make. Caterpillar's 21,000-employee manufacturing force, for example, includes no fewer than 250 "finite element analysts"—specialists who subject parts and machines to simulated stresses inside computers. Says vice president for technical services Gerald Palmer: "We want to create in a digital world."

Teams of knowledge workers are the people who make the soft factory go. Ask Wisnosky of Wizdom Systems to identify the seminal thinkers in manufacturing today, and he replies: "There's no Taylor, no Sloan, no Colt. There are teams of people—the work is coming out of information sciences." Himself an innovator in soft factory design, Wisnosky isn't losing sleep over the shortage of skilled labor, which he figures will eventually solve itself. Today's 12-year-olds who are growing up with PCs, he reasons, will surely find the new factories interesting places to work.

Sound far-fetched? Sean McAlinden, a research scientist at the Office for the Study of Automotive Transportation at the University of Michigan, believes the auto industry, for one, is on the verge of a wholesale renewal of its work force. He looks forward to the year 2000, when about half of today's auto workers will have retired and "we can create an automotive labor force consisting entirely of skilled workers—problem solvers." If those problem solvers succeed in helping U.S. automakers expand their global share, adds McAlinden, jobs lost to streamlining will be replaced by jobs linked to growth.

Perhaps the biggest hazard U.S. manufacturers face is complacency with their newfound success. GE's Jack Welch, in a speech before the Detroit Economic Club earlier this year, warned American manufacturers, "That way lies danger, because while we pat ourselves on the back, global competitors are working with feverish intensity to overcome the disadvantages of their economies and their currencies." Japanese CEOs he knows, Welch said, are beginning to execute draconian cost cuts, eliminating 30% to 50% of their production expense. But the best American manufacturers aren't standing still; they are constantly improving their agile systems by utilizing what IBM's Toole calls "America's secret weapon—the microprocessor" and the software that goes with it.

Reprinted with permission November 14, 1994 issue of Fortune, (c) 1994 Time Inc. All Rights Reserved.

THE NEW DEAL: WHAT COMPANIES AND EMPLOYEES OWE ONE ANOTHER

Loyalty? Job security? They're nearly dead. But employers that deliver honesty and satisfying work can expect a new form of commitment from workers.

by Brian O'Reilly

Does this sound familiar? You're expendable. We don't want to fire you, but we will if we have to. Competition is brutal, so we must redesign the way we work to do more with less. Sorry, that's just the way it is. And one more thing—you're invaluable. Your devotion to our customers is the salvation of this company. We're depending on you to be innovative, risk-taking, and committed to our goals. Okay?

It is understandably not okay with legions of workers encountering this widespread replacement of the job compact of the previous era, the one that traded loyalty for job security. That deal is virtually dead, but top managers rarely realize how debilitating their one-sided version of the new deal is. Daniel Yankelovich, the marketing and opinion researcher, is one of many who have observed a vast drop over the past few years in workers' commitment to employers. Says he: "Companies are unaware of the dreadful impact they are having. They don't realize they are violating an unwritten but important social contract they have with workers."

The bill will come due soon. Until recently the brass could regret but tolerate sullen workers. In a recession the folks had no place to go. And Pat Milligan, a partner at Towers Perrin, a human resources consulting firm, observes that there is always a period after a contract is broken when people will try to adhere to the old rules and work hard.

But now, says Milligan, employees are getting restless. "The economy is picking up. Workers are saying to management: 'I have choices now. Tell me what the new relationship is so I can decide if I want to stay.' And companies that don't articulate the new deal beyond the paycheck and the pension won't get the best people."

The encouraging news is that certain companies are crafting a new deal that works—sometimes. It makes no one feel warm and fuzzy, but it seems to minimize debilitating fury and anxiety. In its most naked form it goes like this: "There will never be job security. You will be employed by us as long as you add value to the organization, and *you* are continuously responsible for finding ways to add value. In return, you have the right to demand interesting and important work, the freedom and resources to perform it well, pay that reflects your contribution, and the experience and training needed to be employable here or elsewhere."

For some companies and some workers, that is exhilarating and liberating. It requires companies to relinquish much of the control they have held over employees and give genuine authority to work teams. Companies must work harder than ever to make themselves attractive places to work. Employees become far more responsible for their work and careers: No more parent-child relationships, say the consultants, but adult to adult. If the old arrangement sounded like binding nuptial vows, the new one suggests a series of casual, thrilling—if often temporary—encounters.

For others the arrangement is troubling. Attractive, mobile, young technical experts and professionals may fare well, at least for a while. But down the road, will those folks be cast aside for someone younger, more attractive, more current? Or will wisdom, not technical expertise, be what keeps people employed 20 years hence? No one knows. Says Kevin Sullivan, senior vice president at Apple Computer: "Experience or knowledge? It's a dilemma."

Companies that make explicit the new rules discover they can elicit a new form of commitment and hard work from employees—but relations may be far less warm, loyal, or familial. Says a young project manager at Prudential in central New Jersey: "We're cold and calculating and looking out for ourselves. If the economy picked up, I'd consider a job elsewhere much sooner than before. I wouldn't bat an eye."

Most companies are only edging toward the new deal but already find that winning commitment without the old carrot of lifetime job security can be extraordinarily difficult. Chevron vice chairman James Sullivan knows why he joined the company 33 years ago: "I chose Chevron because the work was interesting and because I'd have lifetime employment." Sullivan was lucky. Chevron reduced its work force by nearly half, to about 50,000 people, after the merger with Gulf in 1984. It cut staff by another 6,500 in the past two years. But the impact on employee loyalty has been severe. "On employee commitment, I'd give us a B-minus," Sullivan says.

Though profitability is up sharply, Chevron decided that isn't enough. The company has bravely posted the results of employee morale surveys in company bulletins and in the lobby of headquarters in San Francisco, and has vowed to improve them by developing a new relationship with workers. "It's not easy," Sullivan says candidly. "Until you try to write about it or talk about it, you don't realize how inept you are." Nonetheless, candor and communication are essential, he has found. Chief Executive Kenneth Derr and other bigwigs hold periodic meetings with employees at facilities far and wide, and toil to explain how business is changing and how this affects career advancement and security.

Some others are more bashful. At a big industrial company in the Midwest, top managers can't bring themselves to declare that the old loyalty-security pact is dead. They have drafted dozens and dozens of unpublished versions of a new compact with employees. They are working on yet another.

Should we mourn the death of the old ties? Anyone disemployed or haunted by memories of the Great Depression will miss lifetime job security, but the security-loyalty-paternalism pact of yore wasn't all that terrific either. The old deal often became stultifying. Corporate tolerance for unproductive workers produced ludicrous, and ultimately demeaning, arrangements. Du Pont would stick surplus executives in window offices and tell them to "count boxcars," a none-too-delicate message that their careers were sidelined. The head of human resources at a publishing company recalls, aghast, how the company used to park unproductive 35-year-old executives in useless jobs and leave them there. "We made no attempt to steer them to something useful."

Although constant anxiety about job loss is unfair to workers and counterproductive, ironclad job security definitely doesn't produce the agile and competitive work force today's economy demands. For decades, until January 1988, a big New York bank promised workers that anyone with 20 years' experience would never be laid off. Imagine what sort of worker such a policy attracted and what behavior it encouraged. Says a human resources executive at the bank: "That was okay when we were clerically intensive and needed the mindset of a grunt. But as the organization changed in the Eighties and technology became important, we found that the people who came for security wouldn't adopt new ways of doing things."

Undoing those bank workers' sense of entitlement "is like moving the Rock of Gibraltar," he says. Once older clerical workers heard they wouldn't get tenure, they agreed to accept training and new methods of working—reluctantly. But their resentment and sense of betrayal lingers. "These are adults, living independent lives with families and mortgages," says the executive. "But they are emotionally and intellectually blocked. Some are still furious and won't go the extra mile for themselves or for customers." Some still don't get it at all, he has found; a bank worker in his 40s who recently lost his job told his superiors that he assumed they would find him another spot. "He acted like we owe it to him to deliver a new job," says the executive. "We don't."

At AT&T, after ten years of upheaval since divestiture and the elimination of more than 100,000 jobs, the new message—that employees are responsible for their own survival—is slowly sinking in. For an electrical engineer who has worked at Bell Labs in Holmdel, New Jersey, for more than 20 years, it requires a stressful and demoralizing adjustment.

He can be notified at any time that his job is "at risk." That means that Bell Labs is cutting back people in his area or discipline, that his skills are obsolete, and that he had one of the poorer job evaluations in recent years. Even if there are no layoffs and his evaluations are good, he cannot relax. His engineering projects typically last a year or two, and when they end he must find another project to work on. If he can't find another job at the company within a few months, he must leave.

Now he hustles all the time, concerned that he won't have the necessary skills to win a berth on a new project when the current one ends. It is a persistent worry but not a paralyzing fear so far. He says, "They don't expect me to see 15 years into the future. But they expect me to recognize that the box I'm working on now will be a microchip in a year, with ten times as much software, and to be ready." His concerns, in order of urgency: "What project will I be on in six months, what will my role in the project be—electrical engineer, software writer, tester—and will I have a job?"

To stay current he tries to take engineering and other courses that AT&T offers, but sometimes work leaves little time. "If I think I need to learn more about power circuits, and my boss says no, he really needs me now, it's still my responsibility. I'll take the course at night or on weekends." And if he chooses to master a technology that AT&T turns out not to need? "It's my problem."

A few miles away, at a big Prudential office, paternalism has died an even harder death. "Five years ago we played softball and basketball on company fields, and it was enough to make us loyal because we had job security," says a young manager there. But the company has eliminated 5,000 jobs nationally since then, and a quarter of the manager's co-workers have been fired.

"The message we're getting now is that the company doesn't owe you anything," she says. "Consultants have told us the company is not there for your emotional support, that they don't owe you raises or job security, just honesty. And that a day's pay for a day's work is honest." The result? "Everyone is shocked. The drones are panicking and looking for somebody to tell them what to do. The better ones are looking for opportunity."

She adds, "The people who will survive have realized we have to look out for ourselves. If you see a good assignment, you have to get it yourself. You have to fight for it. Make contacts... If there's a good assignment opening up and I'm not done with my current project, I'll work on the new one at night or on weekends. If I don't do that, I can't complain about not getting new skills."

She and her peers resent the upheaval Prudential is causing, but surprisingly, it's not a disaster. She is still committed to doing a good job. She is driven partly by her own professionalism and competitiveness. "It's like I'm running a marathon and trying to beat my own time."

Gradually, too, she has realized that she is freer to do her work than before. "The old days could be obnoxious. You had to kiss ass and dress right to get ahead. Now none of that matters anymore. If you work hard, you'll find a place." Maybe not at Prudential, though. Rumors say the company will relocate her operation to another office 20 miles north. She worries about the effect of a longer commute on her family. If asked to move, she will quit and find work closer to home. Any qualms? "I don't owe them anything."

Can companies establish this new-age, no-tenure employment compact without poisoning relations with employees? Intel discovered that it helps if the company never had the old implied contract in place to begin with. Like innumerable Silicon Valley firms, the semiconductor maker was founded and staffed by professionals who swarmed out of other companies. Intel never hinted at lifetime job security and didn't demand lifetime loyalty.

Nevertheless, a big round of layoffs in the early 1980s was traumatic, and even Intel realized it could not be cavalier about employee relations. Particularly useful, the company found, is sharing as much information as possible with employees so they can make intelligent career decisions. Intel has quarterly BUMs, or business update meetings, with all its workers, to outline Intel's recent financial health, and twice-yearly SLRPs, describing strategic long-range plans, for executives. A key part of every manager's job is to help co-workers understand if demand for their skills is shifting, and to encourage necessary training. But the message to employees is clear, says human resources VP Kirby Dyess: "You own your own employability. You are responsible."

Note the wording. Many companies tell workers they are responsible for their own careers. That's what Intel used to say. But "career" implied constant, upward movement through one broad discipline. Intel's organization chart has become so flat, there aren't many upper berths to aspire to. Anybody who wants to keep a job must be prepared to go anywhere. Lest anyone ignore that gospel, it is coming home to its in-house evangelists. After a SLRP last year, Dyess realized her HR operation had been growing faster than the company and would have to be cut back. In April 1993, a year before the cutbacks would start, she met with her staff to explain the cuts and to tell them they should keep an eye out for new work. Says Dyess: "Some people are concerned. Some are excited—it's a chance to get into a whole new line of work."

At Reuters, which had a more conventional contract with workers for many years, managers found that switching to a new employment arrangement requires explanation, sensitivity, and time. "Because we were doing well financially, employees' first reaction was, 'Why are you doing this to us?'" says Celia Berk, who heads employee programs and training for the company's operations in North and South America.

"But we decided that if you measure yourself just by financial results, you can't tell if you're creating an opportunity for rivals." Now the company measures itself on client satisfaction, employee effectiveness and satisfaction, operating efficiency, and contribution to shareholder value, in that order. Employee satisfaction is deliberately not at the top of the list, Berk explains. "You could argue that IBM had satisfied employees. It's obviously not enough."

That new measurement system is changing much of how business gets done at Reuters, and the company is exploring ways to link it to employment security and pay. "But we recognized you can't just announce the end of job security without explaining what you'll do in its place," says Berk. "The company isn't entitled to blind loyalty." The company held workshops to explain the new approach and to teach employees how to think about their careers. Reuters developed a set of explicit brochures that show what is expected of managers (for example "Encourages continuous improvement... Looks beyond the short term"), and another set for senior managers ("Promotes innovation... Defines and implements strategy beyond a 12-month time frame"). It revamped its training programs. "We had to rethink adult learning. Not everybody learns well in a classroom."

Wire service employees, measured and rewarded in part on customer satisfaction—customers are newspapers and financial houses—were sent out to clients' offices to observe how they use the Reuters service. Elaborate evaluation procedures solicited comments from supervisors, peers, and subordinates. Criteria were tightly focused: One manager got nicked in a recent evaluation for "failing to use information technology in strategic ways." Supervisors were required to provide candid guidance to their charges. "If a reporter comes to us and says she wants to study Russian, we owe it to her to explain if she will never be Moscow bureau chief," says Berk.

And yes, she says, they fired people. "A few. You have to. Everybody in the organization knows who the drones are. If you don't deal with them, people gauge how much in control the company is. But you can't line everybody up, tell them to salute, and fire anybody who doesn't respond right away. Some people take time to adapt."

In the absence of job security, it turns out, targeted firings are far more palatable to workers than wide-swath layoffs. Companies should probably do more firing—most employees feel it's necessary. Sirota & Alper Associates, a New York City firm that measures employee sentiment, among other things, found that failure to get rid of nonperformers damages morale. Says David Sirota: "When we talk to employees, one of the biggest complaints we get is that companies do a poor job of facing up to poor performers. It's always the most negative finding. Even in the most militant unions, they complain about it. Workers don't want absolute security."

But firing people fairly means evaluating them fairly, and evaluation and measurement remain large failures of the new employment model. Even the best-intentioned companies flub it. At an AT&T division near Bedminster, New Jersey, employees were told that those with the poorest evaluations over the past two years would have to go. Dozens of workers who had migrated to the division from other AT&T operations in recent years discovered that the grading curves shaping their earlier evaluations were all different. In some operations, B's were rare and C's were common. In others, B was average and C was for comatose. But the rule held firm. Some of the worst workers were kept, some of the best lost their jobs. Says a survivor: "This year, at evaluation time, everybody is going to be hysterical."

Can this new, more entrepreneurial employment arrangement really work in the long term? Hardly any companies have enough experience with it to say. The new code rests on important assumptions that may be flawed: that workers are professionals, so their current psychological dependence on employers can be redirected to commitment to their craft; that their work will increase their skills; that their skills are highly transferable between companies or industries.

Apple can woo Stanford grads with the prospect of working on the hottest new device because new hires are confident they can move effortlessly to another company down the street. Their confidence seems reasonable, since 75% of Apple employees are engineers, MBAs, or other professionals.

But it may not be justified. In rapidly evolving professions like electrical engineering and biotech, work on the hottest company projects by itself may not keep you up to speed. Many techies have discovered that their skills have peaked five years after graduation and that they will be replaced by more recent graduates. "It's a real problem," says a top manager who asked not to be identified.

And if you're not a hot, young Silicon Valley engineer, the problem may be worse. Philip Breslin, retired manager of labor relations at Bethlehem Steel, says, "Work at most companies is more prosaic and less glamorous than that. For the assistant purchasing manager at a widget factory, it's hard to make the work fascinating enough to substitute for job security." Besides, says Breslin, jobs for many workers aren't transferable even in the same industry, because each company winds up developing unique ways of handling chores.

An antidote for some of those shortcomings appears to be a team-based approach to managing projects. Even if the widget maker can't make purchasing glamorous, says Breslin, "in many situations, team building is a substitute for pay raises and security. Not because it makes me employable elsewhere, but because it provides me with an identification with a group of people all trying to accomplish a set of goals." At Southwest Airlines, pilots sometimes help clean the plane, notes Charles O'Reilly, a Stanford management professor. "It signals a unity of purpose to the cleaning crew—that their work is as important as flying the plane."

The rapidly readjusting manager at Prudential says teamwork is important in other ways too. "My motivation comes from my co-workers," she says. Pay and job security are tied in part to how the team performs, and while she feels no loyalty to management, she is willing to work hard to help her teammates.

Including teammates in arriving at an individual's evaluation gives workers a better sense of job security too, says David Noer, a vice president at the Center for Creative

Leadership, in Greensboro, North Carolina. Peers are often a better judge of who is contributing and who is not. "Qualitative, boss-down evaluations are wrong," he says. "AT&T would have been better off with team-based appraisals."

One of the great unanswered questions of the new work arrangement is how 40ish and 50ish workers will fare if continually forced back into in-house or external labor markets to compete with younger, cheaper workers. James Medoff, a labor economist at Harvard, says older workers' generous paychecks are at some risk. For years a tacit agreement was in place in most companies, he says: "You get paid less than you're worth in the first half of your career and more than you're worth in the second half." Workers let go at 45 may find their new jobs don't pay more with age and feel cheated.

Growing old may not be a catastrophe for job-hoppers, though. Don McDermott, head of a human resources consulting company in Red Bank, New Jersey, says many companies that fired older workers are finding that the youngsters put in their place can't handle the job. Kirby Dyess at Intel says she has studied data looking for evidence that older workers have a harder time shifting between jobs there than younger ones, and hasn't found any.

Says Dyess: "The people who have a problem are the ones who never moved out of a job category, who never took a course, never got a degree, never took risks." That doesn't mean that Intel employees automatically get rewarded for getting old. "Salaries are variable. If I switch jobs in the company, I may find my new position doesn't pay as well as the last one. Nothing guarantees that my paycheck keeps getting bigger."

Will anyone ever spend 30 years with the same company again? Yes. Even the most aggressive exponents of the new employment contract say there will be plenty of lifers. Argues Hal Burlingame, executive vice president for human resources at AT&T: "People will have very long careers here. It just won't be static."

Not everyone gets a gold watch. What may evolve are two or three classes of employees, all with varying degrees of connectedness to the organization, and each getting a very different package of compensation and reward. Peter Moore, managing partner of Inferential Focus, a social trends think tank in New York City, says every company must identify "the critical intellectual strengths it needs to be successful over the long term. You lock those people in—make them captive to the organization, fully employed, compensated, and benefited." Even they may not be retained forever, says Moore. "I have one client where 80% of its revenues comes from businesses it wasn't in three years ago. So who is core in that company?"

Other tasks, advertising or data processing perhaps, get farmed out to a regular stable of individuals or organizations who are paid on a contract basis for results. And a third set of workers—telemarketers, widget assemblers, clerks, and so on—come in part time or as needed.

Whar many companies find is that if they won't offer security, they'd better offer freedom, and lots of it. American Express surveyed workers and found what they wanted more than anything else was free time. Some customer service agents and credit analysts there are now free to set their own hours and work dusk to dawn if they choose. Amex travel agents often work at home on computer terminals, answering calls from customers who don't have a clue. Michael Connors, a senior vice president (and full-timer), says their productivity has not diminished at all. Workers who want to improve job skills can drop in to career resource centers at several Amex facilities.

Intel discovered the best way to keep valued workers is to set them free occasionally. Every seven years Intel employees get an 11-week paid sabbatical. Yes, there is a seven-year itch, says Dyess, and workers run the risk of burnout if they can't get away.

Is there a place in all this for loyalty—workers devoted to the company instead of their own resume, or companies carrying workers whose contribution has peaked? Probably. Companies in anything but the rankest commodity business will always have to ask workers to invest in skills that are virtually useless elsewhere. Says Robert Paulson, head of McKinsey's aerospace practice in Los Angeles: "Companies are forced to make what they cannot buy. And what they make or do that others cannot is what makes them unique and gives them competitive advantage." A genuine commitment by companies to retrain workers with unusual skills is helpful, but not everyone can be recycled. Companies that fail to demonstrate some sort of fidelity to those workers won't find many new recruits for similar assignments.

There aren't any easy answers to problems caused for employees by competition and the rapidly changing skills that companies need to survive. But all workers deserve at least an honest explanation of how that change will affect them and what their employer will or won't do to help. "Employees don't expect the impossible," says Robert Levering, co-author of *The 100 Best Companies to Work for in America*, "but they do demand the possible. And good, two-way communication is probably the most important thing companies can do."

It's not just fair, it's practical too. Chevron has discovered that when it candidly explains its problems to employees, their commitment to the company and their work increases, even if the news is bad. And managers who demonstrate they care about their workers might just find they get loyalty in return.

Reprinted with permission June 13, 1994 issue of Fortune, (c) 1994 Time Inc. All rights reserved.

Leading-Edge Distribution Strategies

Neil S. Novich

The idea that a corporation's future may hinge on the quality of its distribution system is not always apparent. Yet leading-edge companies are discovering the hidden value of strong distribution systems.

Neil S. Novich is Vice President of Bain and Company, Inc., in Boston, Massachusetts. He leads the distribution and advanced logistics specialty group.

Like many textile companies in the United States, Milliken & Company faced the danger of being driven out of business by low-priced imports. To survive and even prosper, Milliken used a competitive weapon of increasing importance: high-quality logistics. The company managed to cut its turnaround time from six weeks to one week and increase its on-time delivery from 75 percent to 95 percent. In doing so, it was able to retain old customers and attract new ones.

Milliken is not alone. After focusing on product quality for nearly a decade, manufacturers have reached a critical transition point. No longer can they rely on quality improvements and competitive pricing alone to expand market share or even to hold on to existing market share. They must now include superior logistical service as a critical, integral part of their competitive strategy.

This development is a result of manufacturing's own success. In the early 1980s, leading-edge manufacturers began to realize they could not compete on price alone—quality had to enter the picture.

Consequently, the major focus of management attention in the last decade has been improving quality and productivity. But in the 1990s, quality has improved so broadly over so many product categories that it is no longer an adequate differentiator for customers.

There are now enough substitute products available, functionally equivalent in quality and features, that customers are free to consider other factors in their purchase decisions.

Manufacturers' decisions are therefore being driven not only by price and quality but also by service. Customers of manufacturers define good service as good logistics, including timeliness and reliability of deliveries, ease of placing orders, accuracy of shipments, and so on. Defects in these logistical services are as critical to customers as product defects.

Corporate Futures May Hinge on Logistics

Companies that realize the emerging importance of logistical service will be positioned to ride the crest of a new wave of growing market share and financial performance. Those that do not are likely to be caught in the undertow.

The idea that corporate futures may hinge on logistics is not always apparent to most executives. That is because companies view logistical service in a fundamentally different way than their customers do.

Manufacturers tend to rank the importance of functions in terms of cost—and logistics-related costs are typi-

Novich, Neil S., "Leading-Edge Distribution Strategies," *The Journal of Business Strategy*, November/December 1990, pp. 48-53. Reprinted with permission from *The Journal of Business Strategy*, November/December 1990, Copyright 1990

cally 10 percent or less of total costs. Not surprisingly, that is probably the percentage of management attention logistics receives. Compared to sales, marketing, product design, and manufacturing, logistics are perceived as a relatively unimportant component of the total approach to customers.

Yet this is not at all the way customers think about service. Research done by Ohio State University shows that service level is now as important as, or more important than, product quality and price in making manufacturer selections. In this study, customers in specific industries were asked to rate the importance of over one hundred characteristics in choosing a manufacturer.

Of those few characteristics rated most important in service, logistics were the most numerous, frequently appearing at the top of the list. Those logistical factors include meeting promised delivery dates, avoiding long lead times, filling orders accurately, and providing advance notice of shipping delays.

Why do customers place such an emphasis on service? Mainly because the cost of poor service can equal or exceed the actual purchase price of the product. If manufacturers' shipments are occasionally late, customers try to avoid being caught short by holding excess inventory and ordering too far in advance of need.

Nevertheless, a very late shipment can shut down a production line. In addition to paying for excess inventory, the customer bears the cost of double-checking shipments and invoices and correcting shipment and billing errors.

It is easy to underestimate the cost of such problems: One case study calculated the magnitude of such costs for hospitals. Even though manufacturers had delivery service levels in excess of 90 percent, the hospital's total cost of handling such materials as tubing and intravenous bags, as well as dealing with service-related problems, more than doubled the total purchase cost of products for the customer.

Since substitute products, equivalent in features and quality, are often available, customers can vote with their feet on service. A comprehensive study sponsored by the University of South Florida rated the availability of substitute products of a variety of manufacturers over a broad spectrum of industries. In general, substitutes on a product basis were readily available, leaving superior service as a major decision criterion in choosing manufacturers.

Providing good service does not just help customers—it also helps manufacturers. Just as the cost of poor service to customers is frequently underestimated, so the cost of poor customer service to manufacturers is also underestimated.

Higher Profits

Good service reduces customer turnover, which yields higher market share and reduces the acquisition cost of new customers. In fact, poor logistics are the cause of roughly 50 percent of all customer complaints from manufacturers and can be responsible for turnover levels as high as 15 percent to 20 percent. This has a direct effect on profitability.

Indeed, the Profit Impact on Market Strategy (PIMS) study by the Strategic Planning Institute reveals that companies rated as providing superior service achieve, on average, 7 percent higher prices than their competitors and grow 8 percent faster than low-service companies. On average, they are also twelve times as profitable.

Furthermore, the emerging need for service—and the fact that many manufacturers do not provide it adequately—has prompted many customers to rely on wholesalers, who tend to be more service oriented than manufacturers.

Wholesaling is growing almost 50 percent faster than manufacturing. From 1980 to 1990, the portion of products moving through wholesalers increased nearly 20 percent. This means that some profits originally captured by manufacturers are now being captured by distributors and that a manufacturer's market share and customer base are increasingly under the control of its distributors.

Caterpillar sets the standard for understanding and responding to its customers' needs. It realizes that the unavailability of a spare part can keep an expensive piece of equipment idle, costing Caterpillar's customers much more than the price of the part.

The firm's parts distribution network can deliver the right part anywhere in the world within forty-eight hours. The system is so reliable that Caterpillar receives an average of only two to three complaints per year.

Good service like this leads to outstanding financial performance for four reasons:

☐ **It enhances customer loyalty.** This accelerates growth of the customer bases, lowering acquisition costs for new customers and increasing the sales to each customer since long-term customers tend to buy more.
☐ **It increases referrals.** Many customers are searching for good logistical support, and long-term customers tend to speak well of manufacturers distinguished by good logistics.
☐ **It supports price premiums.** Since good logistics lower overall costs (the purchase price *and* the cost of handling the product), customers are willing to pay a higher purchase price in return for good logistics.
☐ **It reduces operating costs.** Less time and money are devoted to correcting faulty orders.

While improving logistical service is a complex process, some manufacturers have developed a service strategy as explicitly as they have developed manufacturing and marketing strategies. Development of such a service strategy centers on four essential steps:

- Understanding and measuring your customer service needs;
- Determining where and how the service system breaks down;
- Benchmarking your system against that of your competitors; and
- Simplifying the service system to meet needs better than competitors do.

Step 1: Understand and Measure Customer Service Needs

Most manufacturers have a poor idea of what customers consider to be good service. Frequently, customer service is measured in a way that is convenient for the manufacturer but not relevant to the customer.

Take back-order rates, for example. When manufacturers measure back-order rates—the portion of orders that cannot be filled immediately—they do not usually include customers who did not place an order because the product was not immediately available. In one example, internal back-order systems indicated 95 percent of customers were able to order what they wanted immediately. But that measure did count customers who decided not to place orders after they discovered the products had to be back ordered.

When the company carefully tracked and counted these customers, the successful order rate turned out to be 75 percent. In other words, the manufacturer's success rate (95 percent) was artificially high because it had not been counting the 20 percent of customers who figuratively walked out the door.

One manufacturer and distributor of building products typically served customers who were primarily concerned with the rapid availability of its products. In the past, the company took rapid availability to mean "available in a few days."

This, however, was not the right measure for most customers. The company's research revealed that half of all customers defined "availability" as "twenty-four-hour availability"—that is, available on an overnight basis.

One powerful method for understanding the customer's service needs is measuring customer turnover and determining the root cause for defections. Although customer turnover—new customers and customers who defected to other businesses—may represent a small proportion of total sales, low turnover is critical to profitability and growth.

Average nominal revenue growth of publicly held manufacturers, for instance, is about 5 percent per year. But for many companies, the 5 percent figure is actually the net result of growth rates of 10 percent or more in new customers revenue, minus a 5 percent or more decline in current customers revenue.

If all such defections could be stopped, real growth would leap to 10 percent or more—a doubling of growth, with an accompanying improvement in profitability and shareholder value.

Another method to understand customer needs is analyzing potential customers. Most manufacturers and distributors attain only a fraction of their total potential markets. Some noncustomers may indeed be unsuitable, but many may not be customers for reasons that can be corrected.

These correctable problems often center on service requirements that are not currently being met but could be. Problems can also center on the mere perception that such requirements are not being met. Looking at customer needs across an industry can add further insight into a broader spectrum of service that manufacturers should address.

Cablec, a leading manufacturer of electrical and electronic wire and cable, was not commonly used as a supplier for certain customer segments that required very fast order turnaround. By streamlining the manufacturing process, it was able to successfully service this high-profit group of customers and simultaneously reduce total inventory levels.

Of course, manufacturers may find that the services some potential customers want are too difficult or costly to provide. But most manufacturers can find some service improvements that are relevant, feasible, and attractive to customers.

Black & Decker has taken the understanding of customer needs one step further. The company focuses not only on customer needs but also on *future* customer needs. By surveying customers annually on how their needs may change, Black & Decker's logistical system is ready to respond immediately.

Step 2: Determine Where the Service Process Breaks Down

For a service problem to be corrected, it must be well defined. One method of accomplishing this is to understand exactly where the service process breaks down in specific instances. One case study, for example, showed that although a company attracted new customers, many went elsewhere after trying to place an order.

This was because telephone representatives lacked a ready way to cross-reference their own products to those of other manufacturers. After discovering the reason for this loss of customers, the company installed an on-line system that corrected it.

The best way to obtain relevant information on most service problems is by understanding the customer's purchasing process in detail. This means analyzing the ordering process from the customer's perspective and finding out when problems occur.

In doing so, a manufacturer should measure customer defections at each step, since sales are lost when a manufacturer "fails" one of the steps. In areas where defections are high, corrections have the potential to yield high profits.

Step 3: Benchmark Yourself Against Competitors

Caterpillar keeps its edge on parts availability by periodically benchmarking itself versus the competition. Every few years, the company performs a Competitive Parts Availability Test, which measures availability from competitors and provides information to correct weaknesses in Caterpillar's own distribution network.

In general, competitive weaknesses are uncovered by finding sections in the purchasing process where customers defect to competitors. Identifying and correcting these problems decrease customer turnover.

At each step in the purchase process where customers are lost to competitors, it is vital to understand where customers are going. If there is a pattern of frequent defection to specific competitors, those competitors should be carefully studied. This process can identify specific process improvements, which can be copied and used to stop particular types of customer defections.

L.L. Bean, for example, has defined seven key service objectives, called "Key Result Areas," which are as follows: ease of order placement, response to complaints, order representative courtesy and competence, return policies/guarantees, in-stock levels, shipping costs, and fulfillment time.

L.L. Bean not only monitors its own performance in these areas but also tests competitor performance as well. In this way, the company can be continuously assured that its service is the highest of any of its immediate competitors'.

Manufacturers should also look at the service of their indirect competitors: wholesalers. As mentioned earlier, wholesalers have managed to grow rapidly and take a significant part of the direct market share away from manufacturers by providing superior service.

Benchmarking should not stop with the immediate competitive set. Once the purchase process has been defined in some detail, there may be companies well outside the industry that have developed specific ways of handling customers at relevant steps which can be applied to other industries.

Step 4: Simplify the Whole Service System

The previous steps have involved mostly improving specific elements in the customer's purchase process. This alone may provide significant benefits, but it will not allow a company to achieve its full service potential. To do that, a company must work on the service system as a whole.

Most administrative and logistical processes for dealing with customers are unnecessarily complicated. First of all, the results produced by these systems are highly variable, because many transactions require handling on a case-by-case "exception" basis, and the amount of time it takes to complete a process is often inconsistent.

The systems are also inefficient. Many departments do not communicate and cooperate when resolving problems. The same activity, such as an approval for return, must often be duplicated by more than one person. The result is that the time required to process a transaction or issue is longer than it needs to be.

Of course, there is a reason for everything. But while complexity in service logistics may begin as a way to ensure consistency and contain service costs, it almost always ends up creating more inconsistency and costs. From relatively

...mple beginnings, processes appear to ...olve in the following way:

Accountability becomes unclear. Responsibility, authority, and accountability become delegated vertically, while approval authority is not delegated to the necessary degree. With too many layers of management approval, no one level is held accountable for decisions.

Responsibilities become vague. At the same time, power diffuses horizontally, and the understanding of which department is responsible for what becomes unclear. Confusion and internal competition ensue.

Reward system becomes incompatible with goals. Departmental goals and evaluation systems end up not supporting common goals, so the value/reward system is often incompatible with common goals.

Information becomes inconsistent. Information between, and even within, departments becomes inconsistent, moving on an ad hoc basis. Therefore, the information relevant to specific areas is spread over too many reports. Information about on-time deliveries, for example, is often available to the transportation departments but not to the customer service or sales departments.

Black & Decker attacked this problem by integrating its departments under one logistical system. Sales, marketing, manufacturing, distribution, transportation, and customer service all coordinate efforts toward improving the logistical system.

By simplifying processes and avoiding ...plication of effort among employees ...d departments, order cycle times can ... shortened and error rates drastically ...t. This results in vastly improved ser...ce, customers captured from competi...rs, and substantially improved market ...are and profitability.

Consider exceptions—the day-to-day transactions that, because of some problem or complication, do not turn out as the customer and company had hoped. Exceptions are usually more common than generally believed.

When each of hundreds of transactions by a specific company was examined in detail, the actual exception rate was found to be 70 percent. In other words, only 30 percent of actual transactions between the company and a customer conformed to a uniform standard and did not require intervention.

One company that successfully attacked complexity is Motorola. It now authorizes field service personnel to make repairs for customers without additional approval if the cost is less than $1,000. This has significantly decreased repair time and increased customer service and satisfaction.

L.L. Bean is again a good example. The company's goal is to resolve 90 percent of all customer problems while the customer is on the phone, and the operators are given considerable authority and a good information system to allow them to do so.

To reduce complexity in the whole service system, one must identify the key processes that are important to customers and then reduce inefficiencies by eliminating departmental overlap, avoiding duplicative steps, and shortening cycle times. One must also eliminate variability by reducing exceptions and standardizing cycle times.

Service is a critical element in the marketing mix, and it is rapidly becoming the most critical. Responding will not be easy; superior service means developing and managing a world class logistical organization. But many manufacturers are not experts in logistics.

Logistics require a very different set of capabilities than what makes a company superior in manufacturing. So manufacturers that are determined to improve their logistics have a lot to learn—and they need to start now. ■

BRACE FOR JAPAN'S HOT NEW STRATEGY

After a mighty effort, top U.S. companies are closing the quality gap. But their toughest rivals—guess who?—have moved on to *flexibility***. It's catch-up time again.**

by Thomas A. Stewart

Here's the good news: American business's campaign to improve quality is paying off so well that in many areas the Japanese no longer enjoy a clear lead. Now the bad news: While the quality gap narrows, the world's best competitors are suiting up for an even more challenging contest. It's called flexibility, and its watchwords are change fast, keep costs low, and respond quickly to customers. In the race between the U.S. and Japan, guess who's ahead. Says Aleda Roth, a manufacturing expert at Duke University's business school: "Most American companies are a generation behind—as far behind as they were on quality."

The theory behind flexibility is simple. If you and I are competing and I can read the market quicker, manufacture many different products on the same line, switch from one to another instantly and at low cost, make as much profit on short runs as on long ones, and bring out new offerings faster than you—or do most of these things—then I win. I can parry your every thrust, attack niches in your market that you're too bulky to squeeze into, improve faster, and maintain or even fatten profits while forcing you to follow my lead on prices.

Manufacturers and service companies alike will have to play the game to prosper. Many manufacturers will have to install a sophisticated battery of machine tools called a flexible manufacturing system (FMS), which in a single factory turns out immense varieties of product with computer-controlled robots. All companies will have to overhaul their information systems, methods of developing new products, and other techniques to respond to customers in a quick, versatile, and economical way.

To see flexibility in action, look east. That's the message of a revealing study released in July by Deloitte & Touche consultants. They asked 900 U.S. and Japanese companies to describe their key manufacturing strategies. Among the findings:

♦ **The Japanese stress flexibility.** While American manufacturers emphasize product quality (durability, conformance to specifications, and on-time delivery), the Japanese take those as a given. Their focus: more and better product features, flexible factories, expanded customer service, and rapid outpourings of new products.

♦ **They rate themselves ahead in nearly all aspects of the game**, including rapid changes in production methods and the number of new products they can create. That advantage will grow: Japanese manufacturers are about a third more likely than Americans to say increased flexibility figures importantly in their plans.

♦ **They are committed to staying ahead through advanced technology.** From a list of 38 technologies, such as computer-aided design, automated material handling, and robotics, Deloitte & Touche turned up just six in which Americans claimed more experience. Looking toward the future, Japanese companies are 25% more likely to emphasize leading-edge manufacturing, and have bigger investment plans for 33 of 42 advanced techniques.

Eventually, flexibility means dramatically changing one's ideas about how to run a business. In a visionary study that drew on people from 77 U.S. companies, the Iacocca Institute of Lehigh University concluded, "We stand at the threshold of a new era in manufacturing. "Beyond mass and lean production beckons "agile production," where factories are small and modular and machinery is reprogrammable to make an almost infinite variety of new or customized goods at low unit cost. Says the institute's operations director, Roger Nagel: "Whatever you thought your break-even could be, that figure can be a lot smaller today—usually less than half." In an age of demanding consumers, mass production won't cut it.

Many top-flight U.S. companies are working hard to develop these abilities—Figgie International, General Electric, and Motorola, for example. Baxter Healthcare is testing the ultimate in modularity—an intravenous solutions factory that can be shipped anywhere, set up in a week, and moved anytime—and considers itself one of the world's standard-bearers in a mind-boggling technology called "rapid prototyping." In Deerfield, Illinois, Baxter routinely makes working prototypes of complex medical instruments for its Belgian design center, shipping them just 24 hours after receiving the specs.

As a group, however, the Americans are no match for their transpacific rivals. The Japanese have invested in flexibility for the better part of a decade, but it's only now becoming clear how strong a weapon it is. Says MIT professor Charles Sabel: "The strategy is becoming more and more explicit—to make progress by splitting markets. The goal is a totally plastic production system, one that—within some reasonable area—allows a factory to turn out anything." Even more exciting (or alarming, depending on whose ox is gored), some manufacturers—Toyota, for one—have begun to learn about flexibility what they taught the world about quality: It can actually save money.

Japan's flexibility drive was fueled by a boom in capital spending—$3 trillion in domestic plant and equipment from 1986 to 1991, says Kenneth Courtis, senior economist of Deutsche Bank in Tokyo. Though Japanese investment leveled off as the economy slowed, private industry bought new plant and equipment worth $5,320 a person in Japan last year, vs. $2,177 in America. Those figures are adjusted to reflect the fact that Japan's capital-equipment market is so competitive that prices are 30% lower than in the U.S.

No one knows how much of that money went into flexibility, because investments can serve more than one end. But an analysis by Taka Ananuma of the Tokyo office of the A.T. Kearney consulting firm shows that in one area—spending for information technology—three out of four manufacturers cited as one of their aims flexibility enhancement through such means as FMS and computer-integrated manufacturing, almost twice the number naming the next-leading purpose (office automation).

Flexibility is an explicit goal at Toshiba, whose $35.5 billion in sales last year came from products as diverse as appliances and computers, light bulbs and power plants. Okay, so the slogan "synchronize production in proportion to customer demand" probably made few hearts leap when Toshiba workers first heard it in 1985. The idea, explains Toshiba President Fumio Sato, is to push Toshiba's two dozen factories to adapt faster to markets. Says Sato: "Customers wanted choices. They wanted a washing machine or a TV set that was precisely right for their needs. We needed variety, not mass production."

Sato hammered home his theme in an almost nonstop series of factory visits. The key to variety: finding ways to make money from ever shorter production runs. Sato urged managers to reduce setup times, shrink lead time, and learn to make more products with the same equipment and people. He says: "Every time I go to a plant I tell the people, 'Smaller lot!' "

If that's your creed, says Lester Thurow, dean of the Sloan School of Management at MIT, a visit to Toshiba's computer factory in Ome, 30 miles from downtown Tokyo, "is like being in heaven." Toshiba calls Ome an "intelligent works" because a snazzy computer network links office, engineering, and factory operations, providing just-in-time information as well as just-in-time parts. Ome workers assemble nine different word processors on the same line and, on an adjacent one, 20 varieties of laptop computers. Usually they make a batch of 20 before changing models, but Toshiba can afford lot sizes as small as ten.

Workers on the lines have been trained to make each model but don't need to rely on memory. A laptop at every post displays a drawing and instructions, which change when the model does. Product life cycles for low-end computers are measured in months these days, so the flexible lines allow the company to guard against running short of a hot model or overproducing one whose sales have slowed.

Sato's next goal: to get managers thinking about how to ship small lots fast and cheaply, with quicker feedback from stores, so sales and distribution are as flexible as the factories.

He could do worse than check out Kao Corp., Japan's biggest soap and cosmetics company and the sixth largest in the world, with 1991 sales of $4.7 billion. James Abegglen, chairman of Gemini Consulting (Japan), says no company can match the flexibility of Kao's distribution. It derives from a stunning information system that allows the company and its wholly owned wholesalers to deliver goods within 24 hours to any of 280,000 shops, whose average order is for just seven items.

The goal at Kao isn't flexible manufacturing per se. Rather, says Masayuki Abe, a systems development manager, "the purpose is to maximize the flexibility of the whole company's response to demand." That's done by collecting and distributing data with an Orwellian obsessiveness—ten gigabytes of it at any one time, enough to fill 128,000 pages of text. One system links everything: sales and shipping, production and purchasing, accounting, R&D, marketing, hundreds of shopkeepers' cash registers, thousands of salesmen's hand-held computers. According to Abegglen, Kao boasts that the information is so complete that its accountants can turn out a year-end closing statement by noon of the first day of the new year.

Some American consumer products companies collect point-of-sale data—executives may receive information on the previous day's sales, for example—but at Kao the split-second linkage extends back to the factories and labs as well. Brand managers see daily sales, stock, and production figures. Within a day they can learn if a competitor is running a sale, and adjust accordingly. When Kao brings out a new product, it melds point-of-sale information from 216 retailers with a test-marketing operation called the Echo System, which uses focus groups and consumers' calls and letters to gauge public response faster than market surveys do. Says William Best of A.T. Kearney's Tokyo office: "Kao can know if a product will be successful within two weeks of launch. They know who's buying it, whether the packaging works, whether to change anything." That helps explain how Kao stormed into the highly profitable cosmetics business, going from nowhere to No. 2 in Japanese market share in less than ten years.

Kao's network virtually eliminates the lag between an event in the market (Ms. Watanabe buys a bar of soap) and the arrival of the news at the company. That makes Kao less dependent on sales forecasts and buffer inventory. As George Stalk of the Boston Consulting Group, an expert on Japanese corporations, has shown, speedy information lets a company even out production levels and increase variety without drowning in stock; indeed, though Kao makes 564 household products today, vs. 498 in 1987, average inventory as a percent of sales is down to 8.6% from 9.2%.

As Toshiba and Kao demonstrate, flexibility comes when information feeds the ability to exploit it. A flexible factory is useless if you don't know what's selling, and it doesn't help to know the market cold if you can't react to it back in the plant.

The plunging cost of computing power, combined with low-cost capital, put flexibility within reach even of second-tier companies in Japan. Take Fuji Electric, Japan's fourth-largest maker of electrical machinery (after Hitachi, Toshiba, and Mitsubishi Electric). Fuji's investment in FMS and the like soared starting in 1987—the effort consumes 30% of the capital budget—as come-hither prices for computers and numerically controlled machine tools coincided with cheap money. Says Takashi Kurihara, senior engineer for production technology: "We set a target of reducing lead time 30%, labor costs 70%, and work-in-process inventory 50%. We had to, because these are our customers' goals too."

When Fuji gets an order for an electric motor switch, 20% of the time the buyer wants—and gets—24-hour delivery. Another 40% must arrive within two days. Fuji didn't narrow its product line: Those schedules are for customized work.

The thanks go to flexible manufacturing. For example, at its plant in Saitama prefecture, Fuji makes magnetic contactors used to control motors in machine tools. Beginning in 1988, Fuji installed flexible, computer-integrated lines where setup, parts selection, and assembly are all automated using bar codes that tell the machines what to do. Before those lines, Fuji filled orders in three days. Now Fuji needs 24 hours, using one-third as many workers and almost one-third less inventory—making about 8,000 varieties, three times more than before.

Investment in flexibility isn't cheap, but over time it can save money. That's counterintuitive for managers raised to seek economies of scale. Flexibility offers economies of scope—the ability to spread costs across many products. Frank Andrusko, vice president of Amoco Fabrics & Fibers, has seen the contrast. His company and Nisseki Plastics, a Nippon Oil subsidiary, are partners in a joint venture to make non-woven fabric used to strengthen foil and paper packaging. "We like long runs," he says. "We use the same equipment, but they make very short runs at higher cost, with more differentiation that lets them get a higher price." The two also approach customers differently: "Their salespeople don't carry data sheets describing what's available. They ask, 'What do *you* want?' then make it. They need more people in research than we do."

Scale will always matter, but economies of scope have awesome, and sometimes superior, power. Explains Joel Goldhar, a professor at the Illinois Institute of Technology business school: "Compared with a million-unit factory, a two-million-unit factory will always be more economical. But a factory that makes 10,000 units of 200 different products can be just as economical—and with customization you can get unique products, which means monopoly prices."

In a flexible factory, scale and scope reinforce each other. No more vivid example exists than the auto industry. Japanese carmakers are rebuilding the heart of their factories to become even more versatile and labor-efficient—an effort that could once again give them fundamental cost advantages and protect their lead in the time and cost of bringing new cars to market.

Both Toyota and Nissan have zeroed in on the body assembly process, the stage where the separate stampings that make up underbody, side panels, cowl, and roof are welded together. This "body in white" is then rustproofed, painted, and sent to final assembly, where the engine, seats, and controls go in. Body assembly is the least flexible stage of production and therefore the point of greatest leverage; it is also a big user of time and money in model changes. For example, Ford shut two truck plants for the summer to retool for new models.

While many American auto plants still devote a production line to a single model, Toyota began installing flexible lines in the mid-Eighties. Toyota director Mikio Kitano, a bearded, voluble production engineer, says there is no theoretical limit to how many body types these lines can handle, "but four is good enough." Counting sunroofs and other options, that might mean 20 variations. The secret: "intelligent pallets," computer-controlled fixtures each programmed to hold the panels for a different model. The pallets work in rotation, picking up parts for various models as they come down the line and holding them together to be tack-welded by robots. A line can weld a Camry one minute, a Lexus the next, then a Crown, with no pause.

Setting up for a new model takes half the man-hours it used to, just four months—vs. nine of old—while the line continues to manufacture other cars; when all is ready, only one shift is needed to get a new model rolling with the others. As these lines went in, Toyota's capacity utilization climbed steadily, from 75% in 1982 to 95% today. The main reason, says Kitano: the one-shift model change.

Nissan's high-tech Intelligent Body Assembly System, or IBAS, accomplishes the same thing, though its ultimate ambition is more vaulting. Japan's No. 2 carmaker installed its first IBAS in Tochigi, north of Tokyo, in 1989; now it's in place at three other factories in Japan and in Smyrna, Tennessee. The heart of the IBAS is a cluster of 51 robots that grasp body parts, line them up to an accuracy within 0.1

millimeter, weld them, and inspect them, all in 46 seconds. In principle, they can be of any kind; on average, Nissan builds three models in each IBAS, some with several body types.

It takes three months to prepare a Nissan factory for a new model (it used to take 12), mostly to program robots and set up peripheral operations while the line keeps running. Says Yoshitada Sekine, engineering general manager at Nissan's plant at Zama, near Yokohama: "It will one day be possible for data created in Japan to be transmitted by phone or satellite and begin production of a new model simultaneously in any plant in the world."

Nissan describes its strategy as "five anys": to make anything in any volume anywhere at any time by anybody. IBAS is a big step toward the goal, says Sekine: "Minimum economic scale is now linked to the total output of a plant, not the individual model." That is, an IBAS can handle about 20,000 cars a month, but it doesn't much matter which models use the capacity. As U.S. automakers think about dropping whole car lines, Nissan is gearing up to fill market niches with *more* lines.

In 1981, Honda, its supremacy in motorcycles challenged by Yamaha, countered by introducing 113 new or revamped models in just 18 months. Yamaha cried uncle after managing 37 changes, announcing it was content to be No. 2. Will a similar "variety war" break out in cars? Says George Stalk of BCG: "I don't think they can stop. The war's destroying Saab, Renault, and Volvo. For GM and Ford, it's come down to new products—if they blink, they're gone."

The Ministry of International Trade and Industry (MITI) has prodded Japan's carmakers to slow their model changes. With all Asia before them like a ripening honeydew, why risk worse political heat in the U.S. and Europe? But model changes mean less as more cars are built to customer specifications. And history suggests that the Big Three ought not to count on their rivals' forbearance.

Even without a variety war, the Japanese will gain immensely from flexibility. The new lines cost more to build (10% more at Toyota, 20% at Nissan), but a single model change pays more than the difference due to lower tooling and other costs. Toyota claims a 60% saving compared with its old lines. Greater capacity utilization has saved Toyota the cost of building five production lines, and the company predicts that the number of workers on the body lines will fall 30% by 1994 from its level in 1986. By then, Toyota says, total savings will top half a billion dollars.

When it comes to hardware for flexible manufacturing, the Japanese lead is, if anything, widening. Okuma Corp., which makes the world's broadest machine-tool product line in two factories in the hills outside Nagoya, sells 14 flexible manufacturing systems in Japan for every one it exports to America. Though U.S. purchases of industrial robots are at record highs, Japan has already installed 390,000 to America's 45,000, according to Donald Vincent, executive vice president of the Robotic Industries Association. Brian Carlisle, CEO of California robot maker Adept Technology, says this represents a 15- to 20-year lead unless the U.S pace picks up dramatically.

Eric Mittelstadt, CEO of GMFanuc Robotics, a U.S.-Japanese joint venture that makes robots, says that when American companies automate, they tend to favor fancy, special-purpose lines to speed mass production rather than flexible systems or inexpensive robots that can be configured to serve many purposes. The $40 billion that GM spent on automation in the 1980s is a classic example but not unique. It took a major effort by managers and employees at GE Appliances in Kentucky to coax versatility out of inflexible labor-saving equipment bought a decade ago.

Just having the right equipment isn't enough, though; more important is how you use it. Six years ago Harvard business school professor Ramchandran Jaikumar reported that the typical American company with an FMS used it to turn out ten different items, Japanese companies 93. Says George Stalk: "We're still seeing that in spades. If you spend $700,000 on a big machining center, the factory manager wants to get his utilization rate up. So he uses it for his highest-volume products, defeating the purpose of the investment."

That wouldn't happen if U.S. companies saw flexibility as a strategic asset. Most don't, says Eric Mittelstadt, the robot maker: "Few of our customers have thought this through. They usually have a specific project in mind, like a model change, rather than a plan to use robotics to make the whole process flexible."

For a flexible manufacturer, the focus of competition begins to shift. Capital spending matters less when a factory can change its product line by upgrading and reprogramming existing equipment rather than by replacing it: Witness the 60% drop in the cost of tooling up for a new model on Toyota's body assembly lines. The savings show up in lower prices or enhanced features, or can be directed upstream to R&D and downstream to customer service.

Japanese companies surveyed by Deloitte & Touche plan to emphasize both lower-priced products and those with high R&D content—a formidable pairing. Hitachi, Toshiba, Fujitsu, Canon, and others now spend more in R&D than on plant and equipment. They can afford to because of flexible factories, says Fumio Kodama, professor of innovation policy at Saitama University near Tokyo: "The introduction of FMS has paradoxically brought about the situation in which we will not have to worry about manufacturing anymore." Follow the money, economist Courtis says: "The objective of the unprecedented level of investment in innovation and R&D is clearly to become the world's new-product laboratory—the role the U.S. had in the Fifties and Sixties."

Can America catch up? Absolutely, say Craig Giffi, Gregory Seal, and Douglas Shinsato, who conducted the Deloitte & Touche study. And now's the time. They say manufacturing follows an unavoidable progression from product quality (doing it right) through reliability (always doing it right) and only then to flexibility—adding variety and speed.

Many U.S. companies can take that step. Says Adept Technology's Carlisle: "We spent the Eighties on the basics—inventory management, quality control, reducing bureaucracy—stuff the Japanese did in the Sixties and Seventies. Most of that is out of the way now."

Just in time, as a window of opportunity opens. Fortunately for their competitors, Japanese companies have pushed the pause button as their economy struggles and industry adjusts to a post-bubble financial market. Also, says Paul-Josef Lantz of Baring Securities in Tokyo, the flexibility of Japan's industry has overwhelmed its transportation network. Just-in-time deliveries of ever smaller quantities of ever more goods have clogged roads, forcing some companies to curtail variety proliferation. In response, the Ministry of Transport says it will spend more than $3 trillion in the next ten years on automated distribution centers and rail, harbor, and road improvements—encouraged by the U.S. government in the mysterious belief that the investment will help America compete. (At least it isn't corporate investment, the theory goes, and U.S. contractors might win some business.) When Japan catches its breath, its companies will roar back.

To exploit this fleeting moment American companies must acknowledge that quality is just a start. The flexibility wars are coming. It's not hard to know you're in one, says Eric Mittelstadt: "You see your competitor making lots more products, but he's still meeting you on price, and he's still making a profit, and he's starting to beat you on the content—to get a technology lead—because he can make changes quicker." If that's happening to you—or could—you'd better get going.

Reprinted with permission September 21, 1992 issue of Fortune, (c) 1992 Time Inc. All Rights Reserved

Global Manufacturing Strategies and Practices: A Study of Two Industries

Scott T. Young
University of Utah, Salt Lake City
K. Kern Kwong and Cheng Li
California State University, Los Angeles, and
Wing Fok
Loyola University, New Orleans, USA

Introduction

Recent years have seen the re-ordering of global manufacturing powers. Once dominant, the USA has witnessed an erosion of global market share in industry after industry. At the same time, European manufacturers have been forced into a downsizing posture. Japanese firms have built upon manufacturing strategies in many industries and markets to achieve their current prowess in global competitiveness. Japanese manufacturing has been intensely studied by Western researchers in an effort to understand the transformation of the country's industrial capabilities. Schonberger[1] and Hall[2] studied the tactical aspects of the Japanese success, while Wheelwright[3] described Japanese manufacturing firms' strategic use of capacity, facilities, vertical integration, production processes, the workforce, quality, and production planning and control.

In recent years, South Korea has threatened Japan in several markets, using labour-cost advantage to become the cost leader. Korean manufacturing is now the object of much speculation and interest. Could Korea become the next Japan? Meanwhile, economic policies in the People's Republic of China have loosened to the extent that students of the global marketplace have speculated on the future success of a communist entry into selected markets.

Manufacturing in the USA has experienced significant declines in industries once believed sacrosanct and Western Europe, with the possible exception of West Germany, suffered similar declines in the 1980s.

This study examines the manufacturing practices and strategies of China, Korea, Japan, Western Europe and the USA in two industries: small machine tools and non-fashion textiles. The objective of this study is to compare international production practices within the context of industry capabilities and manufacturing strategy.

Methodology

The Korea Productivity Center and the Sogang Institute for Economics and Business originated a study of the manufacturing practices in Korea[4]. This study interested other researchers in international manufacturing and a team was formed with members including the Shanghai Institute of Mechanical Engineering, IMD (the international business school in Lausanne, Switzerland), and the Business School at Indiana University. The first data collection efforts were in China, Korea, Japan, Western Europe, and the USA. Questionnaires were administered either by mail or by personal interview, translated into the appropriate language and focused on six key areas of production: forecasting, production planing, scheduling, shopfloor procedures, purchasing and materials management. The sample sizes are listed in Table I. Non-response to a mailed questionnaire was initially quite high, so the research team contacted manufacturing managers by telephone and arranged in-person interviews. The intention of the project, first undertaken in 1987, was to determine the current state of manufacturing practices in these countries. This research represents the early phase of ongoing global studies now conducted by the Global Manufacturing Research Group (GMRG) of the University of North Carolina, directed by D. Clay Whybark.

The research teams selected the machine tools and textiles industries because they were present in all the countries. The teams believed single-industry studies would be more instructive than multi-industry studies, in view of the variation of industry-specific practices.

	Machine tools	Textiles
China	44	56
Japan	18	36
Korea	89	33
Europe	34	24
USA	45	50

Machine Tools

Vast differences among the countries' capabilities must be considered. China's machine tools have been described as of inferior quality and technologically primitive. The tools are not carefully engineered and are less durable than those produced in other nations. The machine tool industry has primarily been responsible for providing tools to the Chinese defence industry. Chinese authorities reduced capital investment from 1976 to 1980, resulting in the continued production of outdated tools and the inability to produce higher quality lathes and milling machines. Consequently, little export of Chinese machine tools takes place. The industry is updating technologically and importing advanced technology tools, primarily from Japan, the USA, Switzerland and West Germany[5].

The Japanese concept of "quality at the source" is not a trademark of Korean manufacturing. Kang commented on how the Korean manufacturing attitude of "get started, see how it goes, and fix it later", differs startlingly from the Japanese fervour about quality control[6]. Despite this different philosophy, Korean products have been noted for quality and innovation[7].

Japan is the world leader in machine tools. In 1975, Japan ranked fourth in the world and produced half of the US total. By 1982, Japan had captured the world lead and in 1990 possessed over half of the market share in the USA. The Japanese accomplished this by introducing less expensive and easier-to-operate numerically controlled (NC) machine tools. By being at the leading technology edge, Japan quickly gained the world lead in the industry trends of automated and unmanned systems using new materials[8].

West Germany manufactures 62 per cent, Italy 18.6 per cent, the UK 9.3 per cent and France 8.7 per cent of the machine tools in Western Europe[9]. In the period from 1978 to 1984, these countries suffered an average of 28 per cent reduction in the industry workforce, with that in the UK being 59 per cent. This was caused by business lost to Far-Eastern suppliers and an overall industry recession in the early 1980s. In terms of sales, the UK dropped 27 per cent in this seven-year period, while West Germany, France and Italy slightly increased sales. Also, there were 10 per cent fewer factories in Western Europe in 1984 than in 1975.

With the Western European aims of reducing manufacturing costs, achieving more flexibility, and shortening processing times[9], there was an expected increase in the use of CAD/CAM, NC machine tools, FMS (Flexible Manufacturing Systems) and cellular manufacturing. Within Western Europe, the possible inability of many of the UK firms to meet these challenges was perhaps the most serious concern.

The US machine tools industry, the world leader from the Second World War to the early 1980s, held a global share of less than 10 per cent by 1989[10]. Reasons abound for this decline, but one cause is the cheap licencing of technology to Japanese machine tool makers in exchange for Far-Eastern marketing channels. NC machine tools were invented in the USA, but it was the Japanese manufacturers who became the standard bearers for the technology. The US industry has rebounded somewhat from a perilous low in 1982, but a trade agreement was necessary to limit Japanese imports. Japanese firms have since circumvented the agreements by locating plants in the USA and 30 per cent of the US machine tool capacity was Japanese owned by 1990[11].

Textiles

China is the world's largest textile producer and textiles are its greatest export. China competes against Korea in the lower-quality end of the textiles market and has lower labour costs than Korea. China was fifteenth in the world in textiles in 1973 and sixth by 1983[12,13].

Textiles are also Korea's greatest export. 62 per cent of the textiles produced in Korea are exported. However, structural changes are jeopardizing Korea's global strength. There have been significant technical innovations in the arts of spinning and weaving, while Korea is burdened with older machines. Rising domestic wage rates have also hurt Korea's textile industry, while the average Korean works 2,833 hours per year compared to 2,168 by the Japanese[6]. Quality improvements in the industry have been slow and productivity has diminished.

Korea, Hong Kong, Taiwan and China threatened Japan's textile industry to the extent that they took a third of the Japanese market. Japan lost share primarily in the lower-cost and lower-quality markets and countered by moving to the production of materials requiring technological capabilities beyond the reach of its Asian competitors. Innovative machinery and large investments in research and development are characteristics of the Japanese textile industry[9].

West Germany adopted a textile industry strategy similar to that of Japan. The Germans turned from competition with the low-cost Far-Eastern countries to production of speciality products[12]. The West German industry can be described as highly specialized with high productivity. German banking was very involved in the decisions of German textile manufacturing because of its high equity stake in the industry. Government assistance was minimal.

Among other European countries, only Italy has increased its global market share in recent years. Italy succeeded as a result of factors such as geographical production concentrations which reduced transportation costs, lower labour costs from locations in high-unemployment areas, and the use of modern technology and modern management practices, including computerized inventory control. The UK textile industry has declined since 1973, a victim of recession, Far-Eastern competition and failed strategies. UK productivity in the textile industry is approximately half that in the USA[13].

Imports seriously affected labour-intensive and short-run fabric markets in the US textiles industry[11]. In reaction, US manufacturers de-emphasized products which could not compete with the imports and focused their efforts upon domestics, including sheets, towels and pillowcases. In 1990, domestic mills were operating at capacity, primarily supplying domestic markets. The trade deficit in textiles was enormous. In 1977, 743 million pounds of textiles were exported and 1,286 million pounds were imported. Ten years later, 913 million pounds were exported and 4,417 million pounds were imported.

Manufacturing Practices

This section will discuss production practices in Japan, Korea, China, the USA and Western Europe.

When asked what the two most important uses of the production plan were, the responses differed widely across countries. The Chinese machine tool managers listed subcontracting and material planning, the Japanese, listed operations scheduling and facilities planning, the Koreans, materials planning and operations scheduling, the Europeans, operations scheduling and materials planning, and the US, operations scheduling and manpower planning (see Table III).

Subcontracting was rarely mentioned by the Japanese and Koreans as a use for the production plan. Operations scheduling was of little concern to the Chinese. Since the Chinese tool industry's largest customer was its own defence industry, there was an obvious absence of market pressures. Subcontracting was also most important to the Chinese textile industry, while materials planning was most important to the Japanese and operations scheduling to the Koreans.

	Percentage responding				
	China	Japan	Korea	Europe	USA
Machine tools					
Budget preparation	32	11	19	38	18
Subcontracting	91	6	3	35	2
Manpower planning	0	28	3	15	47
Facilities planning	20	33	11	35	11
Operations schedule	16	61	34	47	49
Materials planning	52	28	57	44	44
Purchasing	7	28	0	24	24
Other	7	6	0	0	2
Textiles					
Budget preparation	57	19	24	33	10
Subcontracting	84	14	6	46	2
Manpower planning	0	3	6	13	38
Facilities planning	7	22	9	58	8
Operations schedule	2	44	36	38	58
Materials planning	30	58	30	38	66
Purchasing	4	25	0	13	14
Other	0	3	0	0	0

[a] Respondents were asked to list at least two from the list.

The US textile managers had a decided preference for using the production plan for materials planning and operations scheduling, while the European managers found the plan more useful for facilities planning and subcontracting.

Clearly, computers were slow to gain acceptance for production planning in Korea and China (see Table III). The Japanese used computers to varying degrees in both industries, but electronic data interchange (EDI) between buyer and supplier was not reported in either industry (Table IV). The US and European machine tools managers reported much more extensive use of computers for production planning and scheduling than the textile industry managers in their own countries.

Lead times varied widely in the machine tool industry. The US machine tool industry has the longest lead time with an average of 166 days, compared to the 42 days for Japan and 54 days for Korea (Table V). US textiles had more competitive lead times of 26 days, the same as the Japanese, while the Koreans lagged behind with 45 days. However, these figures depend on what is being manufactured.

The Korean manufacturers were more customer-driven in both industries than the Japanese, Chinese and the USA according to the determination of delivery dates (Table VI), obtained from the response to the question, "How is the delivery date determined: By customer, negotiated or by the supplier?"

to meet demand in these industries. Primitive production scheduling practices could cause these problems.

Material shortages were cited most frequently by both US industries as the most frequent cause of late orders.

Considering the lack of computer involvement in production planning in the Far East, it was no surprise that there was little use of Material Requirements Planning (MRP). Korea and China were noticeably more involved with MRP than Japan (Table VIII). Seventy-three per cent of US machine tools managers and 50 per cent of the textiles managers reported using MRP. In Europe, 63 per cent of the machine tools managers and 42 per cent of the textiles managers reported some extent of MRP involvement.

Notable is the high percentage of Far-Eastern respondents who had never heard of JIT. This may be explained because they may call it Kanban or something else or as they are not familiar with the concept (Table IX). However, the use of JIT by the Chinese and US machine tool industries seemed unnecessary in view of their lead times. Multiple sourcing was also more frequently reported in both industries than single sourcing (Tables X and XI). European and American managers demonstrated a decided preference for multiple over single sourcing.

	Percentage responding				
	China	Japan	Korea	Europe	USA
Machine tools					
Not at all	68	17	82	6	9
Occasionally	20	22	11	21	9
Moderate	9	39	0	21	38
Extensive	0	17	0	41	44
No response	3	5	7	11	0
Textiles					
Not at all	89	50	79	12	34
Occasionally	7	25	9	21	18
Moderate	2	19	0	42	34
Extensive	0	3	0	17	14
No response	2	3	12	8	0

	Percentage responding[a]				
	China	Japan	Korea	Europe	USA
Machine tools					
Orally	11	22	13	6	38
Written	98	89	78	85	80
Computer	0	0	0	26	22
Other	9	22	0	6	11
Textiles					
Orally	27	50	9	25	46
Written	89	56	79	67	74
Computer	0	0	0	17	6
Other	25	11	0	5	14

[a] Responses total more than 100 per cent due to multiple forms of purchase order transmission.

The Koreans were heavily slanted towards the customer in both industries, while only the Japanese and US textile industries had a similar orientation.

When listing the causes of late orders (Table VII), the Chinese machine tool industry highlighted lack of labour capacity and material shortages, while their textile industry listed transport problems and lack of labour capacity. The popular belief has been that Chinese manufacturing has had an almost infinite source of labour, but here we discover that they sometimes lack enough labour

	China	Japan	Korea	Europe	USA
Machine tools	142	42	54	163	166
Textiles	27	27	45	43	26

	Percentage responding				
	China	Japan	Korea	Europe	USA
Machine tools					
Mostly by customer	14	33	65	18	24
Negotiation	70	33	19	59	22
Mostly by us	14	33	9	23	42
No response	2	1	7	0	12
Textiles					
Mostly by customer	34	44	45	38	40
Negotiation	52	42	18	42	20
Mostly by us	11	6	12	20	38
No response	3	6	25	0	2

	Percentage responding				
	China	Japan	Korea	Europe	USA
Machine tools					
Machine capacity	25	39	39	12	9
Lack labour capacity	41	28	22	32	29
Product bottlenecks	9	44	13	47	29
Transportation	11	0	0	35	0
Material shortages	34	11	25	26	51
Quality problems	16	17	44	9	29
Due-date changes	23	33	0	21	9
Other	20	0	13	0	31
Textiles					
Lack machine capacity	11	36	39	8	32
Lack labour capacity	50	11	15	46	24
Product bottlenecks	25	36	15	33	38
Transportation	70	0	0	42	2
Material shortages	32	28	18	38	48
Quality problems	16	17	45	17	20
Due-date changes	7	83	9	17	8
Other	11	28	0	0	10

[a] Respondents were asked to list two.

	Percentage responding				
	China	Japan	Korea	Europe	USA
Machine tools					
Never heard of it	48	67	49	24	7
Benefiting from it	7	6	9	44	38
Using, not benefiting	9	17	8	3	2
No need for it	7	0	0	12	20
Beginning to implement	7	0	0	9	24
Difficult implement[a]	20	6	30	3	9
No response	2	4	4	3	0
Textiles					
Never heard of it	55	83	39	46	26
Benefiting from it	0	0	9	38	20
Using, not benefiting	7	8	18	4	0
No need for it	7	0	0	8	24
Beginning to implement	7	0	0	8	0
Difficult implement[a]	20	6	30	4	18
No response	4	3	8	4	12

[a] "Difficult implement" means that a difficult implementation of MRP is in progress.

	Percentage responding				
	China	Japan	Korea	Europe	USA
Machine tools					
Never heard of it	48	11	39	9	4
Benefiting from it	0	22	1	18	13
Using, not benefiting	0	6	0	3	2
No need for it	23	0	0	32	42
Beginning to implement	0	39	9	12	18
Difficult implement	27	11	47	24	18
No response	2	11	4	2	3
Textiles					
Never heard of it	55	47	36	50	22
Benefiting from it	0	0	0	13	24
Using, not benefiting	0	6	12	0	4
No need for it	5	22	0	25	22
Beginning to implement	0	6	9	8	18
Difficult implement	23	17	42	4	8
No response	17	2	10	5	2

	Percentage responding				
	China	Japan	Korea	Europe	USA
Machine tools					
Long-term contract	59	50	9	47	29
Hedging	48	0	3	9	13
Single sourcing	2	17	0	15	18
Large-quantity purchase	20	17	0	15	13
Multiple sourcing	41	56	0	59	67
Sister plants	39	6	0	15	2
Textiles					
Long-term contract	66	56	12	75	58
Hedging	21	11	6	17	16
Single sourcing	5	6	0	8	16
Large-quantity purchase	11	17	0	13	26
Multiple sourcing	39	75	0	46	54
Sister plants	38	3	0	8	4

[a] Respondents chose one or more.

	Percentage responding				
	China	Japan	Korea	Europe	USA
Machine tools					
One	5	17	44	21	13
Two or three	34	61	19	68	73
Four +	61	6	13	6	11
No response	0	16	24	5	3
Textiles					
One	2	22	30	17	16
Two or three	34	67	9	63	74
Four +	52	8	24	13	10
No response	12	5	37	7	0

prohibited from this practice by Item 807 of the Tariff Schedule of the USA, although this does not prohibit offshore manufacturing for the apparel industry.

The machine tools industry is one in which the Japanese are in the forefront of technology and innovation, with firms in other countries following their lead. In Europe, there were decided differences in the strategic use of the workforce between the UK and West Germany. West Germany employed a formal system of vocational training which led to a lifetime career. Vocational training was followed by a two- or three-year apprenticeship. Such a system contributed to an international reputation for skill in manufacturing. The UK's weaknesses in manufacturing were partly attributed to poor development of human resources[12]. Training was carried out within the plant, so the British plant learning curve could be expected to be longer than that of a West German plant.

Government involvement in industry strategies was extensive. Most governments were protectionists for both industries and were involved in recommending global industry strategies. South Korea actually prohibited textile imports unless they were re-exported. The USA limited Japanese imports in the machine tools industry. Only West Germany could be described as *laissez-faire*, welcoming a free market.

Firms within these industries varied their strategies, but industry strategies could be classified into a global competitive scheme, based upon their industry competitive orientation. Porter[21] recommended sharply limiting direct co-operation among industry rivals, arguing that Western governments have misunderstood the role of the Japanese Ministry of International Trade and Industry (MITI). MITI projects work best in stimulating proprietary research and Japanese firms do not contribute their best engineers and scientists to co-operative projects.

Hayes and Wheelwright[16] wrote that firms could be classified into four stages of manufacturing strategy:

(1) *Internally neutral.* Production simply makes the product and ships it.
(2) *Externally neutral.* Manufacturing merely meets the standards set by competition.
(3) *Internally supportive.* Manufacturing attempts to become unique compared to its competition.
(4) *Externally supportive.* Manufacturing pursues uniqueness on a global scale, becoming a world-class competitor.

According to the Hayes and Wheelwright framework, both Japanese industries could be considered to be at stage (4) and the Korean industries at stage (3).

	China	Japan	Korea	Europe	USA
Machine tools	1	4	3	—[a]	2
Textiles	3	4	3	—[a]	3

[a] Not possible to classify because of divergence of national strategies.

Manufacturing Strategy

Several manufacturing strategy areas outlined by Hayes and Wheelwright[16] are pertinent here: quality, production planning, technology and the work force. Japanese quality control is world renowned, with empirical and anecdotal evidence supporting its superiority[1,17]. Korean quality, while not taken as seriously as the Japanese, appears to meet competitive standards[6,7]. Japan was the world leader in machine tools, with quality and technology being the driving reasons. China has struggled to provide adequate tools for its own domestic needs owing to its inferior quality, production planning and technology.

JIT did not appear to be prevalent in these industries. Though the Japanese lead in technology, they appear to be slower to adopt computerized manufacturing information systems than the Koreans.

The Chinese workforce has expected lifetime employment in the past, but in 1986, domestic labour reforms instituted labour contracts in which either the employer or employee can decide not to renew at the expiration of the contract[18]. The typical Chinese worker takes home $45 per month, including a $10 bonus. Chinese managers appeal to the workers' moral and political motivations rather than to material motivations. The state establishes production quotas, and profits are appropriated by the government and allocated to units which experience losses. As a result, state enterprises have little motivation to exceed their quotas[19].

Before the Second World War, the UK's spinning and weaving technologies were the world standard. Since that time, US-based technologies have dominated the industry and today the USA is generally regarded to have the most productive and cost efficient industry in the world[20]. The Far East became strong because much of the textile industry was labour intensive. West Germany succeeded with a strategy of offshore manufacturing to take advantage of the labour cost differential (labour in West Germany is more expensive than in the USA). The UK has not used this strategy as a matter of principle and US textiles were

The Chinese textile industry was at stage (1), but the Chinese machine tool industry at stage (1) (see Table XII). National industrial capability greatly constrains manufacturing in China, as it enhances manufacturing in Japan. Because of the divergence of European strategies, it was not possible to determine a unified strategy. The USA textile industry, with its heavy domestic-market concentration, could be classified as being at stage (3) and the machine tools industry, so late to react to global trends, at stage (2).

Conclusions

The principles of quality and technological innovation which brought the Japanese success in the automobile and electronics industries could be found in both the machine tools and the textile industries. The survey did not reveal any strategic use of production planning practices other than the fact that the Japanese were faster at producing machine tools than the Chinese, Europeans and Americans. However, a competitive advantage was gained by simply outperforming the rest of the industry in production planning.

Korea has increasingly become an exporter to be reckoned with. The Japanese success formulae have been well documented and the Koreans seem to be following a similar pattern. The large-scale entrance of the People's Republic of China into international trade, clouded by the political events of 1989, was years away in the industries we analysed. The unification of Europe in 1992 will result in reduced industry costs, but the final impact cannot be determined. At present, national policies and strategies and firm performances differ substantially among the European countries in these industries and it is difficult to speculate on the global impact.

The relative absence of information systems for production planning in any of these countries could produce a source of competitive advantage for the USA. US manufacturers have more information available for production planning than their Far-Eastern competitors.

This research has described global manufacturing practices and strategies in the machine tool and textile industries. A lesson to be learned from this research is that studying international operations at the industry level is an approach which can yield information quite different from what is expected. Micro studies of individual firms are also needed to provide an in-depth understanding. However, the industries selected for this study were greatly influenced by Government policy. Cultural and language barriers have made an international empirical study difficult, but the only way we can develop a proper global perspective of operations is for researchers to visit plants throughout the world. This research, with the collaborative efforts of the aforementioned groups, is a step in that direction.

References

1. Schonberger, R.J., *Japanese Manufacturing Techniques*, The Free Press, New York, NY, 1982.
2. Hall, R.W., *Zero Inventories*, Irwin, Homewood, IL, 1983.
3. Wheelwright, S.C. "Japan — Where Operations Really Are Strategic", *Harvard Business Review*, Vol. 59 No. 4, 1981, pp. 67-74.
4. Rho, B. and Whybark, D.C., "Comparing Manufacturing Practices in the People's Republic of China and South Korea", Working Paper No. 4, Indiana Center for Global Business, Indiana University, 1988.
5. Davenport, A., "Forging a Modern Machine Tool Industry", *The China Business Review*, May-June 1988, pp. 38-44.
6. Kang, T.W. *Is Korea the Next Japan?*, The Free Press, New York, NY, 1989.
7. Magaziner, I.C. and Patinkin, M., "Fast Heat: How Korea Won the Microwave War", *Harvard Business Review*, Vol. 67 No. 1, 1989, pp. 83-93.
8. Sarathy, R., "The Interplay of Industrial Policy and International Strategy: Japan's Machine Tool Industry", *California Management Review*, Vol. 31 No. 3, 1989, pp. 132-60.
9. "Holding the Lead in the Machine Tool Industry Proves Tough", *Business Japan*, 32, September 1987, pp. 95-104.
10. Holland, M., *When the Machine Stopped*, Harvard Business School Press, Boston, MA, 1989.
11. *Standard & Poors Industry Surveys*, Standard & Poors, New York, NY, 1990.
12. *The World Bank, Korea: Managing the Industrial Transition*, The World Bank, Washington, DC, 1987.
13. Johnstone, B., "Textiles Diversification Helps to Protect Profits", *Far Eastern Economic Review*, Vol. 142, 13 October 1988, pp. 54-6.
14. Commission of the European Communities, *The Social Aspects of Technological Developments Relating to the European Machine-tool Industry*, Office for Official Publications of the European Communities, Luxembourg, 1986.
15. Ghadar, F., Davidson, W. and Feigenoff, C., *US Industrial Competitiveness*, Lexington Books, Lexington, MA, 1987.
16. Hayes, R.H. and Wheelwright, S.C., *Restoring Our Competitive Edge*, John Wiley & Sons, New York, NY, 1984.
17. Garvin, D.A., "Quality Problems, Policies, and Attitudes in the United States and Japan: An Exploratory Study", *Academy of Management Journal*, Vol. 29, 1986, pp. 653-73.
18. Horsley, J.P., "The Chinese Workforce", *The China Business Review*, May-June, 1988, pp. 50-5.
19. Zhuang, S.C. and Whitehill, A.M., "Will China Adopt Western Management Practices?", *Business Horizons*, March-April 1989, pp. 58-64.
20. Toyne, B., Arpan, J., Barnett, A., Ricks, D., Shimp, T., Andrews, J., Clamp, J., Rogers, C., Shepherd, G., Tho, T., Vaughn, E. and Woolcock, S., *The Global Textile Industry*, George Allen & Unwin, London, 1984.
21. Porter, M.E., *The Competitive Advantage of Nations*, The Free Press, New York, NY, 1990.

Young, Scott T., K. Kern Kwong, Cheng Li, and Wing Fok, "Global Manufacturing Strategies and Practices: A Study of Two Industries," *International Journal of Operations and Production Management*, Vol. 12, No. 9, 1992, pp. 5-17. Reprinted with permission from *International Journal of Operations and Production Management*, Vol. 12, No. 9, Copyright 1992.

Capacity Planning Techniques for Manufacturing Control Systems: Information Requirements and Operational Features

William L. Berry*
Thomas G. Schmitt, CPIM**
Thomas E. Vollmann***

ABSTRACT

Substantial interest has been focused on techniques that determine the amount and timing of work center capacity to satisfy the master production schedule. Although several techniques have been developed for preparing work center capacity plans, very little analysis of the operational features and the application of these techniques has been reported. Four techniques, capacity planning using overall factors (CPOF), capacity bills, resource profiles, and capacity requirements planning (CRP), vary substantially in their complexity and the level of detail required to plan work center capacities. All four procedures require the use of the master production schedule to develop a capacity plan, but some have much more demanding data requirements. Important differences are the means by which capacity requirements are estimated by the techniques and the manner in which the bill of material, manufacturing lead time and inventory status information are incorporated into the capacity plan. The purpose of this paper is to describe the operational features of the four capacity planning techniques, the underlying data base requirements, and some key managerial issues in choosing among these techniques.

During the past decade manufacturing firms have made substantial progress in the installation and use of Material Requirements Planning (MRP) systems to plan and control fabrication and assembly operations [4,54].[1] However, two related areas that are frequently cited as major road blocks in managing effectively with MRP systems are those involving the preparation of the master production schedule (MPS) and the development of capacity plans to support that schedule.[2] In many firms the execution of the MPS is handicapped because adequate capacity has not been planned at individual departments or work centers. Although many firms use work center capacity planning techniques, very little analysis of these techniques has been reported in the literature [1]. This paper is intended to fill this gap by providing a comparison of the operational features and data requirements of four medium range techniques for planning the amount and timing of work center capacity to support the MPS.

A CAPACITY PLANNING FRAMEWORK

Before turning to the detailed analysis of the four techniques for capacity planning, it is useful to first look at the various levels at which "capacity planning" is performed in manufacturing firms, and thereafter to address some important issues in system design.

Hierarchy of Capacity Planning Decisions

The relationship of capacity planning decisions to the other modules of an integrated manufacturing planning and control (MPC) system is shown in Figure 1.[3] Also shown is the scope of capacity planning decisions, starting from the overall planning of resources, proceeding to a rough cut evaluation of the capacity implications of a particular

---

* Indiana University, Bloomington, Indiana.
** University of Washington, Seattle, Washington.
*** INSEAD, Fontainebleau, France.

Editor's Note: This is the first tutorial published by the *Journal of Operations Management*. It is the editorial policy of the *Journal* to periodically publish such articles which, in the opinion of the editor, treat topics of current interest to the readership.

---

1. Terms are used which deal with the use of the master production schedule (MPS), MRP system, shop-floor control system, etc. These terms are defined in detail in [2,36].
2. See references 3,6,12,14,15,18,26,38,39,40,43,47,49,52,53,60.
3. See references 3,12,21,23,30,32,39,42,51.

FIGURE 1
Capacity Planning in the MPC System

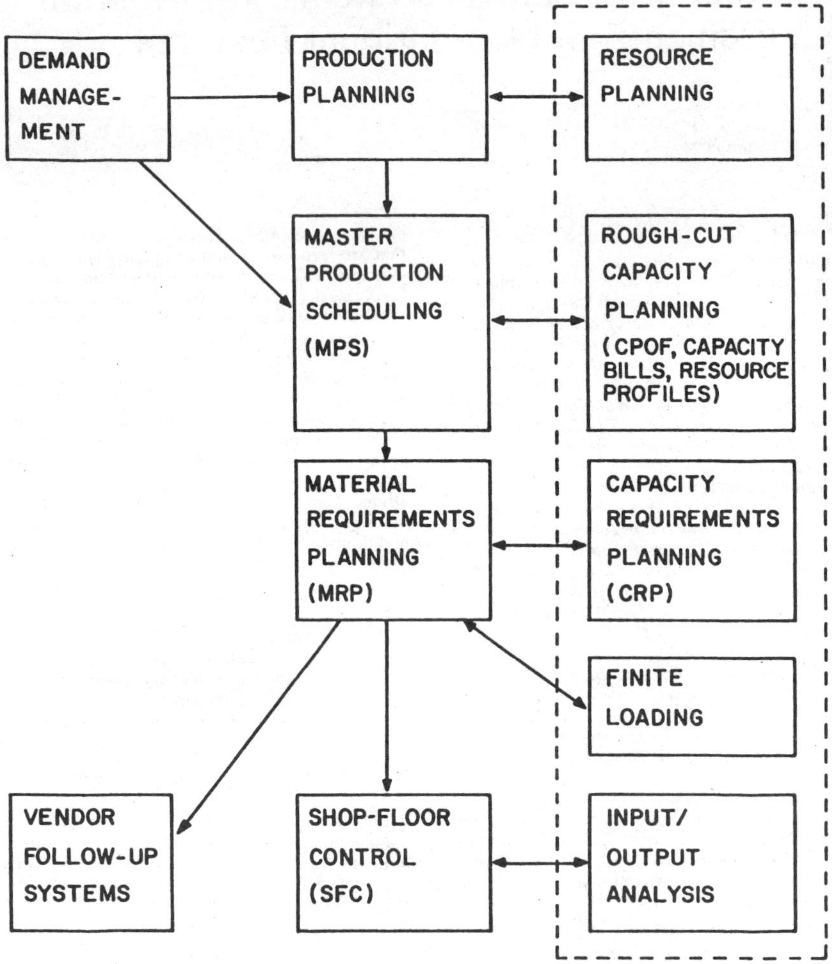

```
DEMAND                                                          
MANAGE-                                                         
MENT                                                            
   |                                                            
   v                                                            
PRODUCTION ──────────────> RESOURCE                             
PLANNING                   PLANNING                             
   |                                                            
   v                                                            
MASTER                                                          
PRODUCTION <────────> ROUGH-CUT                                 
SCHEDULING            CAPACITY                                  
(MPS)                 PLANNING                                  
   |                  (CPOF, CAPACITY                           
   |                  BILLS, RESOURCE                           
   v                  PROFILES)                                 
MATERIAL                                                        
REQUIREMENTS <──────> CAPACITY                                  
PLANNING              REQUIREMENTS                              
(MRP)                 PLANNING                                  
   |                  (CRP)                                     
   |                                                            
   |                  FINITE                                    
   |                  LOADING                                   
   v                                                            
SHOP-FLOOR <────────> INPUT/                                    
CONTROL               OUTPUT                                    
(SFC)                 ANALYSIS                                  
   |                                                            
   v                                                            
VENDOR                                                          
FOLLOW-UP                                                       
SYSTEMS                                                         
```

MPS, proceeding to the evaluation of capacity requirements based upon MRP detailed records, thereafter to finite loading and input/output techniques for short range capacity planning.

These five levels of capacity planning decisions go from large aggregations of capacity in large time periods to very detailed machine scheduling on an hourly or shorter time interval. Resource planning is concerned with long range capacity planning issues typically at an aggregate level.[4] Finite loading techniques and input/output analysis deal with short range capacity planning, and overlap with shop-floor scheduling.[5] The primary focus of this paper is on three rough cut capacity planning techniques and on the technique called capacity requirements planning (CRP) [12,13,37]. They deal with medium term capacity plans at the level of individual work centers, providing indications of capacity requirements over the next three months to two years [5]. The rough cut techniques are capacity planning using overall factors (CPOF), capacity bills, and resource profiles. Each uses the MPS to develop the expected capacity requirements for the work centers. However, CRP makes capacity estimates from detailed MRP plans which are in turn derived from the MPS.

System Design Issues

One stage in the capacity planning process in the medium term is to translate the MPS into its work center capacity requirements using a rough cut technique or CRP. In a following stage, if a mismatch between machine or labor capacity and the capacity required by the MPS is anticipated, a decision to make or buy, subcontract, seek alternate routing, or even hire personnel may be made depending upon the adjustment lead times and additional costs involved [38, pp. 234–238] [39].

This paper focuses on the first stage in the capacity planning process, i.e., the preparation of work center capacity plans. The choice of how the MPS is to be converted into some measure of output and the level of aggregation of that output are important issues affecting the design of the MPC system. If the capacity requirements are assessed using overall capacity planning factors, e.g., in terms of the average labor dollars per sales dollar, the data can be obtained from most finan-

cial accounting systems [12,19,23,42,49,50]. However, the resulting forecast of capacity needs at a particular work center from a set of sales orders can be subject to large errors.

Alternative levels of aggregation include product line groupings of sales and their production data, the capacity profiles of representative products and product options, and the labor requirements of individual end item data [12]. Each of these alternatives represents a choice of input data for capacity planning. Still another alternative is the detailed time-phased piece part requirements, as determined by MRP, routing and time standards data [59].

In order to illustrate the operational features of the four medium term techniques, we use a simplified example. This example allows us to clearly see the issues of aggregation, data inputs, timing, capacity measures, etc. We will also be able to observe the kinds of capacity planning environments that seem more or less appropriate for particular techniques.

Capacity Planning Using Overall Factors (CPOF)

CPOF is a rough cut capacity planning technique that requires data inputs based directly on the MPS rather than detailed time-phased records from an MRP system [13]. The CPOF technique is based upon planning factors involving direct labor standards for end products. When these planning factors are applied to the MPS data, overall manpower capacity requirements are estimated. This overall estimate is frequently allocated to individual work centers on the basis of historical data on shop work loads. CPOF plans are usually stated in terms of weekly or monthly time periods, and are periodically revised as the firm makes changes to the MPS.

Tables 1 and 2 illustrate the two steps involved in developing CPOF plans. The top portion of Table 1 shows an MPS for end products A and B stated over thirteen time periods. This schedule indicates the quantity of each of two end products to be assembled and shipped from the plant by the end of each time period. The first step is to translate the MPS into a capacity plan for the overall plant using the direct labor standards for each end product shown in the lower portion of Table 1. For example, 62.8 direct labor hours are required in time period 1, which is the sum of 33 units of A times .95 standard hours per unit, plus 17 units of B times 1.85 standard hours per unit.[6] This 62.8

---

4. See references 11,12,17,20,42,43,46.
5. See references 10,25,28,29,39,41 for a discussion of finite loading. See references 3,7,8,9,10,24,31,39,44,55,58,61 for a discussion of input/output analysis and lead time management. See references 6,16,34,45 for a discussion of order sequencing at work centers at the time of actual production, i.e., dispatching, when finite work center capacity levels are assumed.
6. A labor productivity rate of 100% of standard is assumed in this example [33].

TABLE 1
Capacity Planning Using Overall Factors (CPOF) Example—Master Production Schedule (in units)

End Product	Time Period												
	1	2	3	4	5	6	7	8	9	10	11	12	13
A	33	33	33	40	40	40	30	30	30	37	37	37	37
B	17	17	17	13	13	13	25	25	25	27	27	27	27

Direct Labor Time Per End Product Unit

End Item	Total Direct Labor in Standard hours/unit
A	.95 hours
B	1.85 hours

hours is shown as the first entry in the row titled "Total Plant Capacity" in Table 2. The other entries in the row are similarly calculated. The second step is that of allocating the overall plant capacity requirements to individual work centers. CPOF does this on a historical basis as is shown in Table 2. The top portion of Table 2 shows the number of direct labor hours per quarter worked at each of the three work centers during the prior year. These data may be obtained from accounting records in many firms. The result is that 60.3%, 30.4%, and 9.3% of the direct labor hours were reported at work centers 100, 200, and 300, respectively, during the previous year. These percentages are thereafter applied to the total capacity estimates (such as 62.8 hours for time period 1) to obtain the estimated direct labor requirements for each work center. For example, in time period 1, 37.87, 19.09,

and 5.84 hours are indicated for the three work centers.

The CPOF technique, or variants of it, are found in a number of manufacturing firms. The data requirements are minimal, involving primarily accounting system data instead of information such as product routing files and detailed time standards. As a consequence, CPOF plans provide only approximations of the actual time-phased capacity requirements at individual work centers.

Capacity Bills

The capacity bills technique provides a much more direct linkage between individual end products in the MPS and the capacity required at individual work centers than does CPOF [13,37]. The capacity bills technique also requires more data than does CPOF. Bills of material, routing, and operation time standard data are all necessary inputs in order to develop the capacity plan using the capacity bills technique.

The example shown in Figure 2 and Tables 3 and 4 illustrates the use of the capacity bills technique. The bills of material for end products A and B are shown as Figure 2. The routing and operation time standard data are shown in the top portion of Table 3 for the assembly of products A and B as well as for the manufacture of component items C, D, E, and F. Combining the data in Figure 2 with those in the top of Table 3 produces the bill of capacity for each of the two end products as is shown in the lower portion of Table 3. The bill of capacity indicates the total standard time per unit

required to produce an end product in each work center used in its manufacture. For example, component item C is produced in lots of 40 units. Operation 2 of 2 requires 1.00 hours of set up time (or .025 hours/unit) and .175 standard hours per unit run time at work center 300. Therefore, the total processing time for each unit of item C at work center 300 is .20 standard hours per unit. Since this is the only component that requires capacity in work center 300 and since item C is only used in the assembly of end item A (on a 1 unit of C per end item of A basis), the bill of capacity for product A shows a value of .20 for

work center 300. The corresponding value for product B at work center 300 is zero. The bill of capacity value of .70 hours per unit of end product A for work center 200 is determined by summing the time per unit for components C and D at that work center of .60 and .10 hours, respectively. When making the calculations for end product B, the multiple component usages per end item are necessarily considered, e.g., .55 hours for work center 200 = .10 for D + .10 × 2 for E + .0625 × 4 for F. (Clearly, alternative methods could be used to allocate the setup time on a per unit basis when there are multiple component usages.)

Once the bill of capacity for each end product has been prepared, the MPS can be used to estimate the resultant requirements at individual work centers. This process is illustrated in Table 4. For example, the quantities in the MPS for products A and B in time period 1 (33 and 17 units respectively) have been used with the bill of capacity data to estimate capacity requirements in time period 1 at work centers 100, 200 and 300. The 23.75 direct labor hours required at work center 100 are the sum of 33 units of A times .05 standard hours per unit and 17 units of B times 1.30 standard hours per unit.

Comparing the capacity plan in Table 4 with that of Table 2 indicates a substantial difference in work center capacity requirements. This difference reflects the period to period differences in product mix. The estimates in Table 2 are based

FIGURE 2
Bill of Material Data

End Product			Level Code
A — B			0
C[1r] — D[1r] — D[1r] — E[2r]* / F[4r]			1
			2

*One unit of component C and one unit of component D are required to produce one unit of end product A. Similarly, one unit of component D and two units of component E are required to produce one unit of end product B. Two units of component F are required to produce one unit of component E.

TABLE 2
Capacity Planning Using Overall Factors (CPOF) Example—Historical Total Standard Direct Labor Hours Worked Last Year

Work Center	1st Quarter	2nd Quarter	3rd Quarter	4th Quarter	Total	Percentage of Total Labor Hours
100	125	90	150	140	505	60.3%
200	55	60	80	60	255	30.4%
300	18	15	20	25	78	9.3%
					838	

Capacity Plan

Work Center	Historical Work Center Percentage	1	2	3	4	5	6	7	8	9	10	11	12	13	Total Hours
100	60.3%	37.87	37.87	37.87	37.41	37.41	37.41	45.07	45.07	45.07	51.32	51.32	51.32	51.32	566.33
200	30.4%	19.09	19.09	19.09	18.86	18.86	18.86	22.72	22.72	22.72	25.87	25.87	25.87	25.87	285.49
300	9.3%	5.84	5.84	5.84	5.78	5.78	5.78	6.96	6.96	6.96	7.91	7.91	7.91	7.91	87.38
Total Plant Capacity		62.8	62.8	62.8	62.05	62.05	62.05	74.75	74.75	74.75	85.1	85.1	85.1	85.1	939.2

TABLE 3
Routing Data

End Items	Lot Size	Operation	Work Center	Unit Work Time	Setup Time	Time per Unit
A	40	1 of 1	100	.025	1.0	.05
B	20	1 of 1	100	1.25	1.0	1.30
Components						
C	40	1 of 2	200	.575	1.0	.60
		2 of 2	300	.175	1.0	.20
D	60	1 of 1	200	.067	2.0	.10
E	100	1 of 1	200	.08	2.0	.10
F	100	1 of 1	200	.0425	2.0	.0625

Bill of Capacity

	A		B	
Work Center	Total Time/ Unit	Unit	Total Time/ Unit	Unit
100		.05		1.30
200		.70		.55
300		.20		0.00
Total Time/Unit =		.95		1.85

TABLE 4
Capacity Bills Example

End Item	Master Production Schedule												
	1	2	3	4	5	6	7	8	9	10	11	12	13
A	33	33	33	33	40	40	40	30	30	30	30	37	37
B	17	17	17	17	13	13	13	25	25	25	27	27	27

Capacity Plan

Work Center	1	2	3	4	5	6	7	8	9	10	11	12	13	Total Hours	Work Center Percentage
100	23.75	23.75	23.75	18.9	18.9	18.9	34.0	34.0	34.0	36.95	36.95	36.95	34.0	377.75	40%
200	32.45	32.45	32.45	35.15	35.15	35.15	34.75	34.75	34.75	40.75	40.75	40.75	40.75	470.05	50%
300	6.6	6.6	6.6	8.0	8.0	8.0	6.0	6.0	6.0	7.4	7.4	7.4	7.4	91.4	10%
Total	62.8	62.8	62.8	62.05	62.05	62.05	74.75	74.75	74.75	85.1	85.1	85.1	85.1	939.2	100%

upon a constant ratio of work in each machine center for each time period, whereas those in Table 4 reflect changes in product mix of the MPS from one time period to the next. These differences will be more important for firms which experience significant product mix variations than for those that have a relatively constant pattern of work. It is useful to note that the total hours shown for each time period (e.g., 62.8 hours in period 1) and for the thirteen period time horizon (939.2) is the same in both Table 2 and Table 4; the differences can be found in the mix of work center loads.

Resource Profiles

Neither the CPOF nor the capacity bills technique takes into account the time-phasing of the projected work loads at individual work centers. In resource profiles, production lead time data are added to the capacity bills data base in order to provide a time-phased projection of the capacity requirements for individual production facilities [3,13,27,37].

For example, the production capacity required at work centers used early in the production cycle for an end product, e.g., in shearing and punch press operations, is offset by the amount of production lead time between these operations and the final assembly of the product. As is true for any capacity planning technique, the size of the time intervals can be varied. However, when time periods longer than one week are used, much of the value of the time-phased information may be lost because of the aggregation of the data.

We now enlarge our example to illustrate the use of the resource profiles technique in preparing a capacity plan. The bills of material for products A and B are given in Figure 2, and the routing and time standard information in Table 3. For resource profiles, an additional data element is required: the lead time for each end item and component part. In order to simplify the example, we use a lead time of one time period for each end item and one time period for each operation for the component parts. Since only one operation is required for components D, E, and F, the total lead time for these components is one time period. For component C, the lead time is one time period for each of its two operations.

In order to use the resource profiles technique, a time-phased profile of resource usage for each end item must be prepared. The operation set-back charts in Figure 3 show this time-phasing for end items A and B. The chart for end item A indicates that the final assembly operation is completed during the current period which ends, by convention, at time 1 in Figure 3. The production of component D is completed one time period prior to the completion of the final assembly as is the production of component C, i.e., at time 0 in Figure 3. Since component C requires two time periods (one for each operation) it is necessary to start the production of this item one time period before the start of component D. In this example, as was the case with previous examples, it is assumed that the MPS specifies the number of units of each end product that must be completed and shipped by the end of each time period. (Clearly, there are other conventions that could be used to define the production time-phasing.)

The operation set-back charts in Figure 3 also contain the total standard time required to make one complete end item when all operations and all components are considered. For example, .25 hours of direct labor are required by component F at

FIGURE 3
Operation Set-Back Charts

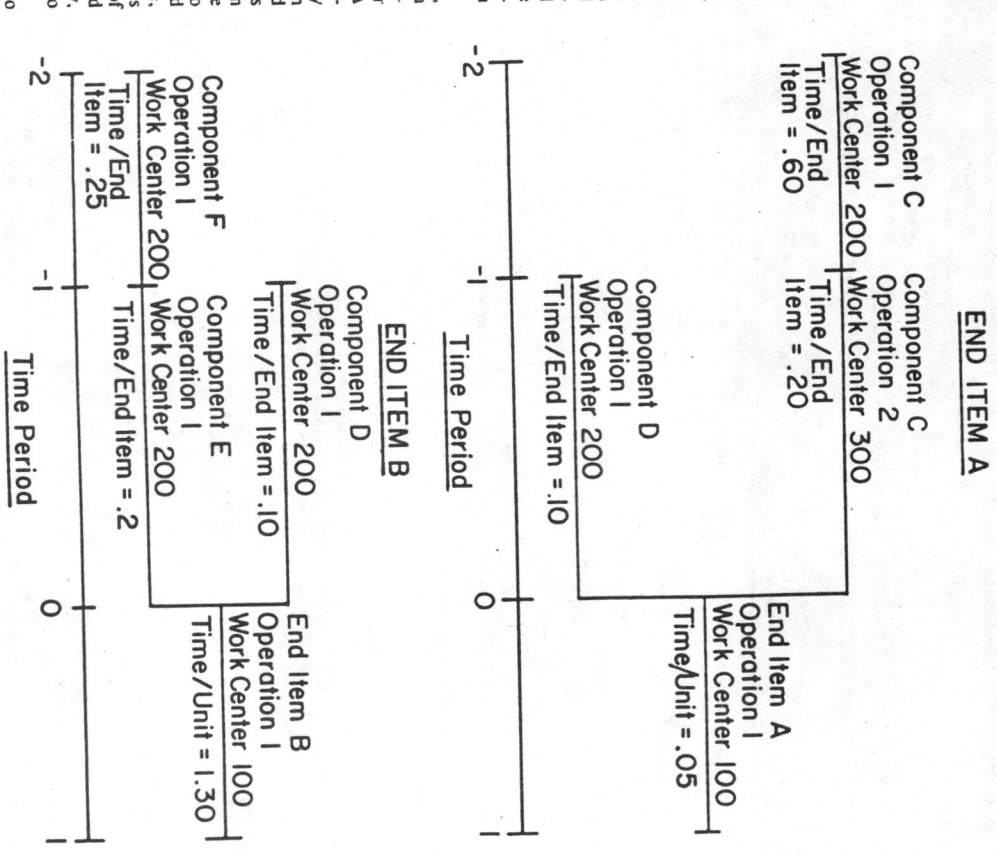

END ITEM A

Component C
Operation 1
Work Center 200
Time/End Item = .60

Component C
Operation 2
Work Center 300
Time/End Item = .20

Component D
Operation 1
Work Center 200
Time/End Item = .10

End Item A
Operation 1
Work Center 100
Time/Unit = .05

END ITEM B

Component D
Operation 1
Work Center 200
Time/End Item = .10

Component E
Operation 1
Work Center 100
Time/End Item = .2

End Item B
Operation 1
Work Center 100
Time/Unit = 1.30

Component F
Operation 1
Work Center 200
Time/End Item = .25

Time Period

work center 200; this time is based on the use of 4 F's per end item B.

The top portion of Table 5 takes the information from Figure 3, and now summarizes it by work center. In the lower portion of Table 5, we show the capacity requirements generated by key MPS quantities for time period 5 (40 of end item A and 13 of end item B). Note that the loads indicated in the section titled "combined A and B" would not be the entire capacity load for each work center. For example, the 7.9 hours shown for time period 4 are only generated by the MPS for period 5. An additional 27.25 hours would be generated for this period by the MPS in period 6. Table 6 provides the capacity plan for the thirteen period time horizon that results from the resource profiles technique.

A comparison of the capacity plans produced by the capacity bills and the resource profiles techniques (Tables 4 and 6) illustrates the impact of the time-phased capacity information. The total work load created by the MPS (939.2 hours) and its percentage allocations to the three work centers remains the same as in Table 4. However, the timing of the work load at work centers 200 and 300 varies substantially. In Table 4 for instance, a capacity requirement of 32.45 hours was planned for work center 200 in time period 2 using capacity bills. In comparison, the resource profiles capacity plan in Table 6 indicates the capacity requirement as 35.65 hours. This difference illustrates the potential benefits of the resource profiles technique in that it accommodates both product mix variations and production lead times in the preparation of capacity plans. However, the lead time offsetting requires additional information and further computations by the supporting technique.

TABLE 5
Time-phased Profile of Resource Usage

	Time Period Ending at Time		
	−1	0	1
End Item A			
Work Center 100			.05
Work Center 200	.60	.10	
Work Center 300		.20	
End Item B			
Work Center 100			1.30
Work Center 200	.25	.30	

Time-Phased Capacity Requirements Generated From MPS for 40 A's and 13 B's in Time Period 5

	Time Period Ending at Time		
	3	4	5
End Item A (40)			2.0
Work Center 100		4.0	
Work Center 200	24.0	8.0	
Work Center 300			
End Item B (13)			16.9
Work Center 100		3.9	
Work Center 200			
Work Center 300			
Combined A and B			18.9
Work Center 100		7.9	
Work Center 200	27.25	8.0	
Work Center 300			

For example, if one looks carefully at Table 5, the .10 hours of capacity per unit of end item A generated for work center 200 one period prior to the current period is based upon operation 1 of component part D. The .10 hour figure assumes a unit run time of .067 hours, a setup time of 2.0 hours, and a lot size of 60. These estimates are based on historical data. But in period 5 end item A is manufactured in a lot of 40, not 60. This creates an actual capacity requirement of 4.68 standard hours (.067 × 40 + 2) instead of the 4.0 hours shown in the bottom portion of Table 5. Thus, any actual lot size for component D which is less than 60 understates the required capacity for work center 200 in the capacity plan, and any actual lot size exceeding 60 overstates the capacity requirement at this work center. Furthermore, if a lot of 40 A's could be made from D's that are already in inventory, there would be no capacity requirements generated by D's. Let us now turn to the capacity planning technique that takes explicit account of component lot sizing considerations as well as all inventory balances and detailed component part schedules.

Capacity Requirements Planning (CRP)

Capacity requirements planning differs from the resource profiles technique in four key respects [13,27,28,39]. First, CRP utilizes the information produced by the MRP explosion process which includes the consideration of lot sizes, as well as the lead times for both open shop orders (scheduled receipts) and orders which are planned for future release by the MRP system (planned orders). Second, the gross to net feature of an MRP system takes into account the production capacity already stored in the form of inventories of both components and assembled items. Third, the shop-floor control system accounts for the current status of each open order, so that only the capacity needed to complete the remaining work on open shop orders is considered in planning work center capacities. Fourth, CRP takes into account the independent demand for service parts, and any additional capacity that might be required by MRP planners reacting to scrap, item record errors, etc.

The CRP technique requires detailed input information for all components and assemblies, including: MRP planned order receipts, on-hand quantities, the current status of open shop orders at individual work centers, routing data, and time standard information. Thus, implementing CRP requires both a far more detailed industrial engineering data base, e.g., work standards and equip-

TABLE 6
Resource Profile Example—Master Production Schedule

End Items	Past Due	1	2	3	4	5	6	7	8	9	10	11	12	13
A	0.00	33	33	33	40	40	40	30	30	30	37	37	37	37
B	56.5	17	17	17	13	13	13	25	25	25	27	27	27	27

Capacity Plan

Work Center	Past Due	1	2	3	4	5	6	7	8	9	10	11	12	13	Total Hours	Work Center Percentage
100	0.00	23.75	23.75	18.90	18.90	34.00	34.00	34.00	36.95	36.95	36.95	36.95	0	36.95	377.75	40%
200	32.45	35.65	35.15	32.15	34.75	34.75	39.45	40.75	40.75	11.80	0	0	470.05	50%
300	6.60	6.60	8.00	8.00	8.00	6.00	6.00	7.40	7.40	7.40	7.40	0	91.40	10%
	63.10	62.80	66.00	66.90	62.05	59.05	74.75	79.45	82.15	85.10	85.10	56.15	36.95	939.2	100%

ing files, but also formal systems for handling transactions on the shop-floor and in the storerooms.

The CRP technique exploits the MRP logic in that the capacity requirements of the MPS are reduced by the capacity stored in the form of finished and work-in-process inventories. That is, CRP only calculates capacity requirements for actual open shop orders and planned orders in the MRP data base. The timing of these open orders and planned orders offers the potential for improved capacity forecasts as compared with the three rough cut procedures. These improved forecasts will be of primary importance in the most immediate time period. In the long term, all components and assemblies have to be manufactured, but in the near term, the requirements planned by the rough cut techniques will be overstated by the capacity represented in inventories. As before, however, these potential benefits are not without cost. An MRP data base is required, as well as a much larger computational effort.

The process of preparing a CRP plan is quite similar to that illustrated in the lower half of Table 5. The main difference is that detailed MRP planning establishes the exact order quantity and timing for each of the component parts. The resultant capacity needs are summarized by time period and by work center. Since this summary is based on all component parts and end items, from the present time period to the end of the MRP planning horizon, one can see the enormity of the calculation requirements. For most firms a computer is essential.

Table 7 partially illustrates the MRP and CRP calculations used to develop the CRP plan. In most MRP systems these records would express the manufacturing schedule in weekly time periods. Table 7 only shows the end item B and one of its components, E. This table illustrates how lot sizes, inventories, gross to netting, and scheduled receipts are taken into account in preparing the capacity plan. The capacity requirements for product B are calculated directly from the MRP record. For example in work center 100, the lot size of 20 units in period 1 for product B requires 26 hours (20 × 1.25 + 1.0) of direct labor capacity. The same capacity requirement can be seen in periods 2 and 4. In periods 6 through 12, the requirements are higher.

The scheduled receipt for 100 units of part E, due in period 2, would also generate capacity requirements. If the shop-floor control system indicated that 60 parts were run, the capacity requirements for the remaining 40 would be added

TABLE 7
CRP Example: Detailed MRP Records and their Capacity Requirements

PRODUCT B (Lot Size = 20, Lead Time = 1)

	1	2	3	4	5	6	7	8	9	10	11	12	13
Gross Requirements	17	17	17	13	13	13	25	25	25	27	27	27	27
Scheduled Receipts													
On-hand	30	13	16	19	6	13	0	25	0	25	0	27	0	27
Planned Order Releases	20	20		20		20	25		25		25		27

Product B's Capacity Requirements at Work Center 100

	1	2	3	4	5	6	7	8	9	10	11	12	13
	26.00*	26.00	00.00	26.00	00.00	32.45	32.45	32.45	34.75	34.75	34.75	34.75	00.00

COMPONENT E (Lot Size = 100, Lead Time = 1)

	1	2	3	4	5	6	7	8	9	10	11	12	13
Gross Requirements	40	40	40	40	50	50	50	54	54	54	56	56
Scheduled Receipts	100												
On-hand	42	2	62	22	22	72	22	72	18	64	10	56	
Planned Order Releases		100		100		100		100	100	100	100		

Component E's Capacity Requirements at Work Center 200

	1	2	3	4	5	6	7	8	9	10	11	12	13
	3.20[a]			10.00[c]		10.00	10.00	10.00					

*20 × 1.25 + 1 = 26 0 hours loaded in period 1, due at the beginning of period 2.
[a]100 × .08 = 3.2 hours loaded in period 1, due at the beginning of period 2. Work center 200 has been set up previously for the scheduled receipt order and 60 units have been completed.
[c]100 × .08 + 2 = 10 hours loaded in period 5, due at the beginning of period 6.

---

to the most immediate period, i.e., 3.2 hours in period 1.

It is worth noting that the lot sizing convention used in this example is lot-for-lot when the net requirements are greater than the specified order quantity. Clearly, other lot sizing methods could also be used. Another convention involves the timing of the requirements. The capacity requirements are calculated here so that the gross requirements (and the MPS) are satisfied by the beginning of the period required. Again, other conventions could be used.

The primary difference in comparing CRP to the rough cut techniques is the determination of the overall level of capacity requirements. In the case of the rough cut techniques, the total hourly requirements for the 13 period example would be the same. However, the overall capacity requirements for CRP would rarely match exactly with that of the rough cut technique. This is because of the rough cut stored in the inventories and the amount of work already completed on open shop orders (scheduled receipts) are taken into account by CRP.

IMPLEMENTING CAPACITY PLANNING TECHNIQUES

The CPOF, capacity bills, resource profiles, and CRP techniques all use MPS data to develop a work center capacity plan. The CPOF technique calculates the overall direct labor requirements for the MPS and allocates this capacity to the work centers on the basis of historically observed work load patterns. By contrast, the capacity bills technique uses bill of material and routing information to plan the capacity at work centers, and thus, more accurately reflects the particular mix of the end items shown in the MPS. The resource profiles technique extends the capacity requirements by the lead times for component parts and assemblies used in the manufacture of the end items.

A related linkage to the overall MPC system is the effectiveness of the shop-floor control system. To the extent that work centers can respond to capacity problems—either with formal systems support or informally—the need for medium or long range capacity planning is less critical [14]. Individual operations which are completed ahead-of or behind-schedule can be identified formally by a computerized shop-floor control system [27], or informally through expediting efforts. For some

firms, several days warning of which operations are completed behind-schedule is ample lead time to increase the capacity levels at the work centers used later in the manufacturing cycle.

Manufacturing operations often require extra effort and premium expenditures when firms choose to respond on the shop-floor to the capacity problems created by dynamic market conditions, product mix variations and design changes [27, 39]. For those firms, the operators frequently are trained at several work centers and are accessible to work overtime with short notice. Also, subcontractors are able to accept overloads with little advance warning. The production control staff and shop-floor supervisors assimilate information regarding short term capacity problems and respond by splitting lots, splitting operations, overlapping operations, rescheduling order releases, etc. [27, ch.6] [38, ch.8–11]. However, while capacity problems often can be resolved on the shop-floor, there are limits to the number of adjustments that can be managed simultaneously [14].

Management Considerations

Any decision on the implementation of the capacity planning techniques has to deal with the use of the outputs. That is, what kinds of decisions and questions result from the analysis? One decision that can result is to change capacity to match the expected requirements [39]. Another is to change the requirements to match the expected capacity [18, 50]. The latter view is much more prevalent in European firms than in the United States because of the costs and constraints they face in adjusting capacity levels [35]. For this reason, an entirely different approach than that examined in this paper is often taken in managing production capacity, i.e., using finite loading methods such as CAPOSS [25].

Our analysis of the four capacity planning techniques indicates that CRP, in accounting for actual shop conditions, is capable of producing more accurate predictions of the MPS capacity requirements. However, computational effort and decision-making turn around time are important considerations in selecting a technique. Rough cut methods produce capacity plans with far less computation time than does CRP. If one anticipates bottlenecks and decides to change the MPS, rough cut analysis can be performed repeatedly to examine several different outcomes. This is not always feasible with CRP because of the computational effort involved. What this means is that extensive "what if" analysis is much more difficult to per-

An MPC System Point of View

In choosing a capacity planning technique, it is necessary to consider the entire manufacturing planning and control system, as well as the environment that the firm faces. In Figure 1, we indicated five distinct areas or system modules that are concerned with capacity planning, but in this paper we consider only the medium term, i.e., rough cut capacity planning techniques and capacity requirements planning (CRP).

To the extent that long range resource planning and production planning are performed effectively, the resultant need for other capacity planning activities is reduced [14, 39]. Furthermore, if a very stable rate of output is designated by the production plan, the MPS will experience relatively few circumstances that require capacity changes.

The Kanban system used by Toyota and other Japanese automobile manufacturers represents a good case in point [22, 48, 57]. The rate of output (cars per day) in the production plan is held very stable. Product mix variations are also substantially less than for other automobile companies because the firm does not permit as many option combinations. Order backlogs and finished goods inventories isolate the factories even more from actual customer orders. The result is an MPC system that is simple, effective, and easy to operate, and the need for rough cut techniques and CRP is reduced.

The CRP technique uses additional information from the MRP and shop-floor control systems to account for the exact timing and quantities of component part and end item production orders. We see that relatively simple accounting system data are required by CPOF. However, capacity bills, resource profiles and CRP require an ever increasing investment in production/inventory control, industrial engineering and shop/floor control data bases, as well as an ever increasing computational cost. The issue is whether the additional costs to support more complex techniques are justified by improved decision making and plant operations.

form when the conventional approaches to CRP are used.[7]

A related issue is the time period for capacity planning and capacity change decisions. Our example indicated that all three rough cut capacity planning techniques produced the same result for the thirteen period time interval in terms of total labor hours. If this is the time period in which the major decisions are made (with overtime, shop-floor control and input/output being used to allocate labor to departments) the choice of a rough cut capacity planning technique is not crucial. Likewise, the differences between CRP (which discounts the capacity stored in the form of inventory) and resource profiles may not be significant under conditions of low inventory levels. Also, if the bills of material are shallow, lead times are short and inventories are low, the differences between CRP and capacity bills tend to be less important.

A final issue of pragmatic interest is the data base design and maintenance. Although the size of the data base required by capacity bills is much smaller than for CRP, the latter data base often already exists if the firm has MRP and shop-floor control systems. For this reason, we find many firms using CRP systems answering questions that could be analyzed at far lower computational cost with rough cut techniques. They do so because there are no additional data base requirements. What is needed, however, is substantially more computer run time. (See the Hyster Company Chapter 11 in [12].) On the other hand, firms without computer-based MRP and shop-floor systems can easily utilize one of the rough cut capacity planning techniques, especially for critical work centers, since the data base requirements are minimal.

---

[7] Some firms have "alterations planning" system capability which can examine the net effects of various schedule changes on capacity requirements [36].

REFERENCES

1. Adam, N. and J. Surkis. "A Comparison of Capacity Planning Techniques in a Job Shop Control System." *Management Science*, Vol. 23, No. 9 (May 1977), pp. 1011-1015.
2. *APICS Dictionary*, 4th Edition. American Production and Inventory Control Society, Washington, D.C., 1979.
3. *APICS Certification Program Study Guide: Capacity Management*. American Production and Inventory Control Society, Washington, D.C., 1980.
4. Anderson, J. and R. Schroeder. "A Survey of MRP Implementation and Practice." *Proceedings of the Material Requirements Planning Implementation Conference*, University of Minnesota (1979), pp. 6-42.
5. Baker, K. R. and D. W. Peterson. "An Analytic Framework for Evaluating Rolling Schedules." *Management Science*, Vol. 25, No. 4 (April 1979), pp. 341-351.
6. Baker, K. R. and J. W. M. Bertrand. "An Investigation of Due Date Assignment Rules With Constrained Tightness." *Journal of Operations Management*, Vol. 1, No. 3 (February 1981), pp. 109-120.
7. Bedfonto, W. R. "Lead Time vs. the Production Control System." *Production and Inventory Management* (2nd Qtr. 1974), pp. 14-22.
8. Belt, B. "The New ABC's of Lead-Time Management." *Production and Inventory Management* (2nd Qtr. 1974), pp. 81-91.
9. Belt, B. "Integrating Capacity Planning and Capacity Control." *Production and Inventory Management* (1st Qtr. 1976), pp. 9-25.
10. Belt, B. "Input/Output Planning Illustrated." *Production and Inventory Management* (2nd Qtr. 1978), pp. 13-20.
11. Belt, B. "Men, Spindles and Material Requirements Planning: Enhancing Implementation." *Production and Inventory Management* (1st Qtr. 1979), pp. 54-65.
12. Berry, W. L. T. E. Vollmann, and D. C. Whybark. *Master Production Scheduling: Principles and Practice*. American Production and Inventory Control Society, Washington, D.C., 1979.
13. Berry, W. L., T. G. Schmitt, and T. E. Vollmann. "A Tutorial on Different Procedures for Planning Work Center Capacity Levels." Indiana University Discussion Paper 155 (September 1980).
14. Bestwick, P. F. and K. G. Lockyer. "The Problem of Capacity—A Speculative Approach." *International Journal of Production Management*, Vol. 1, No. 2 (1981).
15. Colon, J. R. "Is Your Master Production Schedule Feasible?" *Production and Inventory Management* (3rd Qtr. 1977), pp. 32-38.
16. Conway, R. W., W. L. Maxwell, and L. W. Miller. *Theory of Scheduling*. Addison-Wesley, Reading, Mass., 1967.
17. Eilon, S. "Five Approaches to Aggregate Production Planning." *AIIE Transactions* (June 1975), pp. 118-131.
18. Fisk, J. C. and J. Seagle. "The Integration of Aggregate Planning with Resource Requirements Planning." *Production and Inventory Management* (3rd Qtr. 1978), pp. 81-91.
19. Gorenstein, S. "A Loading Model for a Stamping Plant." *Production and Inventory Management* (4th Qtr. 1976), pp. 88-107.
20. Graziano, V. J. "Production Capacity Planning-Long Term." *Production and Inventory Management* (2nd Qtr. 1974), pp. 66-80.
21. Hax, A. C. "The Design of Large Scale Logistics Systems: A Survey and an Approach." Edited by W. H. Marlow. *Modern Trends in Logistics Research*. The MIT Press, Cambridge, Mass., 1976.
22. Hayes, R. H. "Why Japanese Factories Work." *Harvard Business Review* (July-August 1981), pp. 57-66.
23. Holstein, W. K. "Production Planning and Control." *Harvard Business Review* (May-June 1968), pp. 121-140.
24. Huge, E. C. "Managing Manufacturing Lead Time." *Harvard Business Review* (September-October 1979), pp. 116-123.
25. IBM-United Kingdom Limited. *CAPOSS Concepts*. London, 1973, pp. 1-38.
26. IBM. *Master Production Schedule Planning Guide*. GE20-518-0, 1975.
27. IBM. *COPICS*. Chapters 4 and 6, G320-1978, 1972.
28. IBM. *Program Product: Capacity Planning-Infinite Loading, Capacity Planning-Finite Loading Application Description*. GH30-067-2, 1970, pp. 1-74.
29. Irastorza, J. C. and R. H. Deane. "Starve the Shop—Reduce Work-in-Process." *Production and Inventory Management* (2nd Qtr. 1976), pp. 20-25.
30. Kneppelt, L. R. "Implementing Manufacturing Resource Planning/Difficulty of the Task." *Production and Inventory Management* (2nd Qtr. 1981), pp. 59-77.
31. Langford, R. "Short-term Planning of Manufacturing Capacity." *Proceedings of the 21st International APICS Conference*, 1978.
32. Lee, S. M., and L. J. Moore. "A Practical Approach to Production Scheduling." *Production and Inventory Management* (1st Qtr. 1974), pp. 55-67.
33. Lunz, A. G. "The Missing Factors—The Real Keys to Effective Capacity Requirements Planning and Control." *Production and Inventory Management* (2nd Qtr. 1981), pp. 1-12.
34. Maxwell, W. L. and M. Mehra. "Multiple-Factor Rules for Sequencing With Assembly Constraints." *Naval Research Logistic Quarterly*, Vol. 15, No. 2 (1968), pp. 241-254.
35. New, C. "Inventories and Capacity Planning: An Integrated View." Unpublished Paper, Cranfield School of Management, Bedford, England, 1981.
36. Orlicky, J. *Material Requirements Planning*. McGraw Hill, 1975.
37. Osgood, W. R. "How to Plan Capacity Using the Bill of Labor." *Proceedings of the 19th Conference-AIDS*, Atlanta, Georgia (November 1976), pp. 173-179.
38. Plossl, G. and O. Wight. *Production and Inventory Control*. Prentice-Hall, Englewood Cliffs, New Jersey, 1967.
39. Plossl, G. and O. Wight. "Capacity Planning and Control." *Production and Inventory Management* (3rd Qtr. 1973), pp. 31-67.
40. Proud, J. F. "Controlling the Master Schedule." *Production and Inventory Management* (2nd Qtr. 1981), pp. 78-90.
41. Reiter, S. "A System for Managing Job-Shop Production." *Journal of Business*, Vol. 39 (July 1966), pp. 371-393.
42. Rhodes, P. "A Paint Industry Production Planning and Smoothing System." *Production and Inventory Management* (4th Qtr. 1977), pp. 17-28.
43. Ritzman, L. P., L. S. Krajewski, W. L. Berry, S. H. Goodman, S. T. Hardy, and L. D. Vitt. *Disaggregation: Problems in Manufacturing and Service Organizations*. Martinus Nijhoff Publishing, Boston, 1979, Sections 1-6.
44. Schonberger, R. J. "Clearest-Road-Ahead Priorities for Shop-floor Control: Moderating Infinite-Capacity-Loading Unevenness." *Production and Inventory Management* (2nd Qtr. 1979), pp. 17-27.
45. Sculli, D. "Priority Dispatching Rules in Job Shops with Assembly Operations and Random Delays." *Omega*, Vol. 8, No. 2 (1980), pp. 227-234.
46. Silver, E. "A Tutorial on Production Smoothing and Workforce Balancing." *Operations Research* (Nov-Dec 1973), pp. 989-1010.
47. Smolens, R. W. "Master Scheduling: Problems and Solutions." *Production and Inventory Management* (3rd Qtr. 1977), pp. 32-38.
48. Sugimori, Y., K. Kusunoki, F. Cho, and S. Uchikawa. "Toyota Production System and Kanban System Materialization of Just-in-Time and Respect-for-Human System." *International Journal of Production Research*, Vol. 15, No. 6 (1977), pp. 553-564.
49. Taylor, D. L. "From Shipping Targets to a Master Schedule." *Production and Inventory Management* (1st Qtr. 1978), pp. 17-24.
50. Taylor, S. G. "Optimal Aggregate Production Strategies for Plants with Semifixed Operating Costs." *AIIE Transactions* (September 1980), pp. 253-257.
51. Taylor, S. G., S. M. Seward, S. F. Bolander, and R. C. Heard. "Process Industry Production and Inventory Planning Framework: A Summary." *Production and Inventory Management* (1st Qtr. 1981), pp. 15-33.
52. Vollmann, T. E. "Capacity Planning: The Missing Link." *Production and Inventory Management* (1st Qtr. 1973), pp. 61-74.
53. Weeks, J. K. "A Simulation of Predictable Due Dates." *Management Science*, Vol. 25, No. 4 (April 1979), pp. 363-373.
54. Wemmerlov, U. "Design Factors in MRP Systems: A Limited Survey." *Production and Inventory Management* (4th Qtr. 1979), pp. 15-34.
55. Wemmerlov, U. "A Note on Capacity Planning." *Production and Inventory Management* (3rd Qtr. 1980), pp. 85-89.
56. Weston, F. C. "Mathematical Programming and Aggregate Production Planning in a Multi-Organizational System." *Production and Inventory Management* (1st Qtr. 1974), pp. 37-50.
57. Wheelwright, S. C. "Japan—Where Operation Really Are Strategic." *Harvard Business Review* (July-August 1981), pp. 67-74.
58. Wight, O. W. "Input/Output Control, A Real Handle on Lead Time." *Production and Inventory Management* (3rd Qtr. 1970), pp. 9-30.
59. Wilkerson, D. A. "Material Requirements Planning and Manpower Planning." *Production and Inventory Management* (2nd Qtr. 1976), pp. 1-17.
60. Wilson, G. T. "Seasonal Production Planning for Several Products Whose Storage Costs Differ." *Production and Inventory Management* (1st Qtr. 1978), pp. 49-62.
61. Young, J. B. "Understanding Shop Lead Times." *Proceedings of the 22nd Annual International APICS Conference* (October 1979).

Berry, William L., Schmitt, Thomas G., Vollman, Thomas E., "Capacity Planning Techniques for Manufacturing Control Systems: Information Requirements and Operational Features," *Journal of Operations Management*, Vol. 3, No. 1, November 1982, pp. 13-25. Reprinted with permission from *Journal of Operational Management*, Vol. 3, No. 1, November 1982, Copyright 1982.

Saturn: Rising star

Advice to GM: Forget Lopez and PICOS; Saturnize.

Never mind that Saturn hasn't made a dime yet. That will happen, once the third shift gets to cranking out more cars. Not enough cars, that's been the problem to date. Ramping up to full capacity has been agonizingly slow. And sure, there've been a few screwups, like the time when bad engine coolant necessitated the recall of hundreds of cars (1,836, to be exact). But even there, Saturn did the right thing, exchanging them for brand new vehicles. Showed GM how to turn a potential disaster into a public relations coup.

Meanwhile, the cars themselves have been receiving their fair share of accolades ("car of the year," etc.) from the automotive press. More important, Saturn owners are in agreement with the experts. In a recent J.D. Powers survey, Saturn placed well ahead of other domestic nameplates in customer satisfaction. Saturn indeed has made its point.

Those of us with a short memory might recall that only a decade ago, U.S. automakers were all but ready to concede the small car market to the Japanese. That's when GM's Roger Smith (remember him?) announced the Saturn project. It would be GM's first new nameplate since Chevy joined the fold in 1918. Saturn's mission was clear-cut: Beat the Japanese at their own game.

With Saturn, GM is attempting to rethink everything from the way cars are made to its relationship with workers and suppliers. For starters, Saturn negotiated its own labor contract with the UAW, putting all workers on salary and linking pay to productivity. There are no time clocks to punch at the plant in Spring Hill, Tenn.; nor are there any restrictive work rules to inhibit Saturn's self-directed teams.

No less unique is the plant itself. GM invested $1.9 billion to build one of the most integrated auto plants in North America. It is actually a half-dozen plants rolled into one. It has its own foundry (air-conditioned, no less) to cast crankshafts and engine blocks; in fact, the entire powertrain—engine and transmission—is manufactured and assembled on-site. Ditto hoods, roofs, fascias, and door panels—they're all stamped or molded on the premises, as are hundreds of other parts.

Indeed, more parts are made under one roof at Spring Hill than at any other GM plant, approximately 35% of the complete car.

Inside Saturn. Although the Saturn plant is far from the maddening crowd, it is within easy reach of one of several interstate highways. For just-in-time (JIT) deliveries arriving from the east or west, there is I-40; from the north or south, I-65; and from the northwest or southeast, I-24. And for good measure, the state of Tennessee kicked in $30 million to build Saturn Parkway, a 4.3-mile, four-lane highway connecting I-65 and the plant. (The state also generously provided $22 million for a worker training program, though it wasn't exactly farmhands that Saturn was hiring but mostly veteran UAW workers from other GM plants.)

The mile-long, 4.1-million-sq.-ft. complex sits in the middle of several thousand acres of farm land owned by GM. On a summer's day, the sweet smells of alfafa, barley, and other cash crops make it difficult to imagine that inside the plant, cars are being assembled. Saturn, it might be noted, also was the Roman god of agriculture.

Inside the plant the colors, smells, and sounds are pure industry. Giant stamping presses spit out steel hoods and roof panels, while some of the largest injection molding machines in the world create fascias and other large molded parts. All in all, 60 steel parts are stamped on-site, along with some 157 plastic parts of assorted colors that will be delivered in sequence to the assembly line. At other GM plants, these parts are typically produced off-site and shipped to the final assembly plant.

Roger Smith wanted Saturn to be a learning laboratory for GM, and indeed a number of technological innovations were introduced at Spring Hill. The engines, for example, are cast by the "lost foam" pro-

---

PLANT FACTS
OPENED: 1990
LOCATION: Spring Hill, Tenn
SIZE: 4.1 million sq. ft. powertrain manufacturing and assembly complex.
CAPACITY: 325,000 cars/yr.
MODEL: Coupe, sedan, wagon.

cess, so-called because the polystyrene pattern used to make the casting is "lost" (i.e. vaporized) when the molten metal makes contact with the pattern. The technique, which is akin to the old "lost wax" process, with polystyrene substituting for the wax pattern, is capable of producing intricate castings requiring little or no machining.

However, the process had never been tried on such a large scale before; indeed, many believed that it was too risky for mass production. So, before investing millions in the process, Saturn set out to prove the process at GM's foundry in Warren, Mich. Upshot: Saturn saved about $15 million by not having to purchase machines to drill holes in the engine block.

Five components in all are made using the lost-foam process: engine block, cylinder heads, crankshaft, and differential transmission case.

Something else you won't see at any other assembly plant in North America: cars being assembled on moving platforms called skillets. Workers ride along with the cars on these "moving sidewalks" while performing their chores. Saturn engineers discovered the skillet while visiting GM's Opel plant in Russelsheim, Germany. In the Opel plant the cars are positioned on the skillet in the traditional toe-to-heel or road position, but at Saturn they are positioned sideways on the skillet, saving about 40% in floor space.

Nor will you see assembly workers using pneumatic tools. Not after a study showed that electric tools are less likely to cause carpal tunnel syndrome.

Like clockwork. According to Saturn's VP of purchasing, Alec Bedricky, Saturn "runs the tightest JIT system in the auto business." Certainly, no one at GM will argue the point. Indeed, one will find little buffer anywhere in the Saturn plant. For instance, the number of powertrains on the floor between the engine plant and vehicle assembly at any time will be less than 140, or barely enough to cover two hours of production, which is in sharp contrast to the two week float that one likely will find at other GM plants. Elsewhere, it's the same story. Less than 95 space frames will be found in transit at any time between body fabrication and the start of trim operations.

"You can't build out-of-sequence here," says Bedricky. "If there is a hiccup in the powertrain plant, it will be felt immediately on the assembly line."

Saturn's engine and transmission lines offer a perfect example of what is meant by flexible manufacturing. Designed by Ingersoll-Rand, the engine line can accomodate both single- and double-overhead cam formats. Saturn also is the first automaker to build both manual and automatic transmissions on the same line. Upshot: The various engine-transmission combinations can be easily adjusted to meet market demand.

Meanwhile, trucks are continuously pulling up to one of Saturn's 50 docks. In a 24-hour period there may be as many 850 "dock occurrences" (unloading docks are continuously manned at Saturn). Deliveries must be made within a five minute window for them to count as "on time." Tardy suppliers that cause a production delay face being fined $500 a minute.

All material arrives at the Saturn plant directly from the supplier's dock without passing through a consolidation point, which is a typical practice at the Japanese transplants. Production parts are delivered daily, some more frequently (e.g. large items like radiators and front-end modules). Seats arrive in sequence from the seating supplier every 30 minutes. The scheduling of dock times and truck routes is all plotted by Saturn's logistics partner, namely Ryder, from its office inside the assembly plant (see accompanying story on page 49).

Suppliers are paid as the parts are consumed in production ("pay on production" or "POP"). While the supplier community at large generally has resisted such an idea, Saturn's suppliers have bought into the concept, says Curt Gibbs, director of material flow and logistics, because "the pipeline at Saturn is so short."

Saturn's scheduling process begins with a 12-week forecast of the model mix (e.g. sedan, coupe) required each week. The model mix can vary by 10% maximum from week to week up until the fourth week prior to start of the actual build (Week 4), at which time the model mix and the operating plan is fixed. During the next two weeks (Weeks 2 and 3), vehicle orders are leveled, allowing only for a 5% change in options. In Week 1, the option schedule is frozen. The final sequencing of cars in the assembly plant—model, color, options—is based on three days of firm orders. The whole idea is to keep production as level as possible so that there is no buildup of inventory (or any shortages) anywhere in the process.

Once a truck pulls up to the dock, parts are off-loaded and brought directly to the point-of-use in the assembly area. There's no receiving station at Spring Hill; nor are there inspectors to check parts coming into the plant. In fact, there's not even a "quality department" at Saturn. Quality is everyone's responsibility at Saturn, including the workers on the assembly line who are likely to squawk louder than anyone if an off-spec part is shipped to the plant, since bonuses are tied not only to the number of cars produced but also to the number that pass through "inspiration point" (i.e. final testing station in the assembly area) with nary a defect.

Looking Back
Some important dates in Saturn history

November 3, 1983	Saturn project officially announced by GM chairman Roger Smith.
January 7, 1985	Saturn created as an independent operating unit of GM.
July 26, 1985	GM and UAW sign separate labor agreement for Saturn.
July 30, 1985	Spring Hill, Tenn., selected as site for new Saturn plant.
December 7, 1987	GM approves $1.9 billion for plant construction, equipment, and tooling.
July 30, 1990	At exactly 10:57 a.m. (cdt), Roger Smith and UAW president Owen Bieber drove a red Saturn sedan off final assembly line.

The chosen. As Bedricky sees it, the only way for Saturn to build the best small cars in the world is to cultivate genuine partnerships with its suppliers. That means replacing bids with long-term assignments; indeed, Saturn's suppliers can expect to have the business forever as long as they continue to meet world class standards for quality, delivery, and cost. Incidentally, Saturn's goal on supplier quality for 1993 is 25 ppm or less (25 defects per million parts). "Most of our suppliers achieved that level in the last quarter of '92," says Saturn's purchasing boss. "Every production part is single-sourced," he adds.

In comparison with other automotive assembly plants, Saturn does business with a relatively small cadre of suppliers—245 direct, and 22 indirect, suppliers. The latter is an unusually low number; indeed, a plant of Saturn's size is normally serviced by a cast of thousands. The 22 indirect suppliers are, in effect, program managers, responsible for an entire commodity area.

"They're our agents," says James Bovenzi, Saturn's director of indirect materials. "Besides procuring nearly all of our indirect materials, they're also in charge of maintaining proper inventory levels."

Saturn's annual tab for indirect materials is in the neighborhood of $100 million. This covers some 70,000 items.

According to Bovenzi, Saturn has "stretched the comfort zone" of distributors supplying indirect materials to the plant. Distributors traditionally are affiliated with a particular manufacturer and generally aren't permitted to carry competing brands. Take cutting tools as an example. A Kennametal distributor isn't likely to be hawking other brands, say, Valenite cutting tools. This conflict in brand names was resolved by having the distributors sign "Saturn only" contracts that in effect encourages them to procure other brands when the occasion warrants it. "Our cutting tool supplier [Metalcutting Tool Management] happens to be owned by Kennametal," says Bovenzi. "But, for certain applications, they won't hesitate to provide us with cutting tools manufactured by someone else."

Besides MTM, other suppliers of indirect materials include: Airco (industrial gases); Cameron & Barkley (electrical supplies); Joseph Ryerson (steel and other metals); Motion Industries (fluid power); and Yale Materials Handling (mobile equipment).

Postscript: Saturn, under a mandate to break even this year, reportedly posted its first operating profit in May. —*Ernest Raia*

A thousand parts alight

For 20 hours a day, six days a week, hundreds of trailers pulled by yard tractors shuttle from dock to dock in a seeming random game of musical trucks.

Some of the trailers will visit 10 docks before they're emptied. Nearly every one will visit at least several docks. A thousand times a day, trailers unload production material or load empty containers at one of 56 docks at the Saturn auto manufacturing plant in Spring Hill, Tenn.

Out of the apparent chaos emerges a pattern that is as purposeful as a beehive. Nearly all the trailers will arrive at the correct dock within five minutes of the assigned time. Materials arriving from suppliers hundreds of miles distant will go directly to the point they're needed on the production line, and be installed on a vehicle within hours.

The system works in large part because Saturn early on determined that transportation must be a central component of its JIT manufacturing system; important enough that Saturn decided it, rather than its suppliers, must control inbound transportation. "At Saturn, transportation is viewed as an integral part of the materials management function," says John Sonia, general manager of Ryder Dedicated Logistic's operation two miles from the Saturn plant.

The process of designing the system began in March 1989, well before the first Saturn automobile started down the production line. At that time, Saturn selected Ryder, which became what it called its Tier One provider of transportation services.

Ryder's principal assignment: Meet Saturn's stringent delivery requirements for direct materials through a dedicated transportation system. In addition, Ryder manages carriers transporting production materials that it is not carrying itself. "We're responsible for the movement of all direct materials into the plant," says Sonia. "We function as the transportation department. We view ourselves as Saturn."

In April 1989, teams from both Ryder and Saturn sat down to design a transportation process that would mesh with Saturn's manufacturing system. "We had to have a complete understanding of their production system before putting the logistics design and system together," Sonia says.

The system had to be effective not only in delivering materials within narrow windows, but it had to be cost-effective as well. That is, Ryder had to have a fleet that was reliable and productive. Ryder's own profitability hinged on designing a system that made the most of tractors, trailers, and employees.

Starting signal. The process begins with a replenishment signal from Saturn. Ryder receives the signal at the same time as the Saturn suppliers. Those signals arrive once an hour during Saturn's 20-hour factory operations.

Initially, Ryder was plugged into Saturn's entire 12-week planning cycle. But Sonia says that proved both unnecessary and a costly consumer of computer memory. "Their equation on parts is not critical to us," Sonia says. The reason: The routes are designed to supply Saturn operating at capacity, so there is little variation in daily routing patterns.

That doesn't mean the system is static. Sonia says changes occur almost weekly, as suppliers are changed or move, or other elements are fine tuned.

Sonia says a change management committee composed of Ryder and Saturn managers meets once a week. In addition, Sonia is in constant touch with Curt Gibbs, Saturn's director of material flow and logistics at the plant.

Routing for profit. The replenishment signals cause Ryder's computer system to generate routing for Ryder drivers—called route managers by the carrier. Those routes on average require a driver to call on three or four suppliers. Overall, Ryder makes some 475 pickups a day for Saturn from 333 supplier locations.

The routes are designed to take advantage of as much of the cubic capacity of Ryder's trailers as possible. "The pickup end has the maximum dollars for savings," Sonia says. "We have a loading diagram for each route to insure the trailers cube out. We cube out long before we weigh out." On average, Ryder trailers are loaded to about 95% of cubic capacity.

The route design offers an interesting example of supplier collaboration. After the initial design in 1989, Ryder's team met with suppliers one at a time to go over the schedule. As a result, almost every route was changed in some way, Sonia says. For instance, the pickup sequence or time might change to better meet a supplier's production schedule or avoid lunch hours. Actual pickups began in June 1990.

Ryder is required to arrive at each supplier within 15 minutes of the specified time. And each supplier then has a set time for loading,

> **Ryder at Saturn: the numbers**
>
> **Trailers:** 375-380, including 48- and 53-ft. vans, drop frames, refrigerated units, and soft sided trailers.
> **Tractors:** 220 power units, including over the road tractors, shuttle units, and yard tractors.
> **Drivers:** 500.
> **Daily supplier pickups:** 475 at 333 locations.
> **Daily dock transactions at Saturn:** 1,000.
> **Mileage:** 14,000 per day, 40 million per year.
> **On time pickup (15 minute window):** 98.3%.
> **On time delivery (5-minute window):** 96.5%.

which varies according to the product. They are required to load according to Ryder's load diagram.

Receiving at the supplier. At the supplier, the Ryder route manager/driver in effect performs the receiving function for Saturn. The driver checks the part numbers, kanban card, and the number of containers against his own list. "If there's a problem, we know it's out there," says Sonia. "We can go into recovery procedures earlier."

Ryder continues to have the responsibility to get materials to Saturn on time, even if a supplier comes up short for some reason. "We've gone as far as leasing Lear jets," Sonia says, to make a delivery window. Under Saturn's agreements with its suppliers, the cost of expedited transportation is paid by the one at fault—Ryder, the supplier, or Saturn.

Sonia considers the regularity of the routes a key factor in minimizing problems. "Our drivers go on the same group of routes every week. They know where they are going, who to contact, and what are the recovery procedures."

On the phone on the road. The drivers are required to call the dispatch office on a regular basis. They reach a computerized system that asks them for a personal identification number and to verify their location. A missed call automatically sets off both audio and visual signals in the dispatch office. The system also allows the drivers to receive and send messages. Sonia says a satellite tracking system was rejected as too expensive and, in the closed loop system run by Ryder's drivers, not needed.

The route drivers return with their loads to Ryder's facility, two miles from the Saturn plant. The drivers park their trailers in pre-assigned spots in the yard. If their shift isn't over, the drivers then pick up another trailer for another run.

Outbound, the drivers haul either returnable containers for the suppliers or service parts from the Saturn warehouse. The parts are delivered to one of four locations around the U.S. Sonia says integrating the parts distribution was important for keeping costs down.

A little help from their friends. Saturn's suppliers are located throughout the U.S., with several in Canada and Mexico. Several of the North American suppliers are out of cost-effective reach of Ryder's dedicated fleet. For those cases, and for occasional expedited freight, Ryder manages a group of 17 contract, common, and expedited carriers for Saturn.

Those carriers were selected by Ryder and Saturn based on their safety, service, and cost records, Sonia says. In addition, Saturn uses suppliers from France and Germany, who ship material by steam ship. Ryder carries the material from the port to the Saturn plant.

Move on down the road. From the Ryder yard, shuttle drivers haul inbound trailers to the correct first door at the Saturn plant. The shuttle driver takes the tractor to another door to pick up a trailer that has been emptied of inbound goods and loaded with returnable containers. Ryder's scheduling software assigns the pickup at a dock that is as close as possible to the drop-off point.

Serendipity has played a small role in helping Ryder provide reliable delivery of the right loads to the right docks. As a security measure, all drivers' identification cards are scanned both on entering and leaving the Ryder yard. The company discovered that system also provided a nearly foolproof way of tracking loads between the yard and the plant. On leaving the yard, the driver's ID card is scanned. "It makes it impossible for the driver to leave with the wrong rig," Sonia says. "That's a tremendous operational tool we hadn't counted on."

A switch in time. A third crew of drivers, working with yard tractors, takes responsibility for switching trailers from door to door in the proper sequence and at the correct time. Trailers must arrive at the assigned door within five minutes of the assigned time. Even moving empties is important. With little storage space at the plant, trailers assigned to pick up empty containers must conform to the schedule.

Ryder began picking up materials for Saturn in June 1990. For some time, the on-time record for both pickup and delivery approached 99%. That slipped somewhat, to 98.3% on-time pickups and 96.5% on-time delivery when Saturn added Saturday to the production schedule in April. "We're trying to get back to 99% on both," Sonia says.

Like any JIT system, the system at Saturn is in constant flux. That requires Ryder to have the flexibility to adjust within the framework of its transportation system.

Ryder continues to seek ways to improve its service, Sonia says. "Saturn expected good performance from us. That was a given," he says. "How we monitor quality is more important. We're benchmarking constantly against other systems."

—*Peter Bradley*

Reprinted with permission of PURCHASING magazine, September 9, 1993
copyright 1993 by Cahners Publishing Company

SERVICE IS EVERYBODY'S BUSINESS

On the front line of the new economy, service—bold, fast, imaginative, and customized—is the ultimate imperative.

by Ronald Henkoff

The crash scene at the intersection of 40th Street and 26th Avenue in Tampa is chaotic and tense. The two cars are bent and battered. Their drivers and passengers are not bleeding, but they are shaken up and scared. Just minutes after the collision, a young man dressed in a polo shirt, khakis, and wingtips arrives on the scene to assume command. Bearing a clipboard, a camera, a cassette recorder, and an air of competence, Lance Edgy, 26, calms the victims and advises them on medical care, repair shops, police reports, and legal procedures. Edgy is not a cop or a lawyer or a good samaritan. He is a senior claims representative for Progressive Corp., an insurance company that specializes in high-risk drivers, high-octane profit—and exceptional service.

Edgy invites William McAllister, Progressive's policyholder, into an air-conditioned van equipped with comfortable chairs, a desk, and two cellular phones. Even before the tow trucks have cleared away the wreckage, Edgy is offering his client a settlement for the market value of his totaled 1988 Mercury Topaz. McAllister, who does not appear to have been at fault in this accident, is amazed by Progressive's alacrity: "This is great—someone coming right out here and taking charge. I didn't expect it at all."

Welcome to the front line of the new American economy, where service—bold, fast, unexpected, innovative, and customized—is the ultimate strategic imperative, a business challenge that has profound implications for the way we manage companies, hire employees, develop careers, and craft policies.

It matters not whether a company creates something you can touch, such as a computer, a toaster, or a machine tool, or something you can only experience, such as insurance coverage, an airplane ride, or a telephone call. What counts most is the service built into that something—the way the product is designed and delivered, billed and bundled, explained and installed, repaired and renewed.

Product quality, once a competitive advantage, is now just the ante into the game. Says Eric Mittelstadt, 58, president and CEO of Fanuc Robotics North America: "Everyone has become better at developing products. In robotics, the robot itself has become sort of a commodity. The one place you can differentiate yourself is in the service you provide."

Companies that achieve distinctive service often have to redefine their very reason for doing business. Fanuc has transmuted itself from an assembler of robots into a designer and installer of customized manufacturing systems. Progressive no longer simply sells insurance policies; it sees itself as a mediator of human trauma. Toyota's Lexus division has invented not just a new luxury car but a whole new standard of luxury service.

Johnson Controls, a seemingly mature manufacturer of thermostats and energy systems, has discovered startup-style growth in the business of managing other companies' buildings. ServiceMaster, a company that fertilizes lawns, kills bugs, and scrubs floors, has prospered by, in effect, selling people back their own leisure time. Taco Bell has been ringing up juicy profits because it knows that its main business is not preparing food but delivering it—and not just in restaurants but in schools, hospitals, kiosks, and pushcarts.

As a result of epiphanies like these, entire companies are—literally—moving closer to their customers. At Progressive, claims adjusters who used to spend much of their time working phones and pushing papers are ambulatory. At Johnson Controls, design engineers who were once ensconced in cubicles and harnessed to their computers are out in their customers' buildings, managing the systems they helped create. Says Patrick Harker, director of the Wharton School's

Fishman-Davidson Center, which studies the service sector: "Once you start thinking of service as a process instead of as a series of functions, the old distinction between the front office (the people who did the selling) and the back office (the people who pushed the paper but never saw the customer) disappears."

The changing nature of customer relationships demands a new breed of service worker, folks who are empathetic, flexible, informed, articulate, inventive, and able to work with minimal levels of supervision. "Rather than the service world being derided as having the dead-end jobs of our time, it will increasingly become an outlet for creativity, theatricality, and expressiveness," says Larry Keeley, president of Doblin Group, a Chicago management and design consulting firm. It's no coincidence that companies everywhere now profess an ardent desire to "delight" their customers.

For far longer than most of us realize—for most of this century, in fact—services have dominated the American economy. They now generate 74% of gross domestic product, account for 79% of all jobs, and produce a balance-of-trade surplus that hit $55.7 billion last year, vs. a deficit of $132.4 billion for goods. The demand for services will remain strong. The Bureau of Labor Statistics expects service occupations to be responsible for *all* net job growth through the year 2005, spawning whole new legions of nurses, physical therapists, home health aides, and social workers to minister to the needs of an aging population, along with phalanxes of food servers, child-care providers, and cleaning ladies to cater to the wants of harried two-earner families. Also rising to the fore will be a swelling class of technical workers, including computer engineers, systems analysts, and paralegals.

The service economy, despite its size and growth, remains extraordinarily misunderstood, mismeasured, and mismanaged. "We still have this perception that making a product is better than providing a service," says James Brian Quinn, professor of management at Dartmouth's Tuck School and author of the book *Intelligent Enterprise*. That notion, which Quinn traces back to prophets as diverse as Adam Smith and Karl Marx, is reinforced by present-day politicians, economists, trade union officials, and journalists—service workers all—who decry the demise of high-paying manufacturing jobs and rue the propagation of low-paying service positions like burger flippers, floor sweepers, and bedpan changers.

Well, it's not that simple. The service sector, whose cohorts include richly remunerated cardiac surgeons, tort lawyers, and movie stars, is as varied as the economy itself. The gap between manufacturing and service wages is narrowing. (So, too, is the difference between productivity rates in goods and services industries. See story, page 79.) In 1992 the median goods-producing job paid only $19 per week more than the median service-producing job, according to a recently published study by the Federal Reserve Bank of Cleveland. More telling: The distribution of low-paying and high-paying jobs in each sector is virtually identical. The real problem isn't the wage gap between workers who produce goods and those who provide services. It's the wage chasm between employees with higher education and those without.

Despite the steady expansion of the service economy, American management practices, accounting conventions, business school courses, and public policies continue to suffer from an acute Industrial Age hangover. "Most people still view the world through manufacturing goggles," complains Fred Reichheld, leader of the customer-loyalty practice at Bain & Co. "We use an accounting system that was designed to serve 19th-century textile and steel mills." That system tallies returns on equipment, inventories, and other physical assets, but what really matters in a service business is the return a company reaps from its human assets—the brainpower of its employees and the loyalty of its customers. Try reporting something like "return on intellect employed" on your next P&L statement, and see how the analysts and auditors react to that.

Service executives often behave much like belly dancers trying to march to a John Philip Sousa song, subjecting their companies to management theories—both traditional and trendy—that were invented in the factory. Says Leonard Schlesinger, a Harvard business school professor who has studied service companies for two decades: "Old legends die hard. Many service firms have aped the worst aspects of manufacturing management. They oversupervise; they overcontrol."

Even new managerial precepts like total quality management, statistical process control, reengineering, and benchmarking are rooted in manufacturing. "Senior management continues to focus on incremental improvements in quality, on redesigning internal processes, on restructuring, on taking people out of the equation," says a frustrated Craig Terrill, an innovation consultant at Kuczmarski & Associates in Chicago. "That's such a defeatist approach. They should be coming up with whole new ways to serve their customers."

The good news is that an increasing number of companies are inventing new ways to reach those customers. Forcing them to change is that fabled taskmaster—the marketplace. Progressive Corp. used to have a winning formula for coining money in auto insurance, a business with notoriously low margins. The company, headquartered in Cleveland, wrote policies for high-risk drivers that its competitors wouldn't touch, and charged high prices to match. The ride ended in 1988, when two things happened. Allstate outflanked Progressive in the high-risk niche, and voters in California, where Progressive made 25% of its profits, passed Proposition 103, a law that sharply curtailed insurance rates.

Peter Lewis, 60, Progressive's plain-speaking chairman, CEO, and president, saw the double wake-up call as an opportunity both to revise his company's practices and to tame the public's hostility. Says he: "People get screwed seven ways from Sunday in auto insurance. They get dealt with adversarially, and they get dealt with slowly. I said, 'Why don't we just stop that? Why don't we start dealing with them nicely? It would be a revolution in the business.' "

With its round-the-clock Immediate Response program, introduced four years ago, Progressive representatives now make contact with 80% of accident victims less than nine hours after learning of the crash. Adjusters inspect 70% of damaged vehicles within one day and wrap up most collision damage claims within a week. By scurrying to the scene, adjusters obtain accurate information fast, which they feed into PACMan (Progressive automated claims management system). The streamlined process reduces costs, builds customers' good will, and keeps the liability lawyers at bay. At the crash scene in Tampa, even the driver of the other car, Xavia Culver, was impressed: "I think all insurance companies should come out and see what's going on, to help out with all the hassle and confusion."

Lance Edgy, Progressive's man on the scene in Tampa, is the very model of a modern service worker. The lead member of a six-person team of adjusters, Edgy joined Progressive in 1990 after graduating from the University of Florida with a degree in finance. The company has invested heavily in his training, offering him courses not just in the arcana of insurance regulation but also in the art of negotiation and in grief counseling (part of his job involves dealing with the relatives of dead crash victims). Progressive's gain-sharing program, keyed to a formula based on revenues, profits, and costs, gives Edgy an opportunity to increase his base salary of $38,480 a year by as much as $5,400.

Says CEO Lewis: "To the extent that auto insurance is a commodity, our biggest differentiator is our people. We want the best people at every level of the company, and we pay at the top of the market." When a competitor recently tried to hire away three of Progressive's highly paid division claims managers by offering them large pay hikes, Lewis increased the pay scales not just for the three would-be defectors but for all 15 of their colleagues as well. Investing in people pays dividends. Progressive's net income, $267 million last year, has increased at an average annual compound rate of 20% since 1989.

For service companies, retaining good employees is essential to winning and keeping good customers. "It's impossible to build a loyal book of customers without a loyal employee base," says Fred Reichheld of Bain. "It's like trying to build a brick wall without mortar." As obvious as this connection seems, managers of service companies routinely disregard it. The annual rate of employee turnover in department stores and restaurants routinely tops 100%. Says Harvard's Schlesinger: "Most service companies operate with a cycle-of-failure mentality. They assume labor is an expendable, renewable resource, and they create a cadre of poor, unmotivated employees who couldn't care less if the customer is satisfied."

When it comes to the link between employee turnover, customer loyalty, and profits, Lexus understands the nexus. Two-thirds of the people who buy a Lexus have bought one before, the highest repeat purchase rate in the luxury car market. That's an extraordinary statistic, considering that the first Lexus went on sale less than five years ago, and considering that the appreciation of the yen has sent the price of a top-of-the-line LS 400 sedan soaring above $54,000.

For three years running, customers surveyed by J.D. Power & Associates, the industry's leading pollster, have ranked Lexus No. 1 in product quality and dealer service among all cars sold in the U.S. "We try to make it very hard for you to leave us," says Lexus general manager George Borst. "When you buy a Lexus, you don't buy a product. You buy a luxury package."

Wrapped in the package is a style of service crafted with the same precision Toyota put into the design of the car itself. Says Borst: "Our challenge was to get people to buy a Japanese luxury car. The quality of the product wasn't the issue. Everybody knew that Toyota could make a top-quality product. The issue was creating a sense of prestige. And where we saw the hole in the market was in the way dealers treated their customers."

When you walk into the showroom at South Bay Lexus, not far from Toyota's Torrance, California, headquarters, the most striking thing is what doesn't happen. No salesmen—sales consultants, to use the proper title—approach. They don't hover, they don't pry, they don't solicit. Even though they're paid on commission, these guys stay totally out of sight until you tell the receptionist you're ready for a consultation. Says South Bay service manager John Lane: "Customers won't stand for the hustle effect."

Like all employees at Lexus dealerships (including receptionists), Lane regularly attends national and regional training courses to learn about cars, even those made by competitors, and customers. Lane figures he received more training in his first month at Lexus than he did in his entire 18-year career at Cadillac.

But back to the showroom. If you want to buy a car—and most customers make two or three visits before they're ready—your sales consultant will usher you into a product presentation room, an alcove with no doors, no clutter, a semicircular marble-topped table, and three leather chairs that are precisely the same height. The implicit message: There are no traps and no surprises.

The first two regularly scheduled maintenances of your car are free. While you're waiting for the work to be done, you can use an office with a desk and a phone. Or you can stand in the customer viewing room and watch the mechanic—sorry, the service technician—attend to your car in a brightly lit garage that seems devoid of grease. If you need to be someplace, the dealer will lend you a car or give you a ride. When you pick up your vehicle, you'll find that it has been washed and vacuumed by a "valet detail specialist," whose compensation, like everyone else's at South Bay, is pegged to customer satisfaction. The annual employee turnover rate since South Bay opened its doors in 1989 is a lowly 7%.

Okay, it's one thing to provide silky service when you're selling a silk-purse-type product. But how much innovation can you possibly bring to the preparation and delivery of a $1.39 chicken taco or a 99-cent bean burrito? Plenty.

Over the past decade Taco Bell, a subsidiary of PepsiCo, has evolved from a regional quick-service restaurant chain with $700 million in system-wide sales and 1,500 outlets into a multinational food delivery company with $3.9 billion in revenues and more than 15,000 "points of access" (POAs). What, you ask, is a POA? It is any place where people can meet to munch—an airport, a supermarket, a school cafeteria, a college campus, or a street corner. Says Charlie Rogers, Taco Bell's senior vice president for human resources: "We've changed the way we think about ourselves, moving from a company that prepares food to one that feeds hungry people."

Like many business insights, this one sounds insanely simple, almost like a Peter Sellers pronouncement in the movie *Being There*. But don't be fooled. Getting from Point A to Point B necessitated a revolution in the way Taco Bell manages people, information, and machines. The first step, unveiled by President and CEO John Martin in 1989, was called K-minus. (The "K" stands for kitchen.) Martin took the heavy-duty food preparation—crushing beans, dicing cheese, and preparing beef—out of the restaurants and centralized it in commissaries run by outside contractors. The cost savings allowed Taco Bell to slash its prices. More significantly, the company was able to shrink the average size of a restaurant kitchen by 40%, freeing up more space—and more employees—to serve customers. Says Rogers: "Most of the people in our restaurants really worked in manufacturing, not service."

Once Taco Bell got the manufacturing out of its restaurants, it began to get the manufacturing out of its management. Like most fast-food chains, Taco Bell used a command-and-control system of supervision that came straight out of Detroit, circa 1960. There was one manager for each restaurant, one area manager for every six restaurants, and one repetitious, mind-numbing job for each employee. Today many Taco Bell outlets operate with no manager on the premises. Self-directed teams, known as "crews," manage inventory, schedule work, order supplies, and train new employees—make that "crew members." Team-managed restaurants have lower employee turnover and higher customer satisfaction scores than conventionally run outlets.

Regional managers, formerly factory-style supervisors who earned about $25,000 a year, are now business school graduates who oversee as many as 30 POAs. Their pay, closely linked to sales results and customer-satisfaction scores, can top $100,000. "I see myself not just as a fast-food manager but as an entrepreneur who manages a multi-million-dollar corporation with 250 employees," says Sueyoung Georgas, a fortysomething native of South Korea, whose territory in the southern suburbs of Detroit includes five restaurants, five schools, three community colleges, and a catering service that provisions banquets and festivals. With people like Georgas onboard, CEO Martin is aiming to increase Taco Bell's points of access to 200,000—a more than tenfold increase—by the year 2000.

Some of the most exciting action in services is occurring behind the scenes, deep in the bowels of the economy—down in the boiler room, to be precise. Okay, a boiler room isn't an intrinsically thrilling place. But it is for Johnson Controls, an old-line Milwaukee manufacturing company, whose founder, Warren Johnson, invented the thermostat in 1883. Sales of Johnson's traditional products—heating controls, batteries, plastic bottles, and automobile seats—continue to expand at a steady pace. But "facilities management services," which Johnson entered in 1989, is running like a racehorse, with revenues growing at a triple-digit clip.

Controls Group vice president Terry Weaver waxes euphoric when he describes the opportunity in managing the heating, lighting, security, and cleaning operations of office buildings. "It's explosive. It's almost impossible to quantify, a market worth tens of billions of dollars in the U.S. alone. It's a wave. It's a megatrend."

Yep, it's exciting. And here's why: As companies restructure, they are paring costs and focusing on what they do best (their core competencies, in B-school jargon). At the same time, they are ditching the things that they do worst, like managing their computer networks, phone systems, and boiler rooms. Through the magic of outsourcing, one company's cost center becomes Johnson Controls' (or some other firm's) profit center.

Johnson Controls Chairman and Chief Executive James Keyes, 53, says service now drives his entire corporation. "Most of our growth has come from the fact that we do more for our customers." Strictly speaking, Tina Brueckner, 27, an engineer in the Controls Group's Milwaukee branch office, had always been a service worker. But she almost never met the people she was serving. Hunched in front of a computer, she designed heating, ventilation, and air-conditioning control systems to specifications drawn up by the customer or the customer's consultant.

Now, instead of basically filling orders, Brueckner finds solutions to her customers' problems. She spends at least half her time in the field as part of a four-person team that helps schools improve their energy efficiency. Says she: "Before I sat at a desk and engineered. Now I go out and talk to my customers. This makes the job a lot more satisfying."

The outsourcing phenomenon fueling growth at companies like Johnson Controls is also spreading to the consumer world. There the powerhouse is ServiceMaster, a company in Downers Grove, Illinois, that has made a mint by doing things for people that they don't want to do themselves: Dust their bookshelves, care for their lawns, and exterminate their roaches. The company, which also cleans and maintains hospitals, schools, and other buildings, reported net income of $145.9 million on revenues of $2.8 billion in 1993, its 23rd consecutive year of record top- and bottom-line results.

Chairman William Pollard, 56, admits to being miffed that his colleagues in the business community don't always treat his enterprise with the greatest respect: "They say, 'Oh, you're just the mop-and-bucket guys.' But then they look at our financial results and wonder, 'How did they do that?'" How indeed? By carefully selecting employees ("service partners" is what the company calls them), training them thoroughly, and giving them the right tools to do the job. ServiceMaster's R&D center, which is focusing this year on floor care, recently invented the Walk-Behind Scrubber, a self-propelled contraption that helped cut by 20% the amount of time it takes to clean a vinyl surface. Next year, incidentally, will be the Year of the Carpet.

ServiceMaster's real genius lies in the way it manages to instill a sense of dignity and importance in low-paid people doing menial jobs. The company's Merry Maids subsidiary rejects nine out of ten applicants for the entry-level position of "teammate." Every prospective teammate goes through a 45-question interview known as the Perceiver. Managers review the results, looking for WOO words—for Winning Others Over—such as "win," "commitment," "we," "yes," and "us."

Merry Maids' pickiness in hiring teammates stems from a new perception of why it's in business. Says President Mike Isakson: "We used to focus on the process of cleaning, making sure the home was free from dust. Now we understand that the ultimate benefits to the customer are peace of mind, security, and stress reduction." In other words, the customer wants to know not only that her home will be cleaned but that nothing will be stolen, broken, or rearranged. Says Cindy Luellen, 33, a Merry Maids office manager in Indianapolis who started out as a teammate: "This job is very rewarding emotionally, especially for a divorced, single mother with just a high school education. It's nice to have the respect of your fellow employees and your customers too."

Respect, loyalty, security, dignity—old-fashioned qualities for a new-fashioned economy. Earlier this century machines helped liberate our ancestors from the toil of the fields. In this generation, wondrous technology has freed us from the drudgery of the assembly line and enabled us to speed new products to far-off markets. As we approach a new millennium, it is people who will carry us forward. In an economy built on service, the extent to which we prosper will depend on our ability to educate, entertain, empower, and ennoble ourselves—and each other.

Reprinted with permission June 27, 1994 issue of Fortune, (c) 1994 Time Inc. All Rights Reserved.

Reducing Variability — Key to Continuous Quality Improvement

SPC can be a tool to measure process variability and improve quality. Using the famous Taguchi Method is a major step toward this goal.

Gregg D. Stocker, CPM
Quality Manager
Ruska Instrument Corp.
Houston, TX

In recent years, quality has undoubtedly become a strategic focus of companies expecting to do business in the 1990s and beyond. In the summer of 1988, the Department of Defense released the Total Quality Management (TQM) Master Plan to achieve continuous improvement of products and services offered and used by the department. A major component of this philosophy is the concept of variability reduction. As a result of DoD's move, many organizations are beginning to understand that reducing the variability of a process results in improved quality and reduced costs.

The concept of variability reduction has its origins in the 1920s with Dr. Walter Shewhart of Bell Laboratories. It has been expanded through the works of W. Edwards Deming, J.A. Juran, Armand Feigenbaum and Genichi Taguchi. Although variability reduction is only one of many components in a continuous improvement process, it is one whose importance calls for further examination.

The concept of variation

Understanding variability reduction requires an understanding of basic statistics. This fundamental requirement has apparently frightened a number of people away from employing many proven quality improvement techniques. Fortunately, the level of statistical knowledge required to understand the underlying philosophies for quality improvement is not great.

Statistically every process experiences variation in one form or another. It is this variation that leads to quality problems. Methods employed to reduce the amount of variation will, therefore, improve quality and reduce cost.

The philosophy of variability reduction is based on the fact that there is a "best" value for a product's function, fit and appearance.

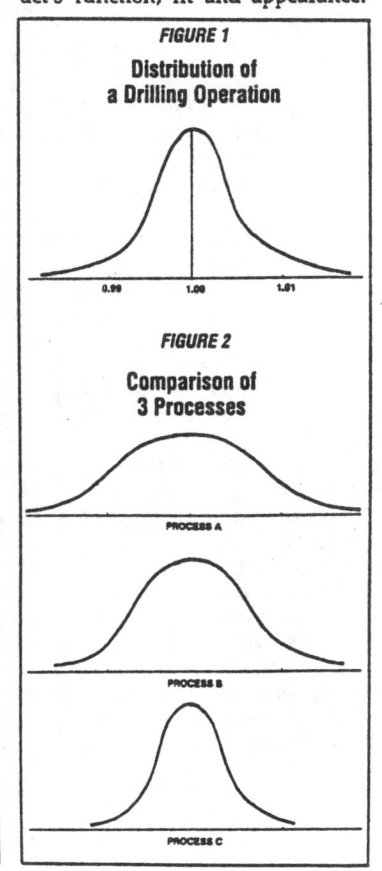

FIGURE 1
Distribution of a Drilling Operation

FIGURE 2
Comparison of 3 Processes

PROCESS A
PROCESS B
PROCESS C

This value is the target that must be achieved to ensure the highest level of quality. To address the existence of variation in a process, traditionally engineering and manufacturing have relied on tolerance or specification limits. This approach must be changed because although parts produced within the specification limits may be functional, their quality decreases and cost increases as the process varies from the target. And this variability can lose business. The company that best meets the needs of the customers within a specific market will gain the greatest share of the market.

Variability is illustrated by the normal distribution, also known as the bell-shaped curve. *Figure 1* presents the output of a process that drills holes to a target value of one inch. The normal distribution states that, as long as the process is operating in a statistical state of control most of the holes will be drilled at exactly one inch. The curve also shows that an equal proportion of parts will vary above and below the one inch target, called the "spread".

Figure 2 presents a comparison of distribution of three different processes. Process A produced a greater amount of variation than process B or C, as shown by the wider and flatter curve. In terms of variability, therefore, process C is the best of the three processes for this particular part, i.e. it is the most centered around the target value.

Process A will produce parts that will be scrapped or require rework. This is indicated by the shaded portions at each end of the curve. Although process B produces virtually every piece within the tolerance limits, the increased variability over process C could result in increased assembly time or possible tolerance stackup problems.

The principles relating to variability of quality and cost are represented by the Quality Loss Function (QLF) which was developed by Taguchi and are discussed later in this article under "Taguchi Methods."

Statistical process control (SPC)

SPC is a tool used to measure the variability of a process and deter-

FIGURE 3

Distribution 60% Acceptable

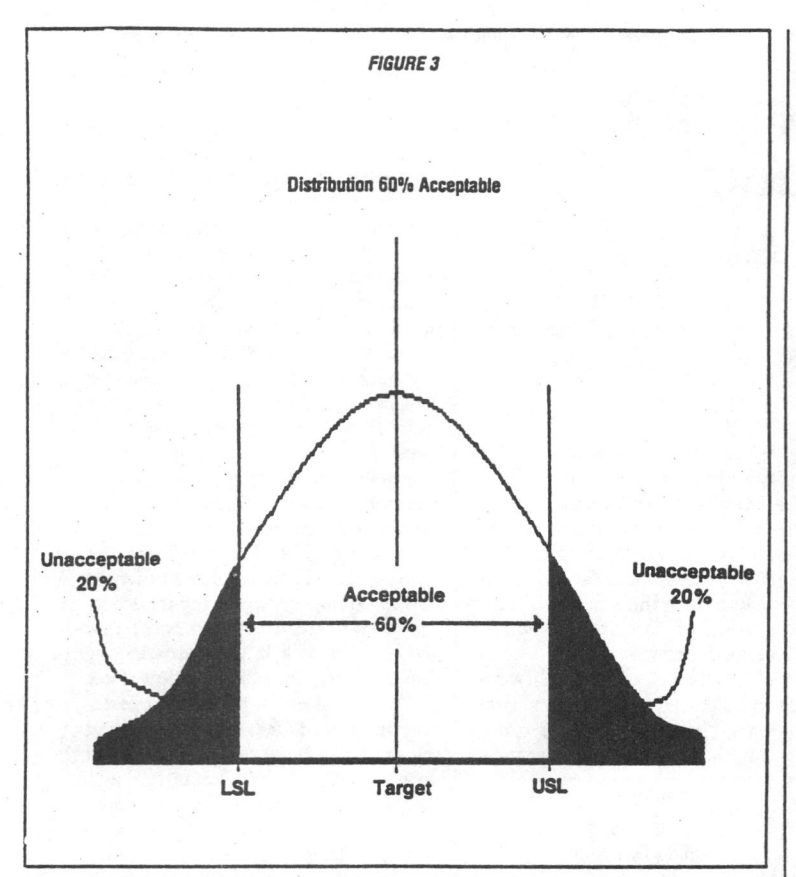

Unacceptable 20% Acceptable 60% Unacceptable 20%

LSL   Target   USL

mine its capability to produce a particular part. The method was developed by Shewhart in 1924 and was used extensively by government contractors during World War II.

A process consistently and predictably producing parts within three standard deviations of the average is considered in a state of statistical control. This means all the special causes of variation within the process have been removed.

A process in a state of statistical control refers *only* to the ability to predict the amount of inherent variation. It does not make any reference to the capability of the process to produce high quality parts on a consistent basis.

Figure 3 presents a process in a state of control, but only able to produce acceptable parts 60 percent of the time. This is because the spread of variation inherent in the process carries outside-the-product specification limits. The measure used to determine if the process can produce acceptable parts on a consistent basis is the process capability (C_p) index.

The C_p index is a measure of the variation of a process with respect to the acceptable tolerance limits for an item. The formula for C_p is:
[Tolerance/Process Spread]
The higher the C_p index, the smaller the variation within the process in relation to the tolerance specifications. As a general rule, any C_p greater than 1.33 is considered acceptable—although statistically the process will continue to produce 66 defects per million.

The problem with the C_p index is that it does not take into account the process average. The process variability may be shifted to one side or the other of the specification limits which will result in a greater number of rejected items than the measure indicates. This situation has led to the development of the C_{pk} index, which is a measure of the process in relation to the item's target value and specification limits. C_{pk} is calculated as the lower of:

$$\frac{(\text{Upper Spec Limit}) - (\text{Process Average})}{\text{Process Spread}}$$

$$\frac{-(\text{Lower Spec Limit}) - (\text{Process Average})}{\text{Process Spread}}$$

The process spread is calculated as 3 sigma. As with the C_p index, the general rule is to consider any process capable that has a value of 1.33 or greater. The higher the C_{pk} value, the less variation inherent in the process, or the larger the specification limits.

As mentioned earlier, any item produced that exhibits a value outside the 3 sigma limit for that process identifies a *special* cause of variation. Statistically, this refers to a problem not attributable to the natural variation causes that can be identified and eliminated on the shop floor by the production worker.

The problems associated with the natural variation within the process are referred to as *common* causes. The common causes, resulting in a flatter and wider curve for the process, can only be eliminated by management action through improvements in the overall system. The philosophy of TQM is based on the premise that the variation must be reduced to improve quality and that a reduction in this variation will automatically result in lower costs for the company.

Companies that use quality levels denoted by sigma are referring to the capabilities of their processes. Motorola, one of the winners of the 1988 Malcolm Baldrige National Quality Award, has targeted its quality level at 6 sigma by 1991. In terms of the normal distribution, this means they are improving their processes to produce less than 3.4 defects per million parts produced.

It is important to note that SPC is only a tool to monitor the process and identify the special causes. Although it is a very important tool for quality improvement, it is not

Reducing Variability

useful in reducing the natural variation inherent within the process.

Figure 4 presents a simple example of the control chart developed by Shewhart. The chart is basically the same as the normal curve except it is presented horizontally and includes a time element. The sample measurements are plotted on the chart, and the process average and control limits (average ±3 standard deviations) are calculated and drawn as straight lines. This chart does not refer to the specification limits in any way. It is hoped that the specifications of the items to be manufactured within that process are well outside the control limits. If not, the process is not considered capable of producing the item(s) in question.

Any point outside the control limits identifies a special cause of variation that can be corrected by the operator. If the part specifications are well outside the control limits the special causes can be identified and corrected before unacceptable parts are produced.

Other signals to special causes of variation include:
- seven consecutive points on the same side of the centerline;
- seven consecutive points that increase or decrease;
- two out of three consecutive points on the same side of the centerline outside the ±2 sigma zone;
- other *non-random* patterns—trends, cycles, etc.

Any efforts to bring the control limits closer to the mean need to address the (common) causes of natural variation. One method proven very successful in the reduction of the natural process variation was developed by Taguchi.

Taguchi methods

The Taguchi Method for design of experiments is a tool used to reduce the inherent variability in a product or process. It combines engineering and statistics to directly address the process variability problem. The tool is employed primarily in product and process engineering to identify and optimize conflicting inputs (factors) to enable improved quality and reduced cost. Developed by Taguchi, it has enabled him to win the coveted Deming Prize in Japan four times.

The factors in product and process design are defined by Taguchi as controllable and uncontrollable. The interaction of these factors has a direct impact on the performance variation inherent in the product. By concentrating solely on the controllable factors, and their resultant effect on variation, the engineer can design a product or process that minimizes variation, thereby increasing quality and reducing cost.

Definition of quality

The Taguchi philosophy is based on the premise that cost can be reduced by improving quality and that quality will automatically improve by reducing variation. This philosophy strongly disagrees with Philip Crosby's statements that quality is solely *conformance to specifications*.

Taguchi believes that tolerance limits are defined to cover up problems in design of the product or process. Minimal variation around the target value is the only true way to achieve high levels of quality. Taguchi states that the difference between an item that is barely within specification and one that is barely out of specification is very little; yet one is considered good and the other is considered bad. Following this philosopohy, Taguchi defines quality as *"the loss a product causes to society after being shipped, other than any losses caused by its intrinsic functions."* Any product characteristic that varies from its intended value causes a loss to society, hence poor quality.

To quantify his definition of quality, Taguchi has developed the Quality Loss Function (QLF). The QLF is a graphic representation of the loss to society caused by product/process variation. The graph is a parabola in which the lowest point represents the minimal loss (expressed in monetary terms) to the customer and company. As the target value is missed in either direction, the cost to society increases. Deviations from the target can also represent an over-designed product—heavier, larger, less efficient, etc. The QLF is a tool to be used during the early stages of design, thereby enabling changes to be made as quickly and efficiently as possible, see *Figure 5*.

By emphasizing a long-term focus on the customer's and society's needs and continuous improvement, Taguchi's philosophy closely follows the teachings of Deming and Juran. In particular, Taguchi's practice of designing a product or process that is insensitive to noise will enable the final product to be of consistent quality, thereby reducing the dependence on inspection as a means to achieve quality.

FIGURE 4
Shewhart Control Chart

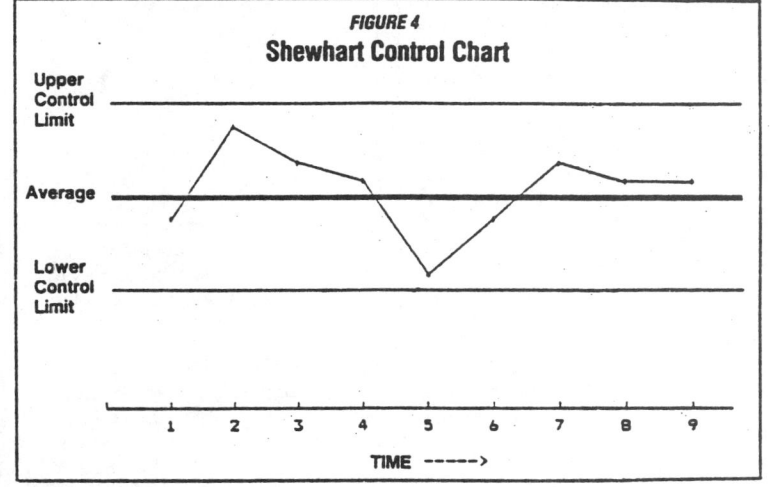

Reducing Variability

Within his method, Taguchi differentiates between the controllable and uncontrollable (noise) factors. These factors consist of any design characteristic that can cause variation in the product's performance. Examples of design factors include tubing wall thickness, screw thread length, wire diameter, cooling method and coating material. Definitions of the two types of design characteristics are as follows:

Control Factors: Factors affecting product/process performance that can be easily controlled during the production of a product.

Noise Factors: Factors affecting product/process performance that are impossible or too expensive to control, i.e. environmental conditions. There are three types of noise factors: external (environmental), internal (wear, shrinkage, etc.), and product-to-product (resulting from part-to-part variation.).

The objective of the Taguchi Method is to reduce the effect of noise factors on variation by concentrating on their interaction with the control factors. Therefore, the control factors are the only factors that can be changed.

Design process

In accordance with the TQM concept, Taguchi has made improvements in product/process design by concentrating on the process itself. He has formalized the design process by defining three distinct stages for all products and processes:

System Design: Determine the product's intended function and build prototype to accomplish objectives. Tentative parameters are defined to construct prototype.

Parameter Design: Determine the factors affecting product performance and distinguish between controllable and uncontrollable. The objective is to determine the combination of factors least sensitive to changes in the noise factors through design of experiments.

Tolerance Design: If the reduced variation determined through parameter design is not acceptable, design changes are made to attempt to achieve objectives. This usually involves increasing manufacturing and purchase costs, i.e. improved grades of material, tighter tolerances, etc.

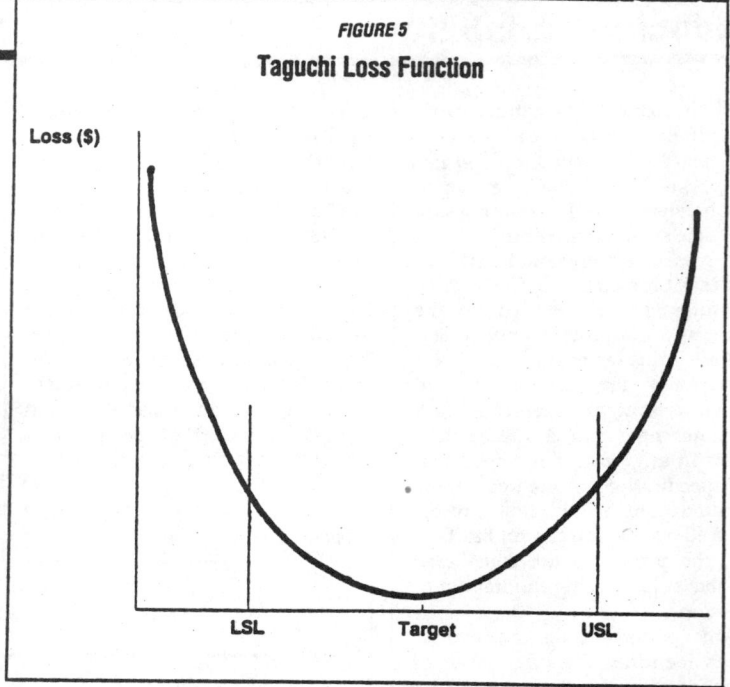

Signal-to-noise ratio

The effect of a specific noise factor on the quality of the design is described by its signal-to-noise (S/N) ratio. The S/N ratio refers to statistical measurement of the stability of a quality characteristic's performance. The S/N ratio objective is usually determined by the QLF, and is the target for the parameter design stage. The larger the S/N ratio, the more *robust* the design, i.e. the less sensitive performance will be to noise. If the actual S/N ratio is less than the target value, tolerance design will need to be performed.

Taguchi uses orthogonal arrays to simulate the results of different factor combinations to greatly reduce the number of experiments needed to complete the design. Statistical analysis, utilizing the arrays, quickly aids the engineer in eliminating the factors that will not affect the quality of the design.

Results

Taguchi Methods are slowly gaining popularity in the United States. In a book published by the American Supplier Institute—the US Center for Taguchi Methods—it was estimated that approximately 5,000 Taguchi Methods case studies are completed annually in the US. Although this number sounds impressive, estimates of the method's use in Japan exceed 100,000. Akashi Fukuhara, one person credited with the implementation of TQC at Toyota, stated that the use of Taguchi Methods is the single most important quality improvement tool used by the company.

Continuing Education in Quality

Deming, W. Edwards, *Out of the Crisis*, MIT Center for Advanced Engineering Study, 1982.

Juran, Joseph A., *Juran on Planning for Quality*, The Free Press, 1988.

Juran, Joseph A., *Juran's Quality Control Handbook—Fourth Edition*, McGraw-Hill, 1988.

Taguchi, Genichi, *Introduction to Quality Engineering*, Asian Productivity Organization, 1986.

Feigenbaum, Armand V., *Total Quality Control—Third Edition*, McGraw-Hill, 1983.

Byrne, Diane J. and Taguchi, Shin, *The Taguchi Approach to Parameter Design*, ASQC 40th Annual Quality Congress Transactions, American Society for Quality Control, Inc., 1987.

FIGURE 5
Taguchi Loss Function

Stocker, Gregg D., "Reducing Variability - Key to continuous Quality Improvement," *Manufacturing Systems*, March 1990, pp. 32-36. Reprinted with permission from *Manufacturing Systems*, March 1990, Copyright 1990.

STATISTICAL PROCESS CONTROL:
What Management Accountants Need To Know

It's complex, but your company may need it for TQM.

BY DAVID E. KEYS, CMA, AND
KURT F. REDING, CMA

U.S. companies are adopting a number of strategies including JIT, TQM, and automation to gain competitive advantage in an increasingly competitive global environment. One such strategy is statistical process control (SPC), a technique designed to improve quality and to control costs. SPC is the mechanism that drives total quality management (TQM) in Japan.[1]

Management accountants need to understand SPC so that they can help companies make valid decisions about whether to adopt SPC and so that they can participate in using SPC to increase quality and decrease costs. We describe here the general nature of SPC, rules of thumb used in SPC, the long-term nature of SPC, and how it relates to JIT, TQM, and Theory Z.

Even after you have gained a general knowledge of SPC you should be aware that SPC is very complex. Someone with a high level of statistical knowledge, usually an advanced degree in statistics, will be needed to help implement the strategy.

SPC THEORY

SPC theory is based on the postulate that process performance is dynamic—that natural up-and-down variation is the rule rather than the exception. Accordingly, performance measurements fluctuate over time, and a single measurement by itself is not meaningful. Proper assessments of process performance require correct interpretations of performance variation over time.

SPC relies on the use of graphic aids or control charts to understand and reduce fluctuations in processes until they are in a state of control (stable). A stable process is subject only to common fluctuations, which result from causes of variation natural to the process. An unstable process is subject to uncommon fluctuations as well as common fluctuations. Uncommon fluctuations result from special causes of variation.

The performance of a stable production process can be improved only by making fundamental changes in the process itself. An unstable production process can be stabilized by locating and eliminating the special causes of uncommon fluctuations. Once the causes of uncommon fluctuations are eliminated, the overall performance of the process can be improved.

The proper implementation of control charts requires a thorough understanding of the process of interest. The management accountant, or whoever is implementing SPC, must select and define one or more measures of performance. Then the appropriate control chart(s) must be selected. Is the c chart, p chart, or x chart most appropriate? Maybe the X-bar and R charts would be better.

Different charts are based on different statistical distribution theories. For example, the decision to use an x chart is based on the assumption that the data points collected are distributed as a normal random variable. The p chart and c chart are based on binomial distribution theory and Poisson distribution theory, respectively.

The performance measure and the appropriate control chart are interdependent. The performance measure selected must be distributed in a manner consistent with the assumptions of a particular statistical distribution. Selection of the proper chart(s) depends on accurate judgments about process performance, that is, about the expected behavior of the performance measure over time. The steps involved in the application of SPC are outlined in Table 1.

A DOLL NAMED EARL

For example, one of the Franklin Company's primary products is a toy doll called "Earl," which is manufactured in lot sizes of 1,000. Franklin has experienced what its management accountant considers to be a high level of unscheduled line stops, which significantly increase costs, decrease quality, and increase the cycle time of Earl production. Therefore, unscheduled interruption in the production process is selected as the performance measure to be studied.

A c chart is selected to track the number of unscheduled interruptions of the production process. Each observation will be the number of unscheduled line stops during the manufacture of one lot of Earls. The c chart is the

Reprinted from Management Accounting. Copyright by Institute of Management Accountants, Montvale, N.J., January 1992

correct chart to monitor this variable because unscheduled line stops with equal lot sizes can be assumed to be distributed as a Poisson random variable, and the c chart is appropriate for analyzing the stability of data distributed as a Poisson random variable. If lot sizes vary, then the c chart normally would be replaced with a u chart. The statistical theory justifying these choices is beyond our purpose.[2]

BUILDING THE CHART

Once the process, performance measure, and control chart have been selected, the control chart must be constructed. First, process performance must be measured and recorded over time. Measurement of performance must be accurate and clearly understood by all personnel who will use the SPC results. If suitable data have not already been recorded, analysis will have to wait until a minimum number of observations are recorded.

After an appropriate number of data points have been plotted, a center line and control limits are calculated. The center line is a measure of central tendency within the process. The control limits define the amount of variation to be expected in a stable process. These statistical calculations are based on equations appropriate for the selected control chart and performance measure.

At the Franklin Company the management accountant plotted 20 consecutive (time-ordered) counts of unscheduled interruptions per production lot on the c chart shown in Figure 1. For this example, only the center line (c) and upper control limit (UCL) need to be calculated. There is no lower control limit because observations less than zero are not possible. The c and the UCL are calculated as shown in the lower part of Figure 1.

The center line (c = 2.6) is the average number of unscheduled interruptions per production lot. The upper control limit (UCL = 7.44) is three standard deviations above the center line. (Note that the variance of a Poisson distribution is equal to the mean.)

INTERPRETING THE CHART

The completed chart becomes the basis for many decisions about process performance. Correct interpretation requires an understanding of the underlying statistical theory and of numerous rules of thumb developed by SPC experts over the years. Does the chart signal stability or instability? What is the risk of an incorrect signal? What are the costs of an incorrect decision? What course of action should be taken? If the chart signals instability, the special cause(s) of variation needs to be identified and eliminated. If the chart signals stability, the process still can be improved. The process needs to be changed fundamentally by altering the level of central tendency or by decreasing the variability of the process.

An incorrect decision that a process is operating in an unstable manner will result in costs of searching for special causes of process variation that do not exist. An incorrect decision that a process is operating in a stable manner will result in failure to search for special causes of variation that do exist. This means that the costs associated with operating in a unstable state will continue.

The c chart presented in Figure 1 signals an unstable process—that is, the process is subject, at times, to excessive uncommon fluctuations resulting from special causes of variation, in addition to common fluctuations. There were 10 unscheduled interruptions during the production of lot 15. This data point is above the upper control limit (UCL = 7.44) that defines the amount of variation to be expected if the process were stable. This signal should prompt management to locate and eliminate the special cause of variation reflected in this observation. Once the causes of uncommon fluctuations are eliminated, attention can be directed at improving the overall performance of the process.

The c chart presented in Figure 2 signals a stable process, which means that the process is subject only to common fluctuations resulting from causes of variation natural to the process. Even if the process is stable, there is room for improvement in performance. Reductions in (or, ideally, elimination of) the number of unscheduled interruptions during the production process would enhance productivity significantly. Also, reducing the variability of the number of unscheduled interruptions would make the process more predictable. Such reductions can occur, however, only after fundamental changes are made in the production process itself.

RULES OF THUMB

Management accountants seeking to understand SPC should realize that while SPC is based on statistical theory, the purpose of this applied methodology is to help organizations improve continuously.[3] Therefore, SPC relies heavily on rules of thumb that have not been proved scientifically. Rather than take the time to prove scientifically which rule should be used, experts develop and use rules of thumb to solve problems. This practical experience then is used to evaluate how well the rule of thumb works. Four of these rules of thumb developed from years of experience in many organizations are discussed below.

1. Control limits are established at three standard deviations (sigmas) from the mean of the variable being monitored. If an observation falls outside these control limits, the process being monitored is presumed to be unstable.

In most situations not enough data will be available to statistically justify the use of three standard deviations rather than some other number of standard deviations. W. A. Shewhart, father of SPC, established this rule because he felt three standard deviations was the point at which the total economic loss from both Type 1 and Type 2 mistakes was minimized. A Type 1 mistake is ascribing an observation to a special cause (process is unstable) when it is the result of a common cause (process is stable). A Type 2 mistake is ascribing an observation to a common cause when in fact it is the result of a special cause.

The use of three standard deviations is not based on hundreds of scientific studies that would be necessary to determine the optimal number of standard deviations scientifically. The use of three standard deviations is based on expert judgments in a wide range of circumstances. If you use SPC you need to decide if you are willing to trust these judgments. In fact, there is some controversy about how many standard deviations to use. For example, Horngren and Foster use two standard deviations.[4] The use of three standard deviations rather than two decreases the probability of Type 1 errors and increases the probability of Type 2 errors. It is justified if the economic loss associated with Type 2 errors exceeds the economic loss associated with Type 1 errors.

Also, the use of three standard deviations implies that a large majority of fluctuations are due to common causes. Because only management can remove common causes, most actions to improve process performance will involve management decisions. Therefore, management personnel rather than nonmanagement personnel are held responsible for a large percentage of problems. This idea is in direct conflict with many managers' and accountants' beliefs that most problems are the result of nonmanagement personnel behavior. The use of three standard deviations is based on the belief that blaming nonmanagement personnel for most problems is not only a waste of time but will lead to negative motivation.

In addition, the use of probabilities associated with the control limits normally is not justified. Most of the time there will not be enough data from an unchanged process to support the assumptions necessary to determine probabilities. Also, the probabilities of Type 1 and Type 2 errors normally are not subject to determination. The philosophy of SPC is to go ahead and make a judgment about these probabilities and improve performance rather than wait for statistical elegance.

2. Observations inside the control limits should be investigated under certain conditions. The second rule of thumb is really three separate rules that aid in the investigation of observations. These rules prescribe situations in which you should investigate observations that are not outside the control limits. They are exceptions to the general rule that only observations outside the control limits should be investigated.

The first exception occurs if an excessive number of observations are close to the control limit. The second occurs if an excessive number of consecutive observations are higher (or lower) than the previous observation, and the third, if an excessive number of consecutive observations are above (or below) the center line. Opinions vary among experts as to what number is excessive in each of these three exceptions. The decisions to establish these rules and to determine what is an excessive number and what is close to the control limit are judgments. These judgments are consistent with common sense even though they violate the general rule. For example, it is intuitive to feel that investigation is warranted after a certain number of consecutive increases (or decreases), even if the observations are not outside the control limits.

3. Seldom is 100% inspection more than 80% effective. Even multiple inspection of all units will not catch all defects. This rule illustrates the need for defects to be prevented rather than identified, a basic tenet of JIT and TQM. Because inspection has limited effectiveness, more effort should be expended in preventing defects before they occur than in trying to identify them after they occur.

4. Only a few processes will account for a disproportionate share of all problems. These processes should be identified, and efforts at improvement should be concentrated on them. This practical recommendation is especially appropriate when organizations first start to use SPC.

These rules of thumb allow SPC to be used in a broader number of situations, allow problems to be solved earlier, help users develop their judgment, and enable the rules to be refined. Until you understand these rules of thumb, you do not understand SPC.

SPC IS PART OF THE WHOLE

Many organizations are implementing SPC in isolation from TQM, JIT, and their organizational management style. Management accountants should realize that SPC, by itself, will provide limited potential benefits. SPC not only should be a part of a quality management program, such as TQM, but part of a general style of doing business, such as Deming's philosophy or Theory Z, as well as part of JIT. If SPC is integrated with the way the organization does business, its potential is unlimited.

For example, a goal of TQM is to stop defects before they occur. A naive user of SPC may think this goal is inconsistent with SPC. After all, SPC waits until data are available to identify problems. However, other methods are used to stop defects before they occur: machine maintenance, operator training, operator responsibility for defects. SPC is used by operators of the process to spot problems that "slip through" as early as possible so that future defects can be prevented. Using SPC will help the operator to understand the process so that he or she can prevent problems before they occur.

In SPC and TQM, management's role is to facilitate the work of the people operating the processes. Nonmanagement personnel will be responsible for observing the process, charting performance, and identifying special causes of variation. These operators have in-depth understanding of the processes, and ideas for improvement will come from them.

It is particularly important for management accountants to understand this approach. Some accountants have an unrealistically high opinion of the accounting system's ability to identify problems. Some even have a Theory X approach to doing business—for example, they use variances to "beat people over the head." In SPC and TQM, ideas from process operators are encouraged and actively solicited. Under Theory Z, these accountants will have

> *Only a few processes will account for a disproportionate share of all problems.*

to listen to people whom they have been "beating on." Traditional attitudes and approaches have to be changed before SPC and TQM can achieve full impact.

Many U.S. companies are adopting JIT while they are using SPC. Adopters of JIT and SPC need to realize that JIT can't be fully successful without a general approach to quality. Japanese companies use JIT along with TQM. They view JIT and TQM as integral parts of a holistic system. This system not only includes JIT and TQM but also Theory Z. Accountants, as information experts, are in a unique position to point this fact out to companies that attempt to implement JIT and SPC in isolation.

SPC IS A LONG-TERM APPROACH

SPC is a complex and long-term strategy. When it is adopted initially, the short-term results will not be impressive to accountants and managers who are used to emphasizing the short run. Therefore, not only management but also accountants and nonmanagement personnel need to understand SPC and how it relates to the overall strategic interests of the organization, a goal that will require extensive training.

A couple of requirements need to be met. First, an expert with at least a master's degree in statistics should be placed in charge of the organization's SPC efforts. At the same time, the people in the organization with the least amount of statistical training—operators of the process—will have to understand SPC well enough to use it. To be effective, people at all levels of the organization need to have a working knowledge of SPC. Therefore, the start-up costs for SPC will be high.

Second, the cost of quality report

(CQR) has to be used consistently with SPC, as an aggregate "after the fact" indicator for some of the costs associated with quality. The CQR is not at a detailed level, its information is not timely, and it does not attempt to calculate all of the costs and benefits associated with quality. If managers and accountants understand these limitations, the CQR can be useful. If not, there is a danger they will use it to cut costs (e.g., training and identification costs) rather than to improve quality. If the CQR is used correctly, it can help improve quality, and the improvements in quality will lead to decreased costs.

Organizations with a long-term perspective, without excessive emphasis on the short run, will have a better chance of educating their people to use the CQR and SPC appropriately as an integrated part of the whole. As organizations adapt to SPC, as well as other changes, they will encounter the natural resistance to change of management and nonmanagement personnel. Organizations with a long-term perspective will have a better chance of overcoming this resistance. ■

David E. Keys, CMA, CPA, is a professor of accountancy at Northern Illinois University. He holds a Ph.D. degree from the University of Illinois at Champaign and is a coauthor of the Bold Step publication, Cost Accounting for Factory Automation. *He can be reached at (815) 753-1538.*

Kurt F. Reding, CMA, CPA, is an assistant professor of accountancy at Northern Illinois University. He holds a Ph.D. degree from the University of Tennessee at Knoxville. He can be reached at (815) 753-6501.

Both authors are members of the Fox River Valley Chapter, through which this article was submitted.

---

[1] For a discussion of some applications of statistical process control to managing the accounting function, see James M. Reeve and John W. Philpot, "Applications of Statistical Process Control for Financial Management," *Journal of Cost Management*, Fall 1988, pp. 33-40.

[2] Irving W. Burr, *Statistical Quality Control Methods*, Marcel Dekker, Inc., New York, N.Y., 1976.

[3] For a more detailed explanation of concepts discussed here see W. Edwards Deming, *Out of the Crisis*, Massachusetts Institute of Technology, Cambridge, Mass., 1986; and Walter A. Shewhart, *Statistical Method from the Viewpoint of Quality Control*, edited by W. Edwards Deming, Dover Publications, Inc., New York, N.Y., 1986.

[4] Charles T. Horngren and George Foster, *Cost Accounting: A Managerial Emphasis*, seventh edition, Prentice-Hall, Inc., Englewood Cliffs, N.J., 1991, p. 841. Moreover, Burr (cited above) suggests that increasing the risk of Type 1 errors (i.e., using "two-sigma" limits) is warranted when there is a relatively long period of time between observations on x charts.

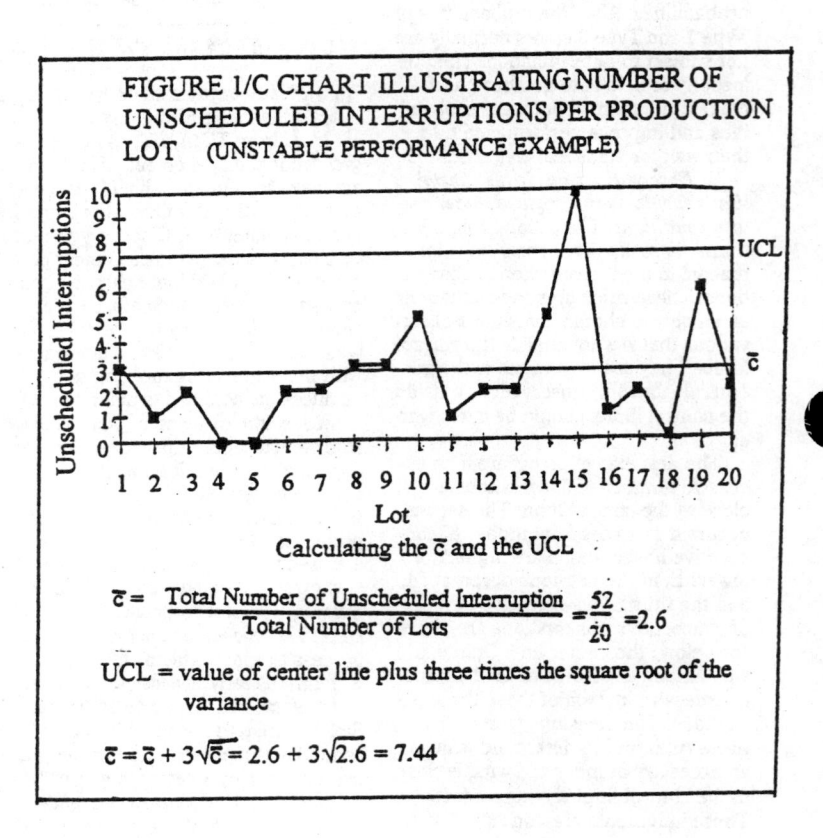

FIGURE 1/C CHART ILLUSTRATING NUMBER OF UNSCHEDULED INTERRUPTIONS PER PRODUCTION LOT (UNSTABLE PERFORMANCE EXAMPLE)

Calculating the $\bar{c}$ and the UCL

$$\bar{c} = \frac{\text{Total Number of Unscheduled Interruption}}{\text{Total Number of Lots}} = \frac{52}{20} = 2.6$$

UCL = value of center line plus three times the square root of the variance

$$\bar{c} = \bar{c} + 3\sqrt{\bar{c}} = 2.6 + 3\sqrt{2.6} = 7.44$$

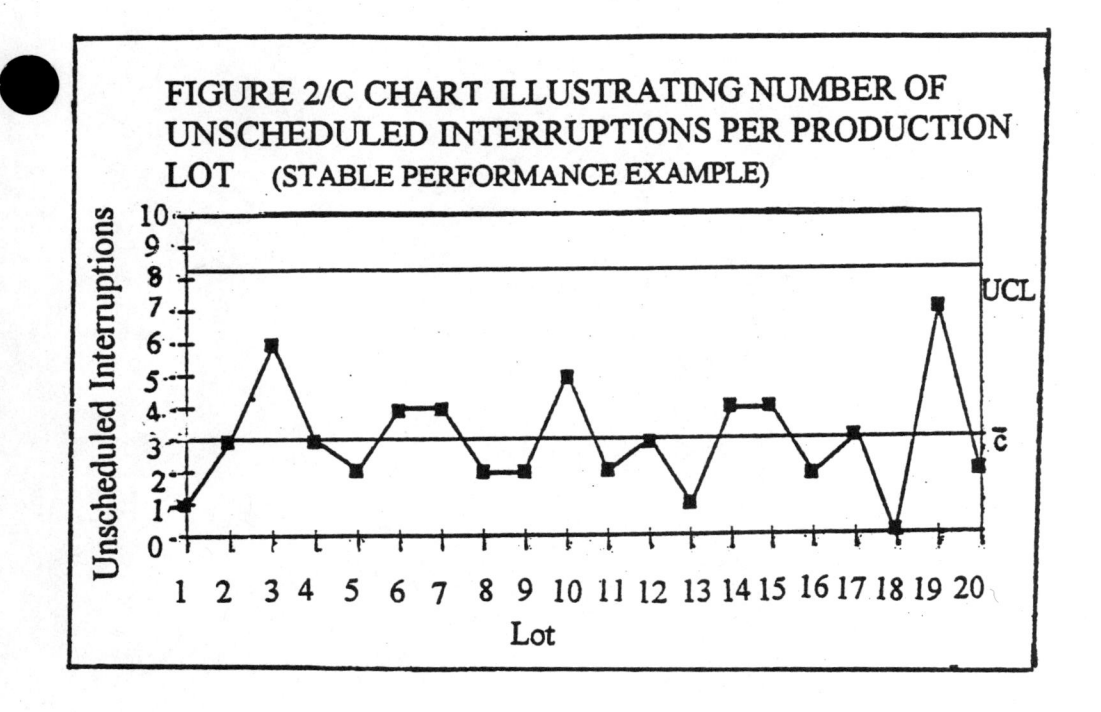

FIGURE 2/C CHART ILLUSTRATING NUMBER OF UNSCHEDULED INTERRUPTIONS PER PRODUCTION LOT (STABLE PERFORMANCE EXAMPLE)

TABLE 1/THE STEPS INVOLVED IN THE APPLICATION OF SPC.

I. Which chart?
    A. Identify the process of interest.
    B. Define the relevant measure of performance.
    C. Select the proper control chart(s) for tracking the performance measure over time.

II. Building the chart.
    A. Collect consecutive measurements over time.
    B. Plot the observations on the chart.
    C. Calculate and plot the center line and control limits after an appropriate number of data points have been recorded.

III. Interpreting the chart.
    A. Make a decision about process performance (i.e., Does the control chart signal unstable performance or stable performance?)
    B. If the process is unstable, identify and eliminate the special causes of variation. If the process is stable, change the process itself to improve it.